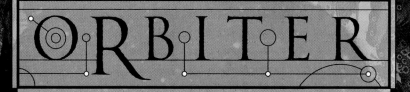

ORBITER

Warren Ellis and Colleen Doran
dedicate this book to
the lives, memories and legacies
of the seven astronauts lost
on space shuttle Columbia
during mission STS-107.

MICHAEL ANDERSON

DAVID BROWN

KALPANA CHAWLA

LAUREL CLARK

RICK HUSBAND

WILLIAM McCOOL

ILAN RAMON

writer WARREN ELLIS
artist COLLEEN DORAN

letterer CLEM ROBINS
colorist DAVE STEWART

DC COMICS Karen Berger VP·Executive Editor · Will Dennis & Heidi MacDonald Editors
Zachary J. Rau Assistant Editor · Amie Brockway·Metcalf Art Director
Paul Levitz President & Publisher · Georg Brewer VP·Design & Retail Product Development
Richard Bruning VP·Creative Director · Patrick Caldon Senior VP·Finance & Operations
Chris Caramalis VP·Finance · Terri Cunningham VP·Managing Editor
Dan DiDio VP·Editorial · Joel Ehrlich Senior VP·Advertising & Promotions
Alison Gill VP·Manufacturing · Lillian Laserson Senior VP & General Counsel
David McKillips VP·Advertising · John Nee VP·Business Development
Cheryl Rubin VP·Licensing & Merchandising · Bob Wayne VP·Sales & Marketing

cover painted by COLLEEN DORAN
logo designed by ASTROLUXEDESIGN

GETTING UP AGAIN

A foreword by Warren Ellis

MY FIRST MEMORY is of being held up in front of a tiny black-and-white TV set by my mother and being told, "Remember this. This is history, this is." July 1969. I was seventeen months old. Neil Armstrong had gotten that sticky hatch open and was making that odd little jump from the end of the ladder to the soil of the Moon.

I didn't sleep much as a kid — probably exacerbated by an insane dog that used to attempt to sleep in the cot with me — and it was probably on those sleepless nights that my father built the Apollo 11 model I treasured for years afterwards. It was the complete stack — the stages unscrewed to reveal each section's engine bells — right down to the tiny Command Module and lander in the top under the escape rocket tower.

I had the bug. Just as my father infected me with SF and comics. The first comic I ever read was one he brought home for me. COUNTDOWN, featuring comics versions of popular SF TV shows of the time. I remember devouring a series of books that I found in the local library a few years after Viking, about children in an invented British space programme. They used children because adults constituted a weight penalty, in the panicky mathematics of chemical thrust against payload mass. My dad's model Apollo stack was brought into focus; that huge bloody thing needed to throw that tiny little capsule to the Moon. And: there wasn't going to be a British space programme. The Russians weren't going to put people on the Moon, and it was putting people out there that was important. We understand environments through experience, not robot telemetry. All my hopes for a science fiction future, for performing the exploration the human being is hardwired for, were pinned on the American space programme.

School stopped for an hour, the day the first Shuttle launched. We watched it on a TV wheeled into the school assembly hall. We didn't do that the first time an Ariane — the European workhorse booster, nominally "closer" to us here in Britain — banged off. It wasn't crewed. It did not have the aura of the future that American spaceflight glowed with.

As I write this, I'm thirty-four years old. I have another Apollo 11 model in my office. Colleen sends NASA astronaut ice-cream packages for my daughter Lilith, who's seven. I came up with the basic concept for ORBITER three years ago. I began writing it in 2001. My father died one year ago.

I wrote the final scene of ORBITER a couple of months ago.

Eight days ago, Kennedy Space Center lost the signal from Columbia as it passed thirty-nine miles above Texas on reentry trajectory, moving at twelve thousand five hundred miles an hour.

I was on the Internet at the time, reading the BBC news, when the ticker flashed up the alert: loss of signal fifteen minutes ago. A Space Shuttle has no abort contingency at that stage in the approach. It's too high and too fast. The control surfaces don't have enough atmosphere to usefully bite into, too deep for OMS/RCS to have any real effect, too fast for attitude jets to correct hard. At eighteen times the speed of sound, escaping into the air off the egress pole would've been like jumping in front of a speeding truck. The Shuttle is infamous for handling like a flying brick in its return mode, as an unpowered glider. Flying Shuttle is — as everyone has learned, once again — experimental flight. Columbia was flying mission STS-107. This means that none of the fleet has been up more than thirty times.

I brought up the webcast NASA TV and BBC News 24 streams on my screen. On the former, KSC Mission Control was appallingly silent. The BBC had footage from Texas, of the plasma-stream "contrail" from Columbia arcing over a perfect blue sky, with a hot flaring light at its apex. The flare was wrong.

Attitude jets were firing off the left wing. Temperature sensors were burning away. Despite a large amount of telemetry being routed away from the cockpit and down to KSC, the crew knew that the bird was sick. A minute is a very long time when you're thirty-nine miles high, the fastest thing in the air, and the laws of nature are scorching their way into the superstructure of your ship.

Florida was just waking up, waiting for the double-boom of supersonics that heralded the return of a Shuttle. And waited.

The flare became two flares. And three. And four.

I called Colleen, not knowing she was in California on business. Hooked up with my friend Matt in Kansas City, and we spent the day working the various news services, keeping each other informed, looking for a sign that, I don't know, someone had gotten out, that Columbia had pulled off an emergency landing, that this was impossible to avoid and there hadn't been Challenger-level incompetence, that crewed American spaceflight hadn't been shot in the heart.

Human remains were found in Texas a few hours later.

My family gave me a lot of space that day.

When Challenger cracked up on launch, the Shuttle fleet was grounded for two and a half years. As I write this, there's talk of the remaining Shuttles staying down for at least a year. And the very sense of human spaceflight is being questioned. As you read this book, you'll find why that gave me an especial chill. After that was said, a business associate in Los Angeles emailed to call me a prophet. I would rather not be. I hope I'm not.

The much-talked-about Prometheus initiative for nuclear thrust currently has application only to robot missions. Going flat-out, in an Apollo-scale manner, it'd take ten years to crew-rate a nuclear-electric mission, where a reactor powers an ion-drive system. A nuclear-thermal system, where a module rides a spike of superhot gas squirted out of the reactor, will, in my opinion, never be crew-rated.

Since I was seventeen months old, space has gotten progressively further away. Even Shuttle was designed only to perform shallow hundred-mile-high orbits.

The current American President is publicly recommitting to NASA. But his father's inauguration address told his nation that they were going to Mars. NASA has always been a political football, and it is entirely possible to re-fund NASA and treat it with respect and still suspend crewed spaceflight for a considerable period of time.

I caught up with Colleen on Monday. I don't think she'll mind my telling you that she cried most of the way home from California. We've both been space freaks from early childhood, and she spent a lot of time at NASA centers, talking with NASA people, in the production of ORBITER. And we both said the same thing.

This book needs to come out now.

It has something to say. Now is the time to get back up. I wrote it in the face of the disappointment of the International Space Station, the wounded Russian programme, the crushed Japanese space initiative, the intellectual poverty of the European Space Agency, and of the site of the beautiful Shuttles never getting further than an eight-minute burn away. There has to be more, I wrote. We're losing space, I wrote, when there is so much out there for us. It meant something huge to Colleen and me; and it means more now.

This is a book about returning to space in the face of fear and adversity. It's a book about glory. About going back to space, because it's waiting for us, and it's where we're meant to be. We can't allow human space exploration to become our history.

Human spaceflight remains experimental. It is very dangerous. It demands great ingenuity. But we are old enough, now, to do these things. Growing up is hard. But we cannot remain children, standing on the shore or in front of the TV set.

Colleen and I have dedicated ORBITER in the names of the seven astronauts lost on Columbia. We also place it in the service of those who will go after, with equal courage and intelligence, to make us great.

And more will go on. Because it's too important a thing to allow it to die in the sky.

WARREN ELLIS
Southend, England
February 2003

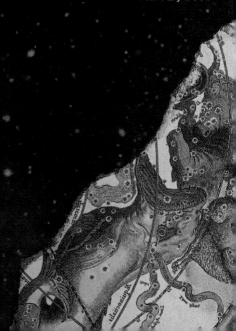

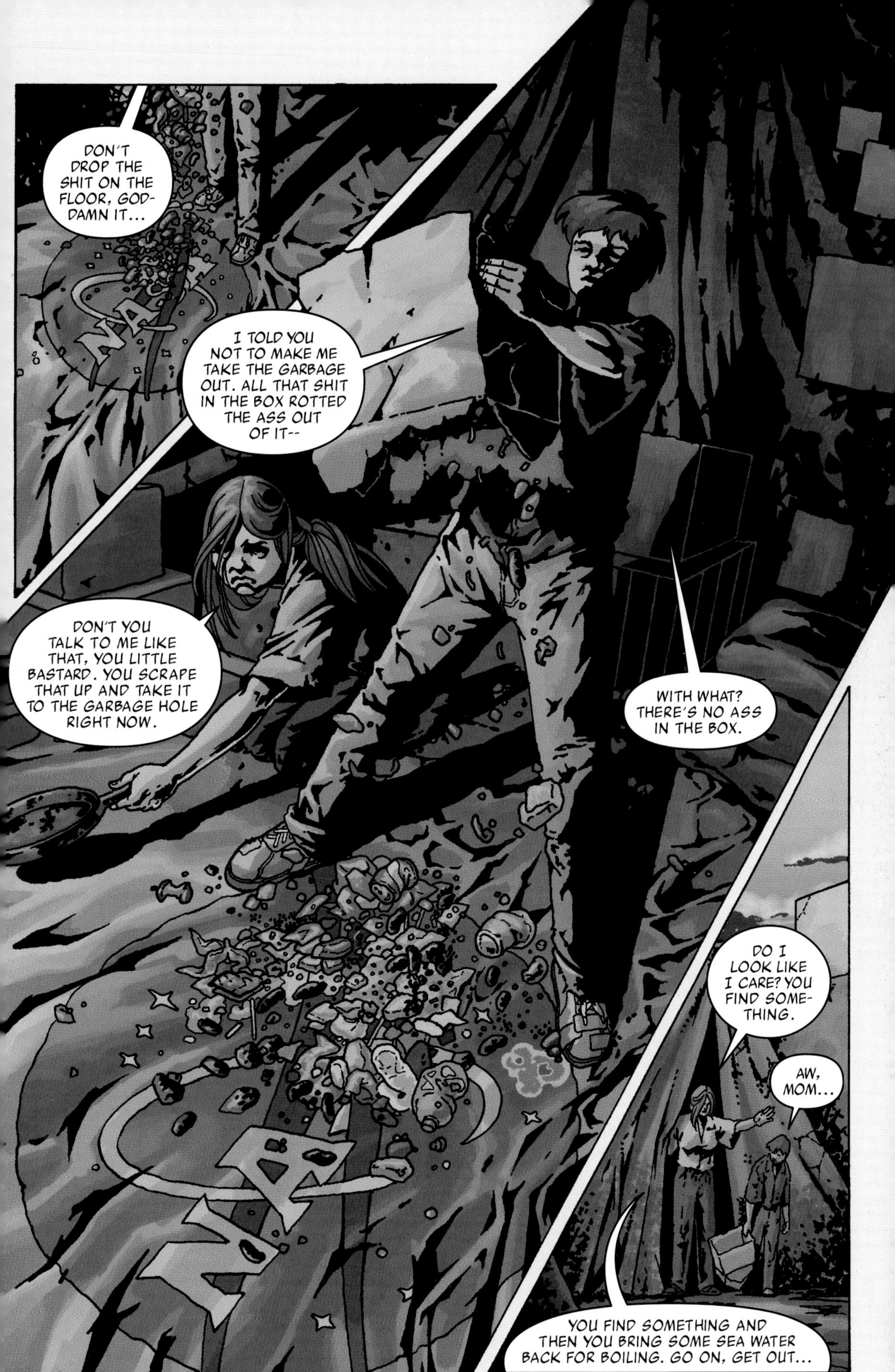
DON'T DROP THE SHIT ON THE FLOOR, GOD-DAMN IT...
I TOLD YOU NOT TO MAKE ME TAKE THE GARBAGE OUT. ALL THAT SHIT IN THE BOX ROTTED THE ASS OUT OF IT--
DON'T YOU TALK TO ME LIKE THAT, YOU LITTLE BASTARD. YOU SCRAPE THAT UP AND TAKE IT TO THE GARBAGE HOLE RIGHT NOW.
WITH WHAT? THERE'S NO ASS IN THE BOX.
DO I LOOK LIKE I CARE? YOU FIND SOME-THING.
AW, MOM...
YOU FIND SOMETHING AND THEN YOU BRING SOME SEA WATER BACK FOR BOILING. GO ON, GET OUT...

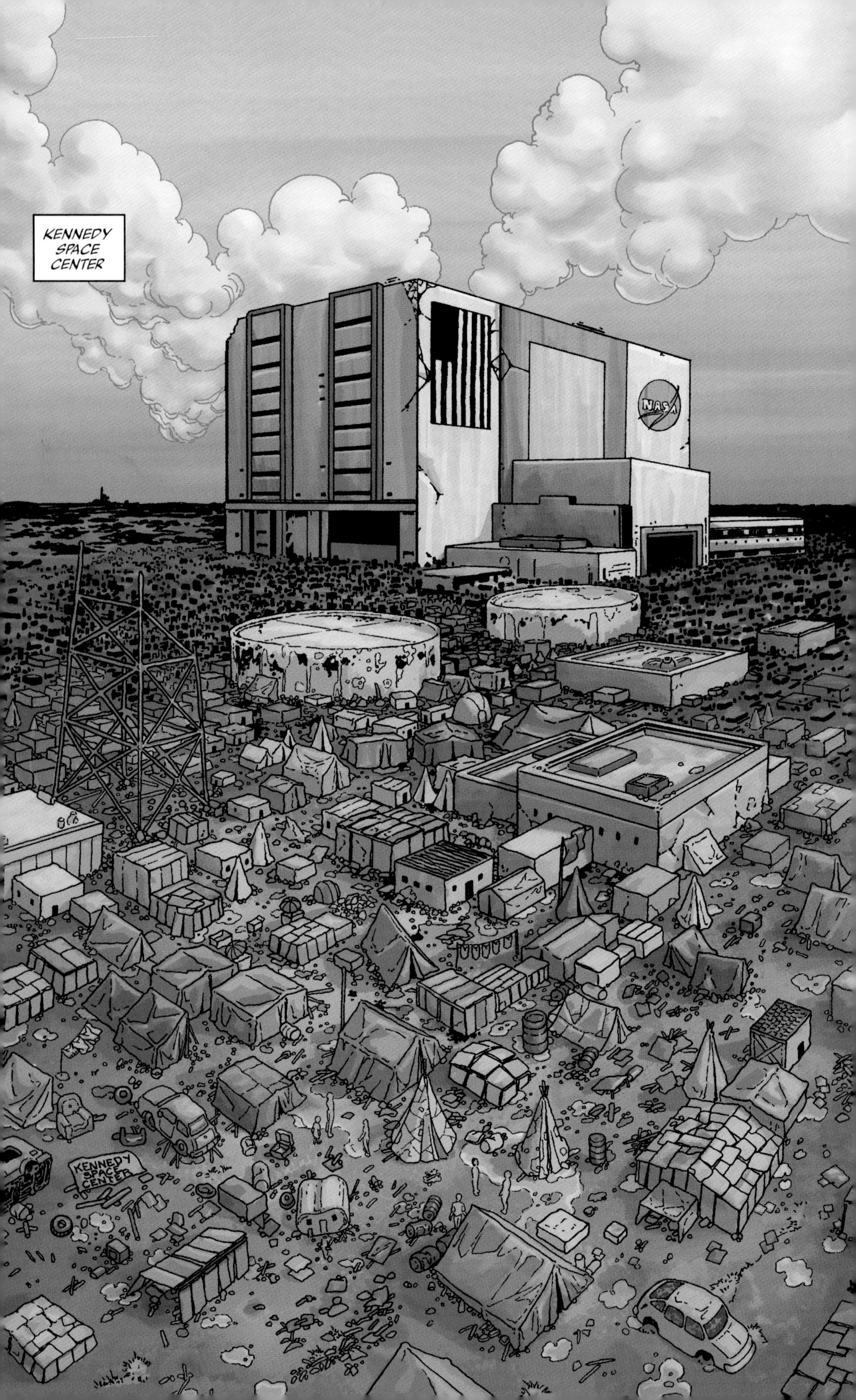
KENNEDY SPACE CENTER
NASA
KENNEDY SPACE CENTER

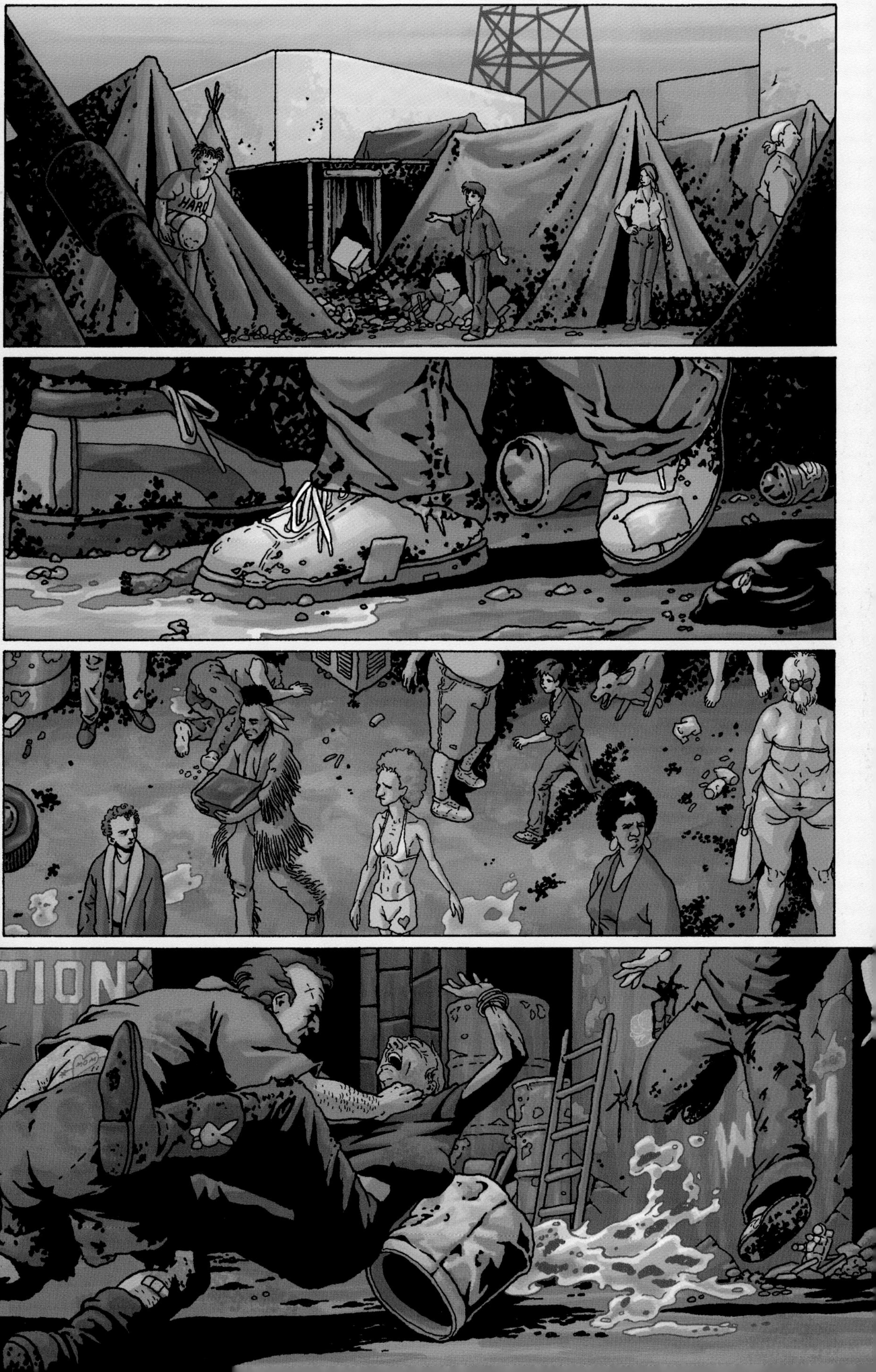

HARD
TION

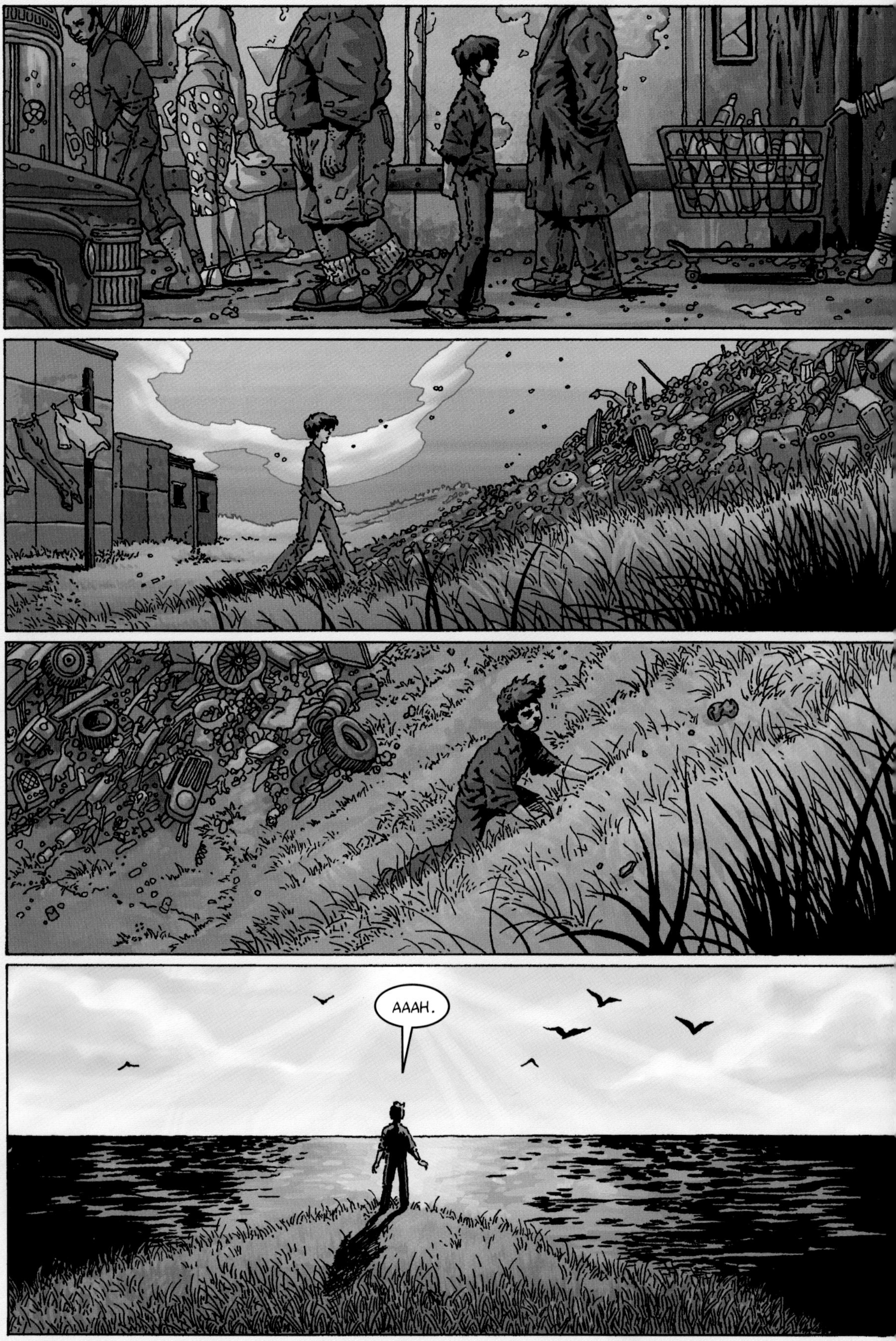
AAAH.

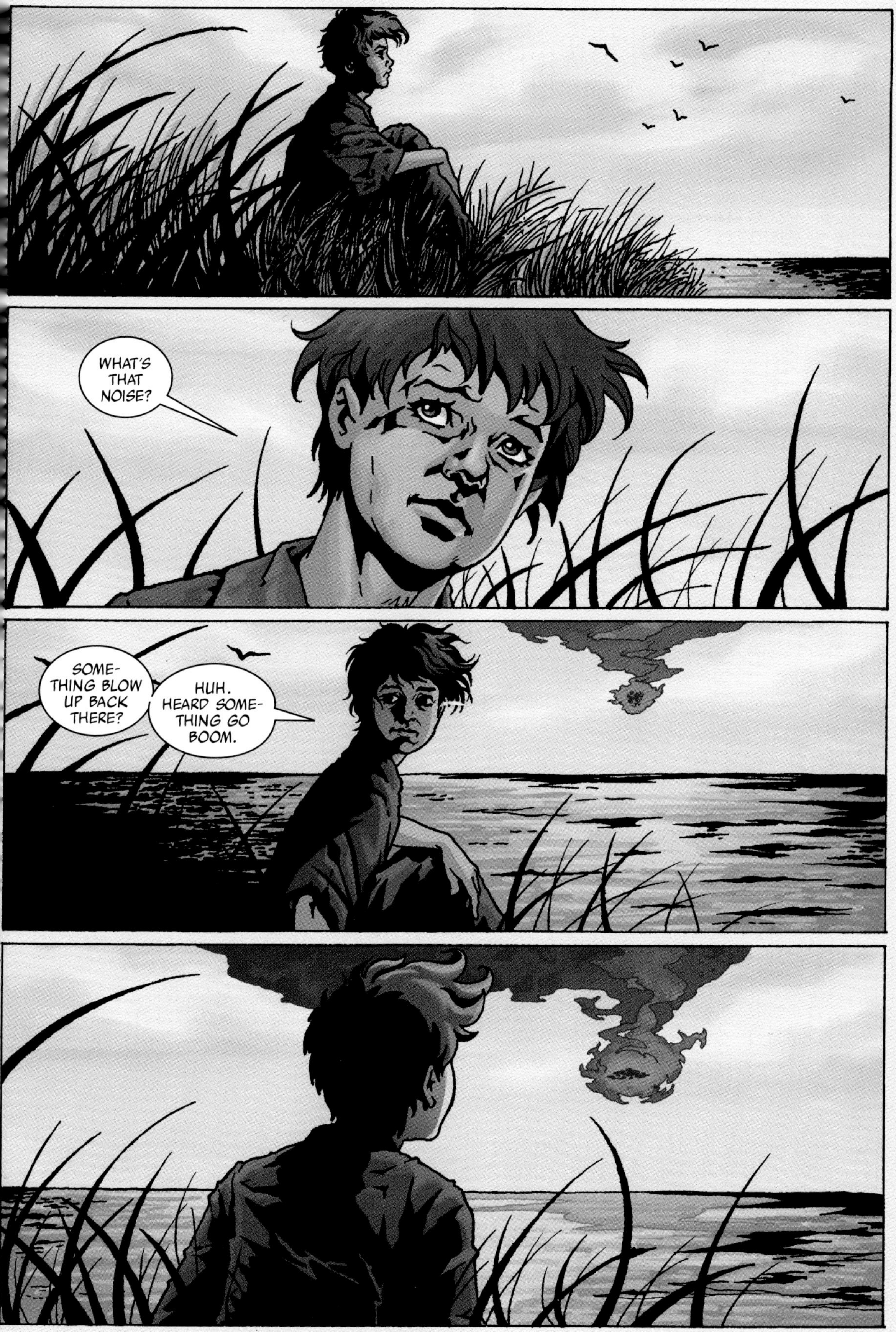
WHAT'S THAT NOISE?
SOME-THING BLOW UP BACK THERE?
HUH. HEARD SOME-THING GO BOOM.

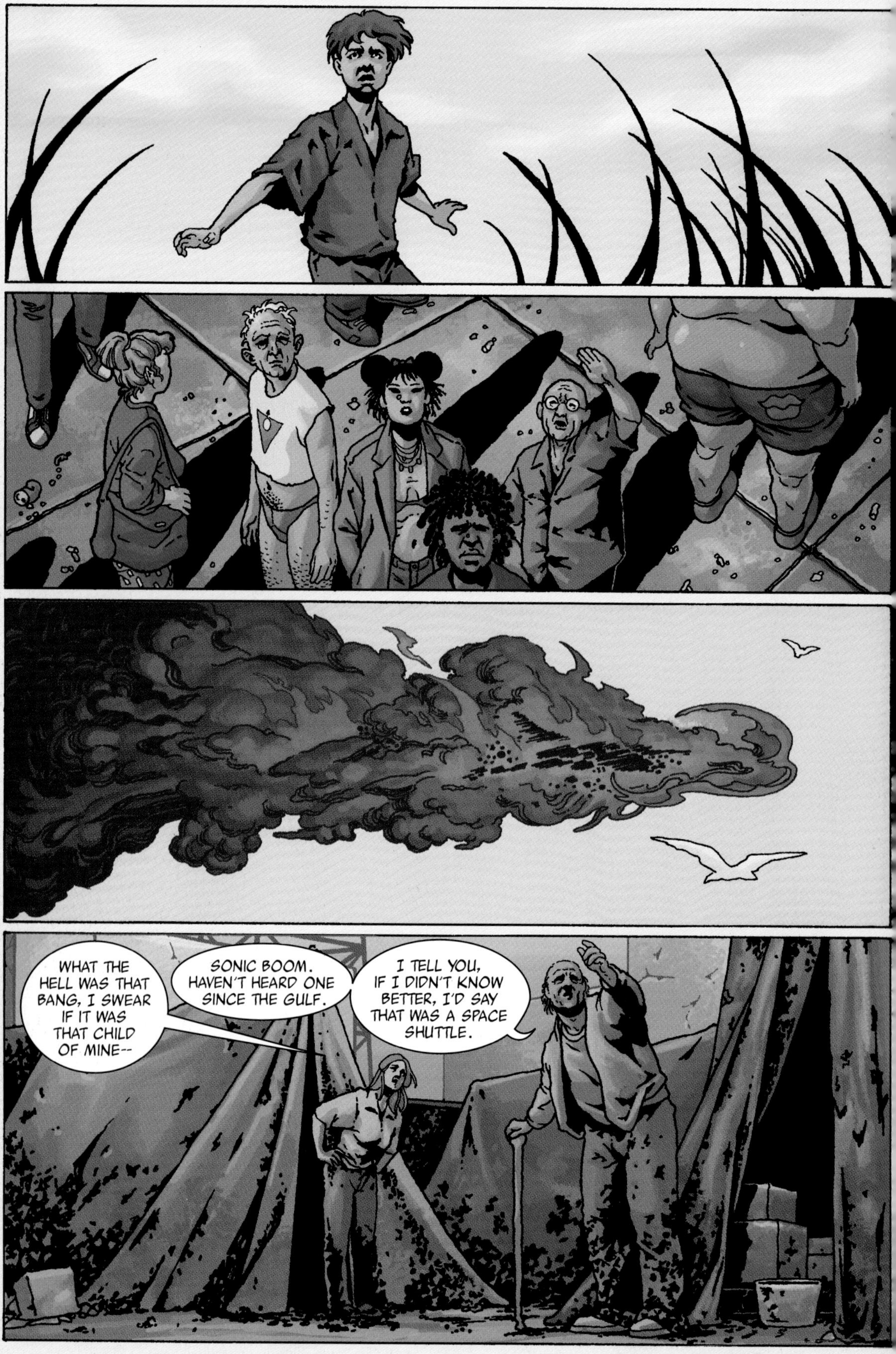
WHAT THE HELL WAS THAT BANG, I SWEAR IF IT WAS THAT CHILD OF MINE--
SONIC BOOM. HAVEN'T HEARD ONE SINCE THE GULF.
I TELL YOU, IF I DIDN'T KNOW BETTER, I'D SAY THAT WAS A SPACE SHUTTLE.

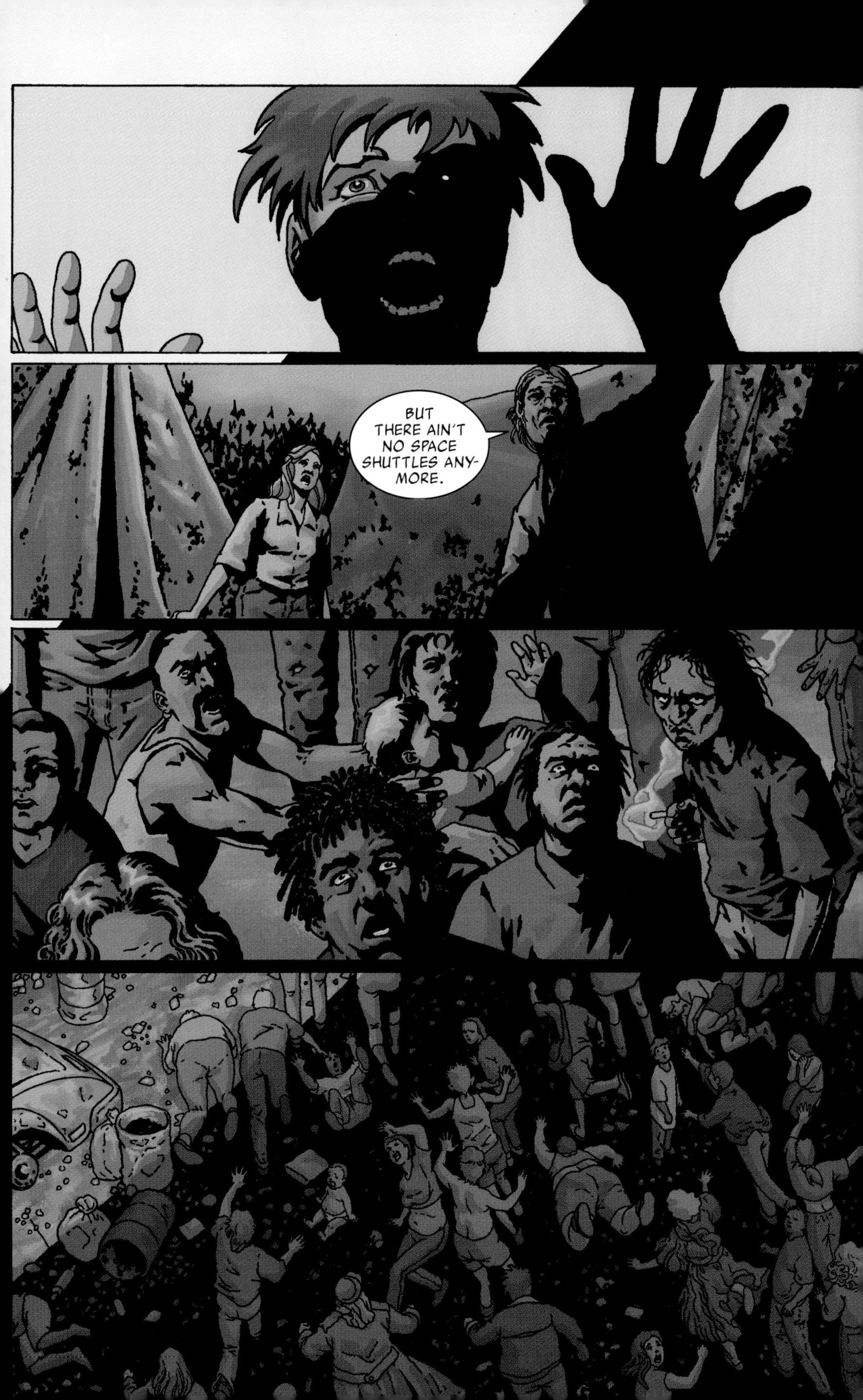
BUT THERE AIN'T NO SPACE SHUTTLES ANY-MORE.

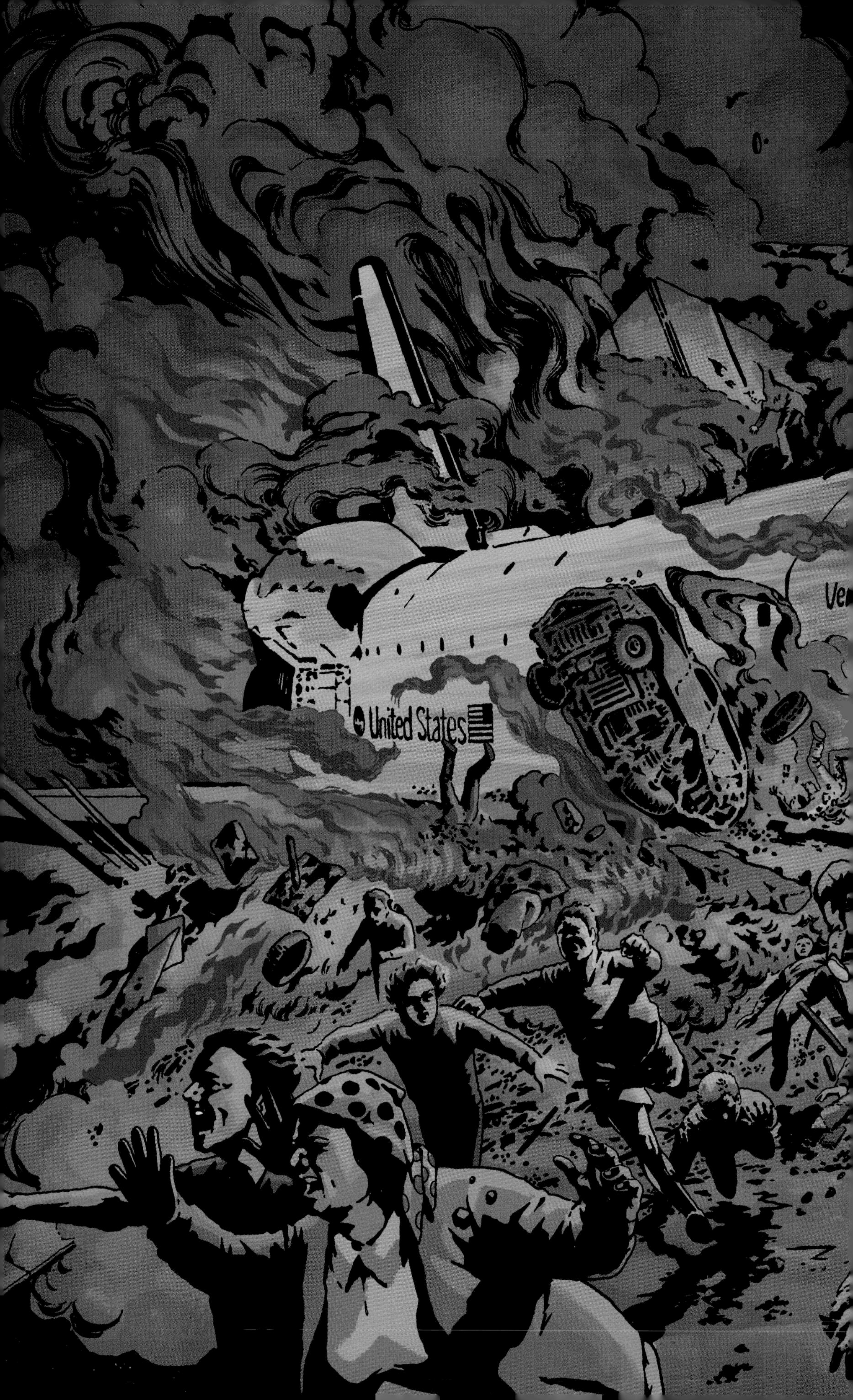
United States

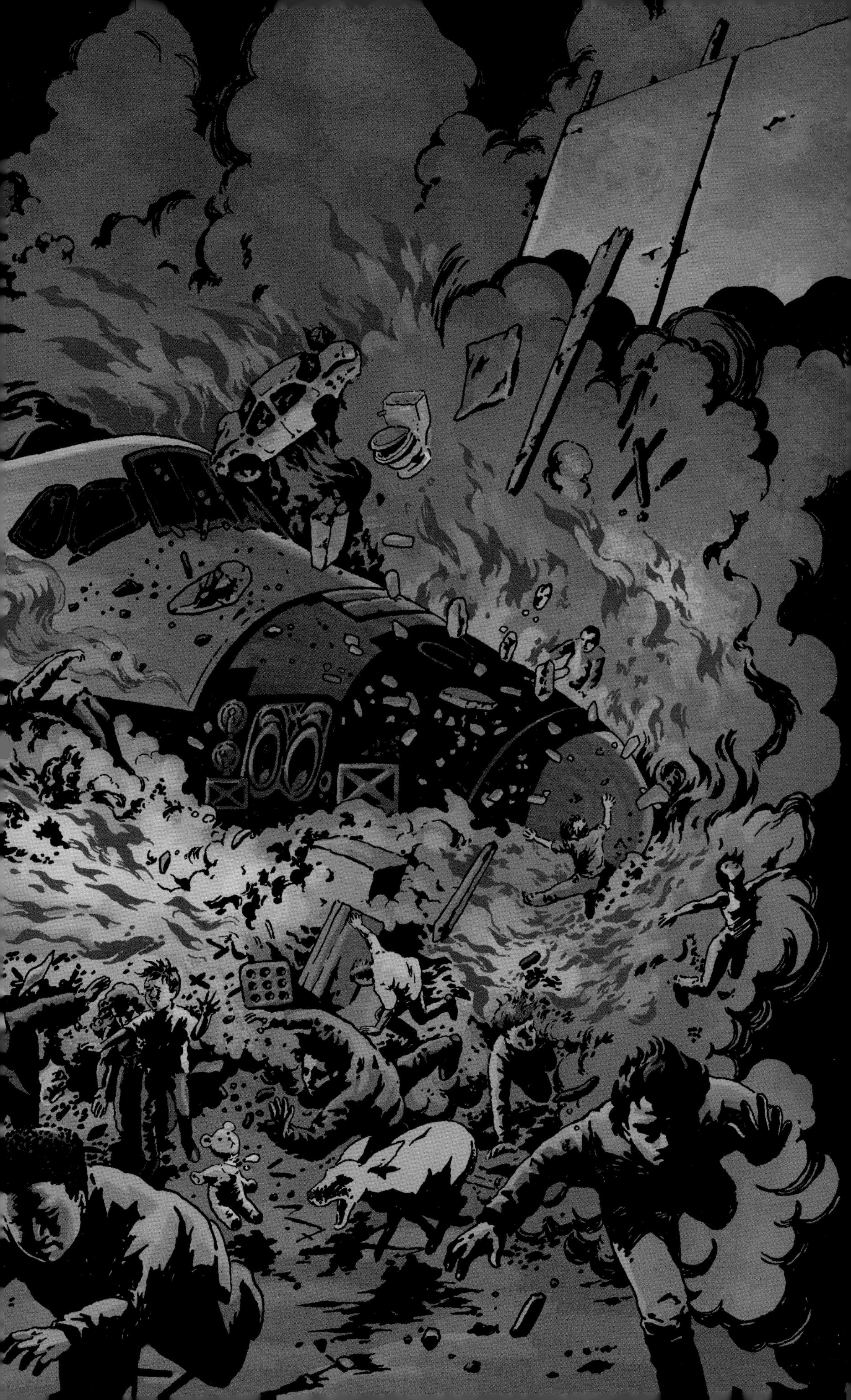

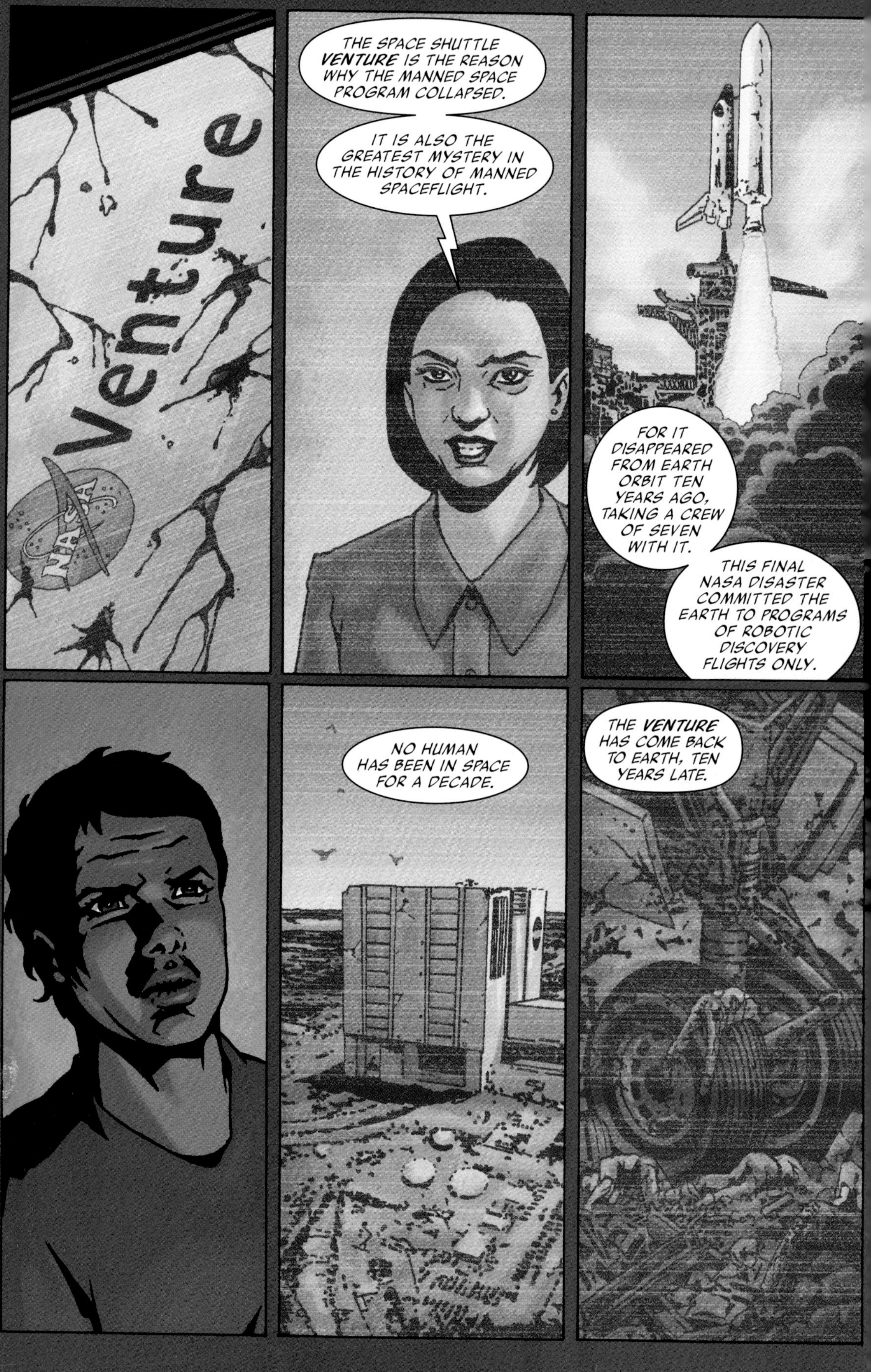
Venture
NASA
THE SPACE SHUTTLE VENTURE IS THE REASON WHY THE MANNED SPACE PROGRAM COLLAPSED.
IT IS ALSO THE GREATEST MYSTERY IN THE HISTORY OF MANNED SPACEFLIGHT.
FOR IT DISAPPEARED FROM EARTH ORBIT TEN YEARS AGO, TAKING A CREW OF SEVEN WITH IT.
THIS FINAL NASA DISASTER COMMITTED THE EARTH TO PROGRAMS OF ROBOTIC DISCOVERY FLIGHTS ONLY.
NO HUMAN HAS BEEN IN SPACE FOR A DECADE.
THE VENTURE HAS COME BACK TO EARTH, TEN YEARS LATE.

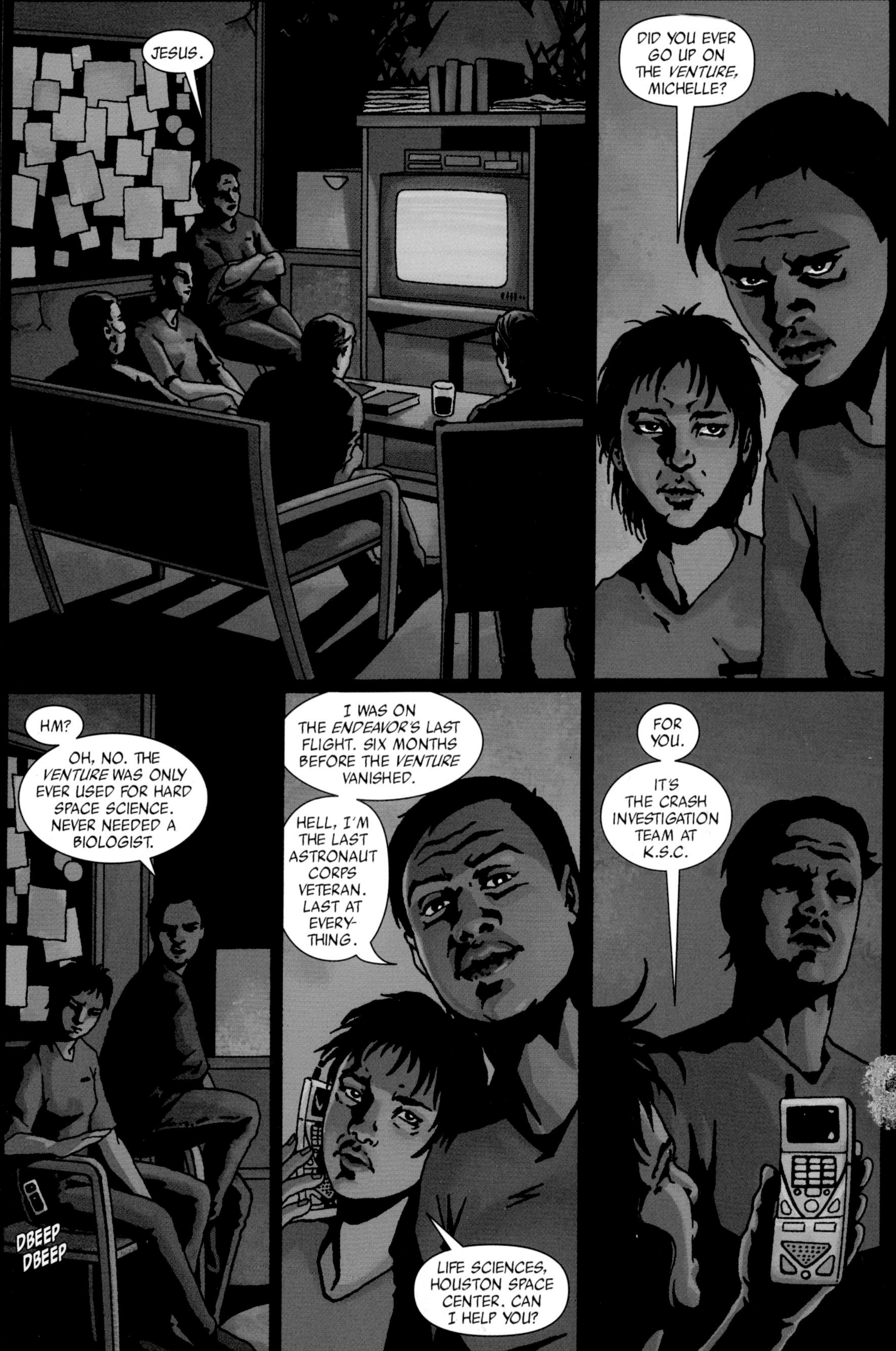

JESUS.
DID YOU EVER GO UP ON THE *VENTURE*, MICHELLE?
HM?
OH, NO. THE *VENTURE* WAS ONLY EVER USED FOR HARD SPACE SCIENCE. NEVER NEEDED A BIOLOGIST.
DBEEP DBEEP
I WAS ON THE *ENDEAVOR'S* LAST FLIGHT. SIX MONTHS BEFORE THE *VENTURE* VANISHED.
HELL, I'M THE LAST ASTRONAUT CORPS VETERAN. LAST AT EVERY-THING.
LIFE SCIENCES, HOUSTON SPACE CENTER. CAN I HELP YOU?
FOR YOU.
IT'S THE CRASH INVESTIGATION TEAM AT K.S.C.

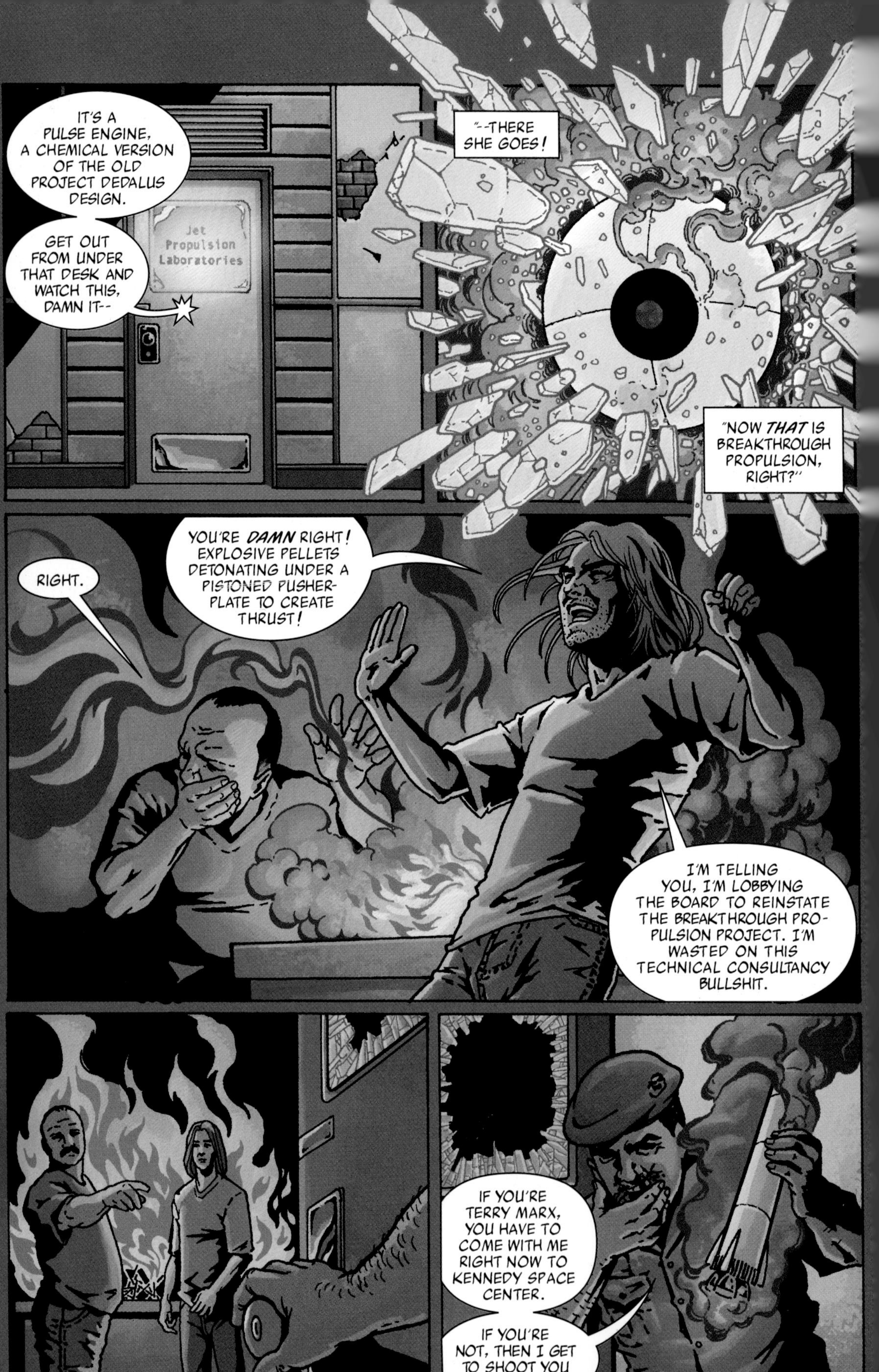
IT'S A PULSE ENGINE, A CHEMICAL VERSION OF THE OLD PROJECT DEDALUS DESIGN.
GET OUT FROM UNDER THAT DESK AND WATCH THIS, DAMN IT--
Jet Propulsion Laboratories
"--THERE SHE GOES!
"NOW *THAT* IS BREAKTHROUGH PROPULSION, RIGHT?"
RIGHT.
YOU'RE *DAMN* RIGHT! EXPLOSIVE PELLETS DETONATING UNDER A PISTONED PUSHER-PLATE TO CREATE THRUST!
I'M TELLING YOU, I'M LOBBYING THE BOARD TO REINSTATE THE BREAKTHROUGH PRO-PULSION PROJECT. I'M WASTED ON THIS TECHNICAL CONSULTANCY BULLSHIT.
IF YOU'RE TERRY MARX, YOU HAVE TO COME WITH ME RIGHT NOW TO KENNEDY SPACE CENTER.
IF YOU'RE NOT, THEN I GET TO SHOOT YOU FOR THIS.

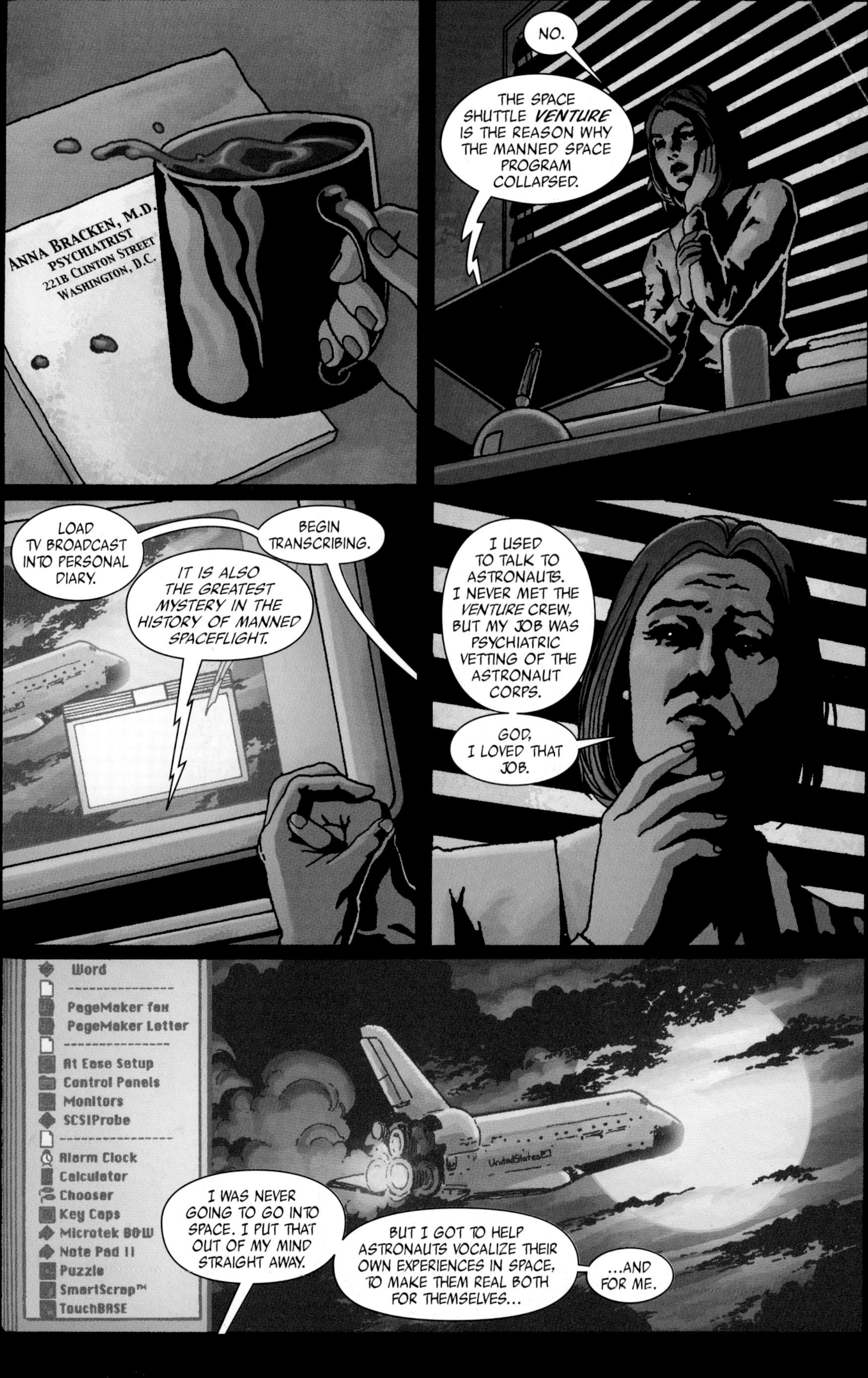
ANNA BRACKEN, M.D.
PSYCHIATRIST
221B CLINTON STREET
WASHINGTON, D.C.
NO.
THE SPACE SHUTTLE VENTURE IS THE REASON WHY THE MANNED SPACE PROGRAM COLLAPSED.
LOAD TV BROADCAST INTO PERSONAL DIARY.
BEGIN TRANSCRIBING.
IT IS ALSO THE GREATEST MYSTERY IN THE HISTORY OF MANNED SPACEFLIGHT.
I USED TO TALK TO ASTRONAUTS. I NEVER MET THE VENTURE CREW, BUT MY JOB WAS PSYCHIATRIC VETTING OF THE ASTRONAUT CORPS.
GOD, I LOVED THAT JOB.
Word
PageMaker fax
PageMaker Letter
At Ease Setup
Control Panels
Monitors
SCSIProbe
Alarm Clock
Calculator
Chooser
Key Caps
Microtek B&W
Note Pad II
Puzzle
SmartScrap™
TouchBASE
United States
I WAS NEVER GOING TO GO INTO SPACE. I PUT THAT OUT OF MY MIND STRAIGHT AWAY.
BUT I GOT TO HELP ASTRONAUTS VOCALIZE THEIR OWN EXPERIENCES IN SPACE, TO MAKE THEM REAL BOTH FOR THEMSELVES...
...AND FOR ME.

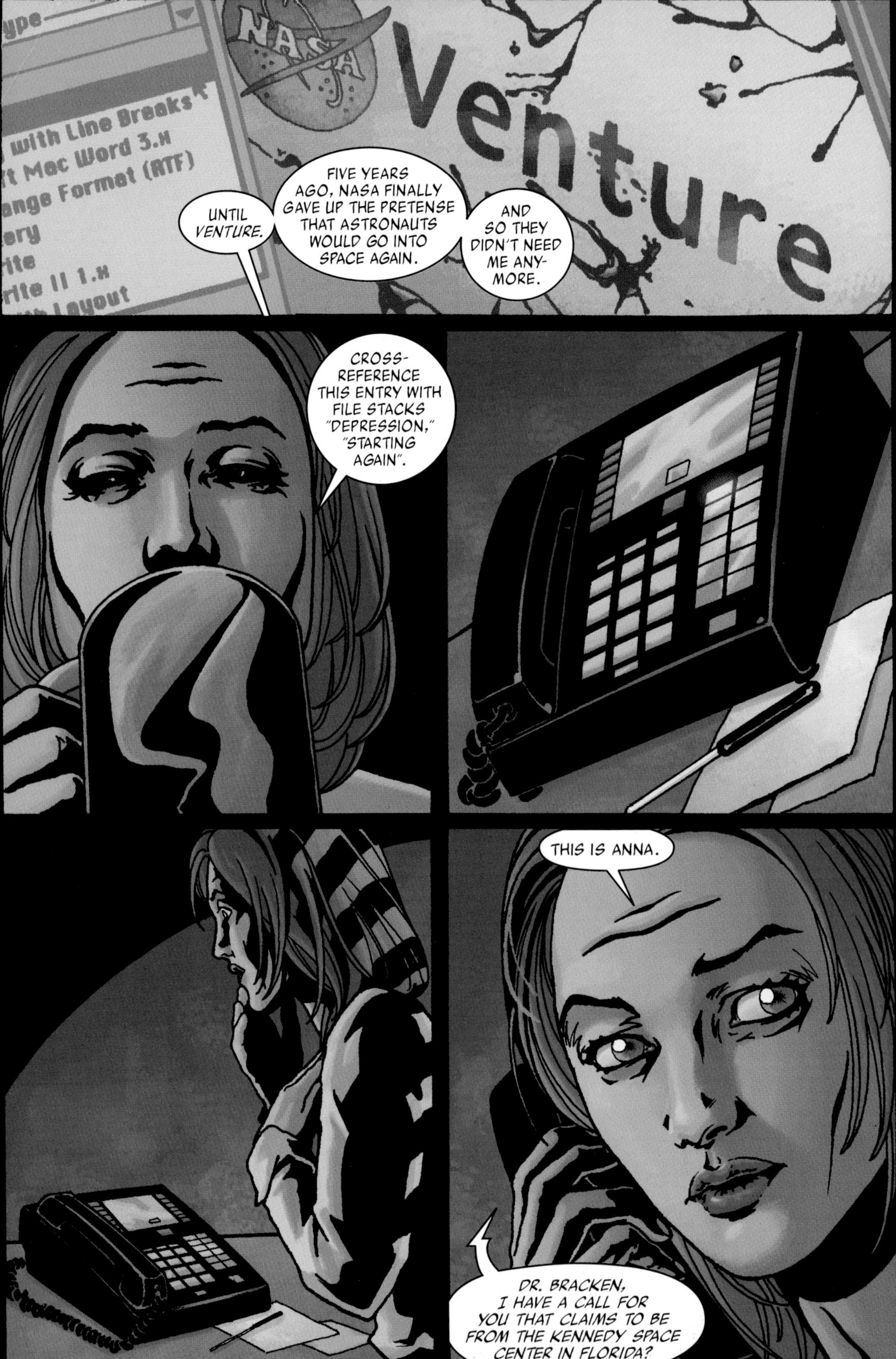
NASA
Venture
UNTIL VENTURE.
FIVE YEARS AGO, NASA FINALLY GAVE UP THE PRETENSE THAT ASTRONAUTS WOULD GO INTO SPACE AGAIN.
AND SO THEY DIDN'T NEED ME ANYMORE.
CROSS-REFERENCE THIS ENTRY WITH FILE STACKS "DEPRESSION," "STARTING AGAIN".
THIS IS ANNA.
DR. BRACKEN, I HAVE A CALL FOR YOU THAT CLAIMS TO BE FROM THE KENNEDY SPACE CENTER IN FLORIDA?

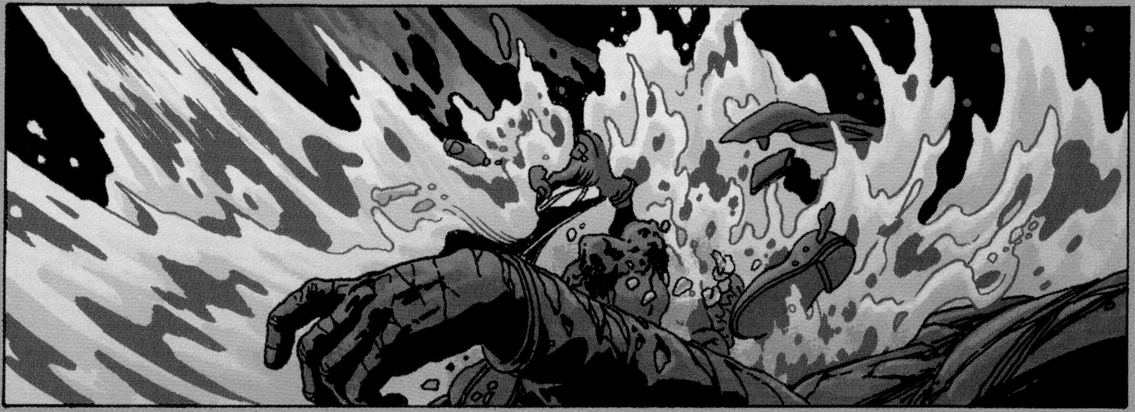

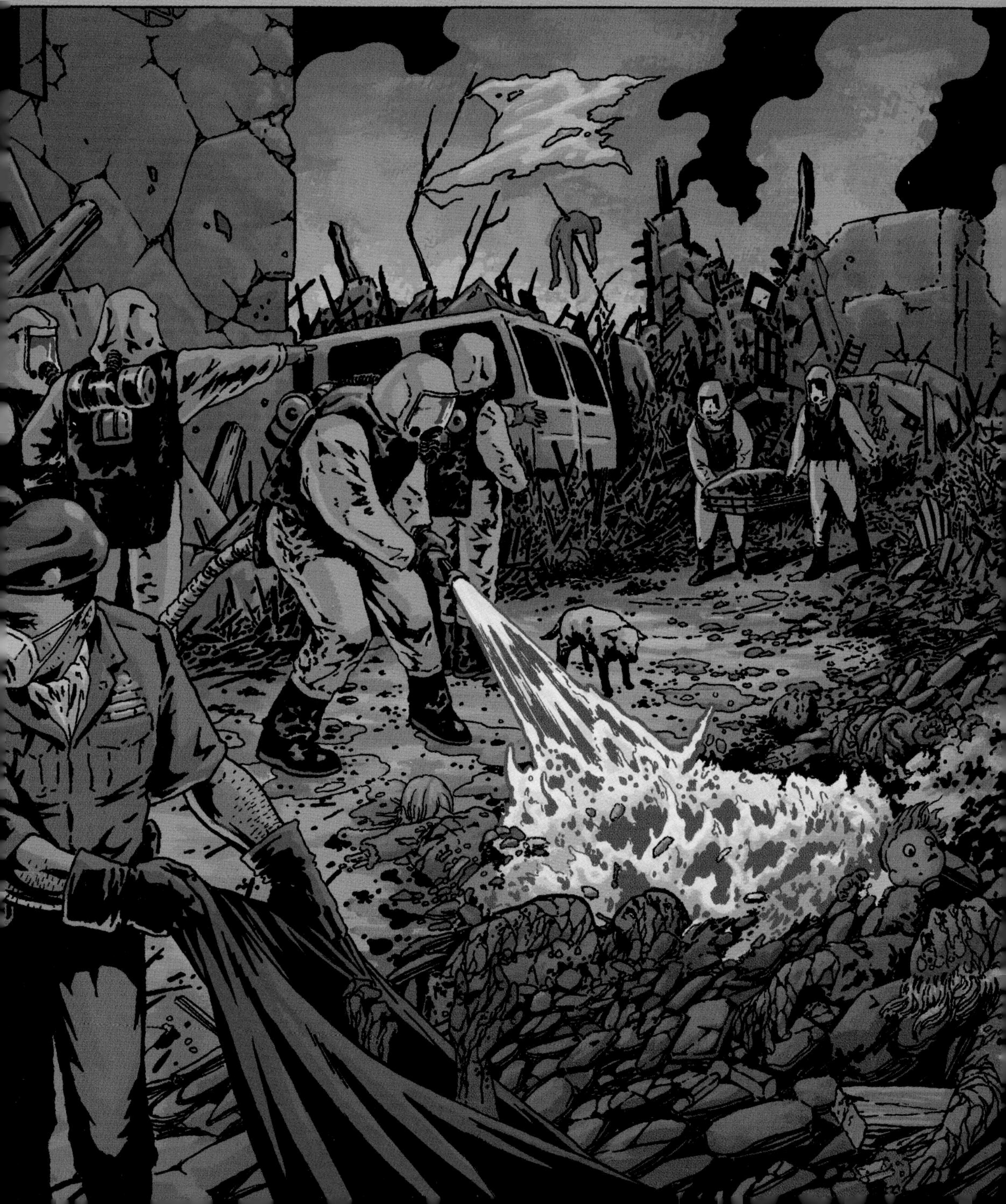

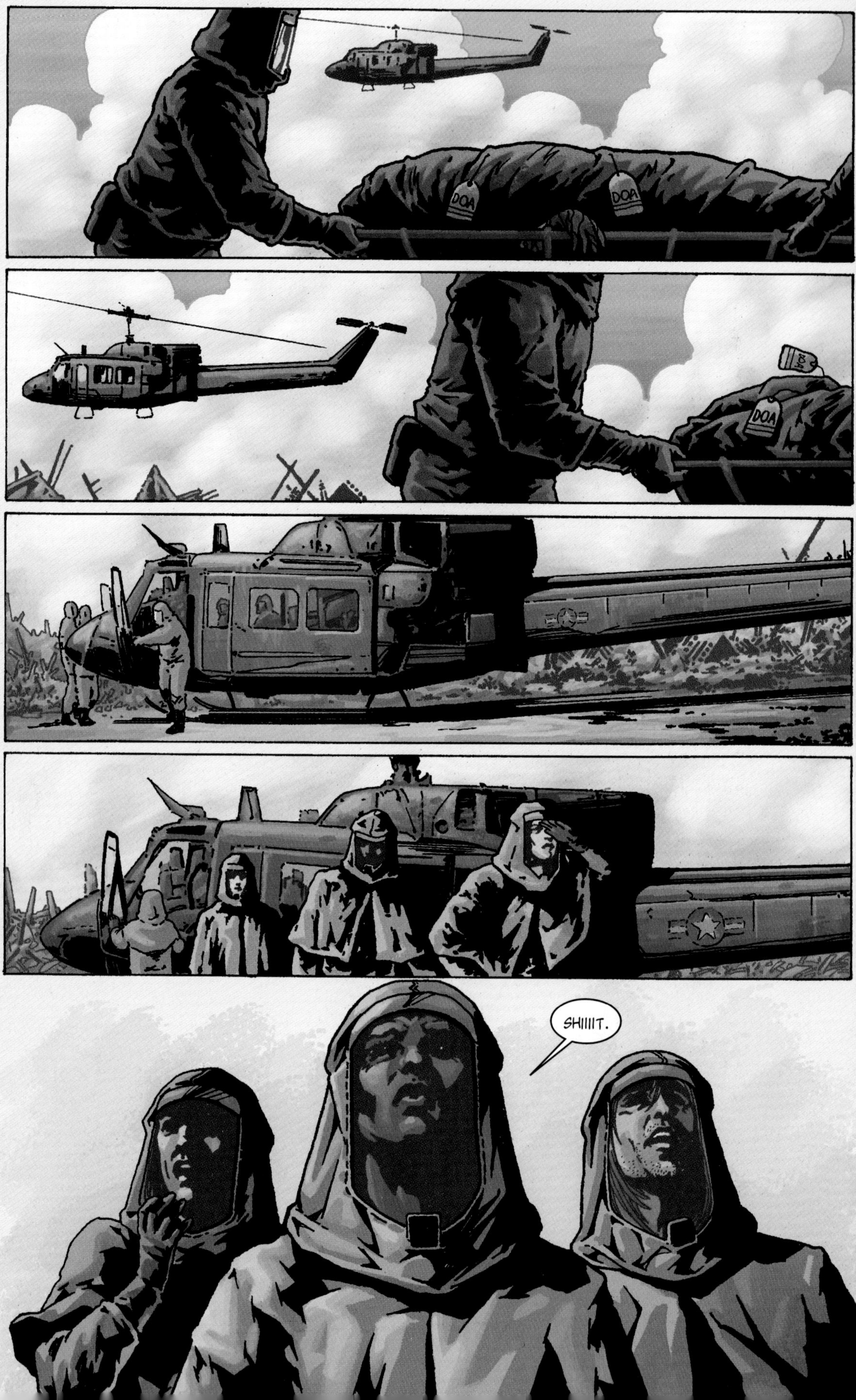
DOA
DOA
DOA
SHIIIIT.

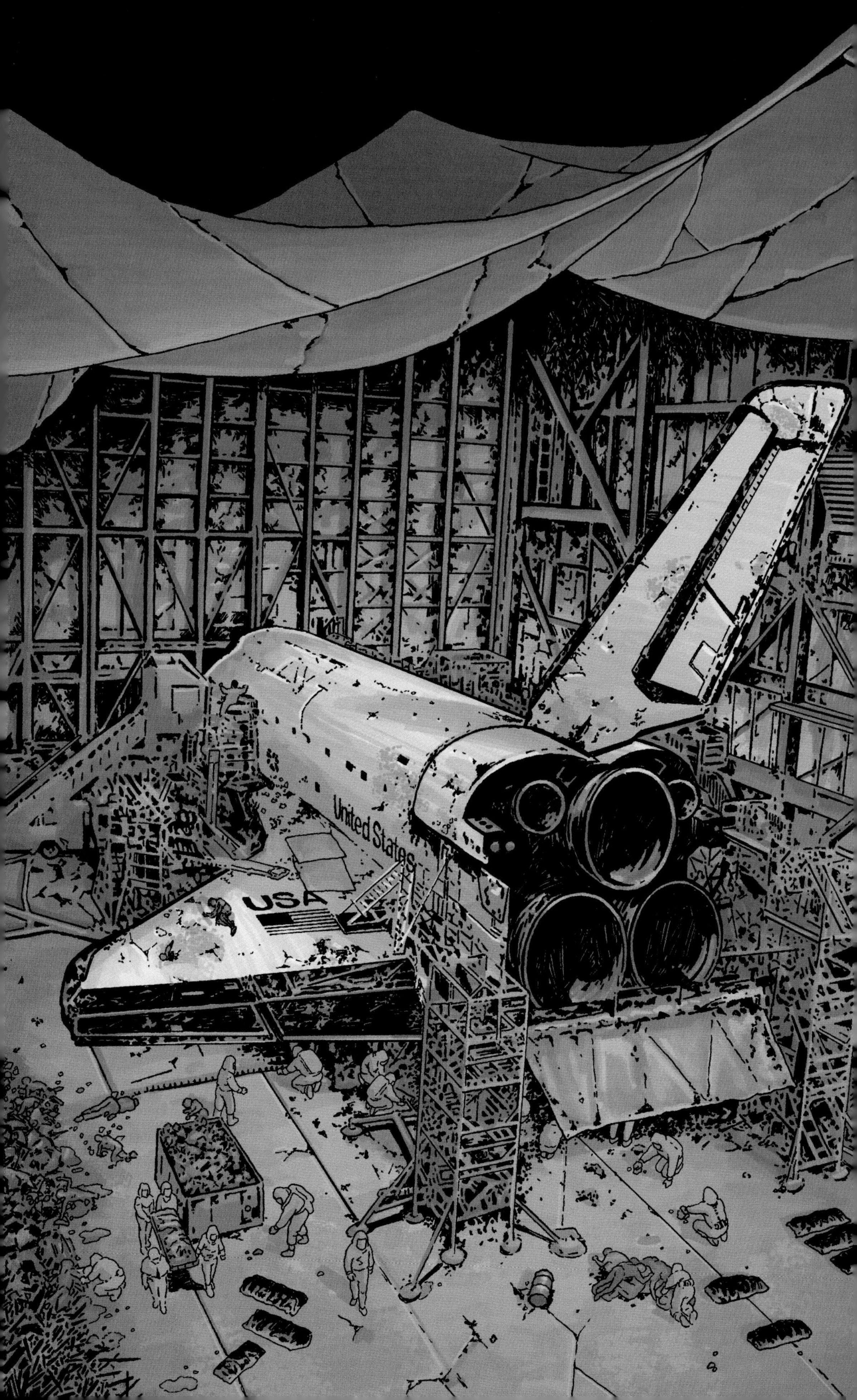
United States
USA

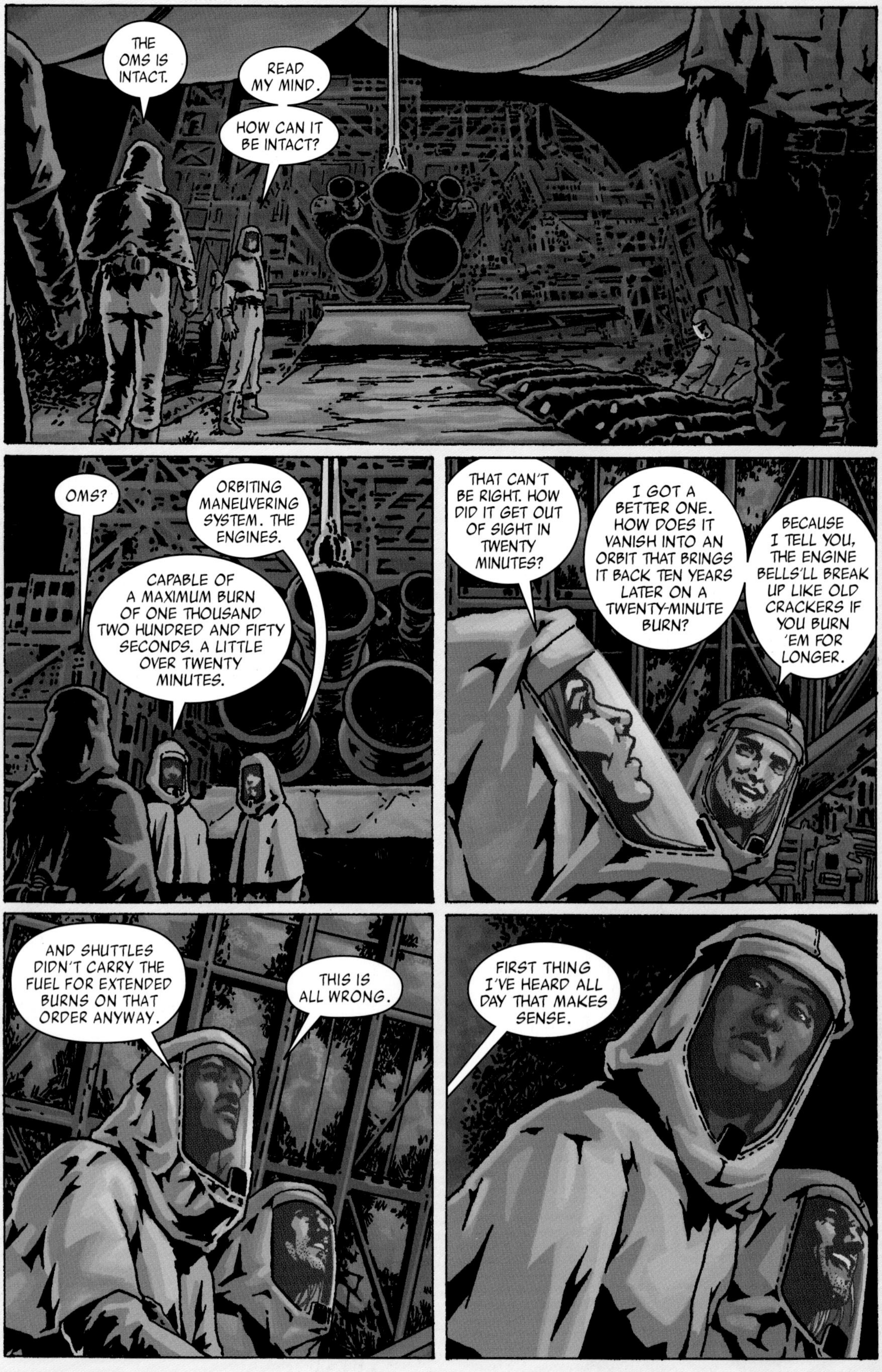
THE OMS IS INTACT.
READ MY MIND.
HOW CAN IT BE INTACT?
OMS?
ORBITING MANEUVERING SYSTEM. THE ENGINES.
CAPABLE OF A MAXIMUM BURN OF ONE THOUSAND TWO HUNDRED AND FIFTY SECONDS. A LITTLE OVER TWENTY MINUTES.
THAT CAN'T BE RIGHT. HOW DID IT GET OUT OF SIGHT IN TWENTY MINUTES?
I GOT A BETTER ONE. HOW DOES IT VANISH INTO AN ORBIT THAT BRINGS IT BACK TEN YEARS LATER ON A TWENTY-MINUTE BURN?
BECAUSE I TELL YOU, THE ENGINE BELLS'LL BREAK UP LIKE OLD CRACKERS IF YOU BURN 'EM FOR LONGER.
AND SHUTTLES DIDN'T CARRY THE FUEL FOR EXTENDED BURNS ON THAT ORDER ANYWAY.
THIS IS ALL WRONG.
FIRST THING I'VE HEARD ALL DAY THAT MAKES SENSE.

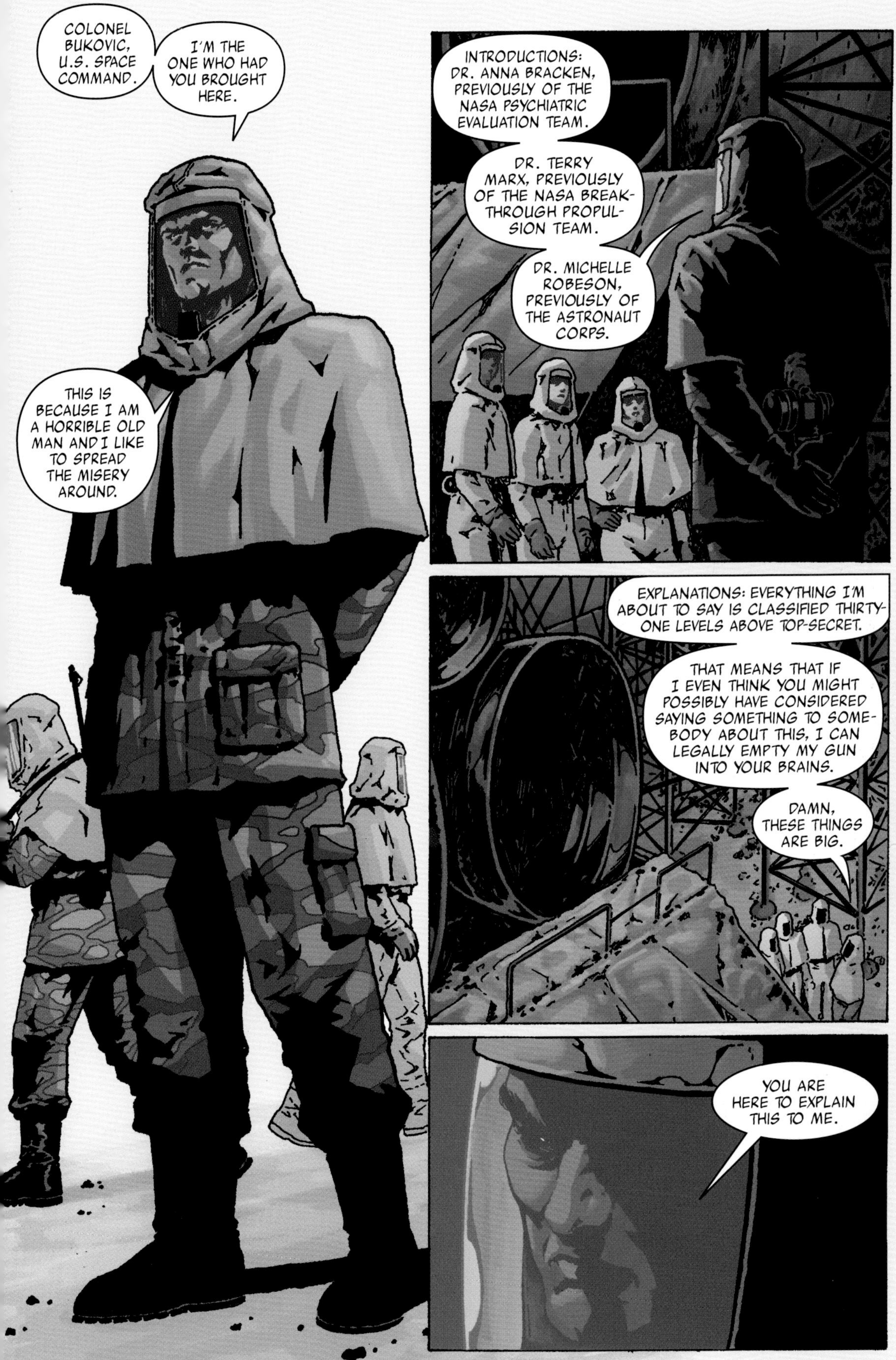

COLONEL BUKOVIC, U.S. SPACE COMMAND.
I'M THE ONE WHO HAD YOU BROUGHT HERE.
THIS IS BECAUSE I AM A HORRIBLE OLD MAN AND I LIKE TO SPREAD THE MISERY AROUND.
INTRODUCTIONS: DR. ANNA BRACKEN, PREVIOUSLY OF THE NASA PSYCHIATRIC EVALUATION TEAM.
DR. TERRY MARX, PREVIOUSLY OF THE NASA BREAK-THROUGH PROPUL-SION TEAM.
DR. MICHELLE ROBESON, PREVIOUSLY OF THE ASTRONAUT CORPS.
EXPLANATIONS: EVERYTHING I'M ABOUT TO SAY IS CLASSIFIED THIRTY-ONE LEVELS ABOVE TOP-SECRET.
THAT MEANS THAT IF I EVEN THINK YOU MIGHT POSSIBLY HAVE CONSIDERED SAYING SOMETHING TO SOME-BODY ABOUT THIS, I CAN LEGALLY EMPTY MY GUN INTO YOUR BRAINS.
DAMN, THESE THINGS ARE BIG.
YOU ARE HERE TO EXPLAIN THIS TO ME.

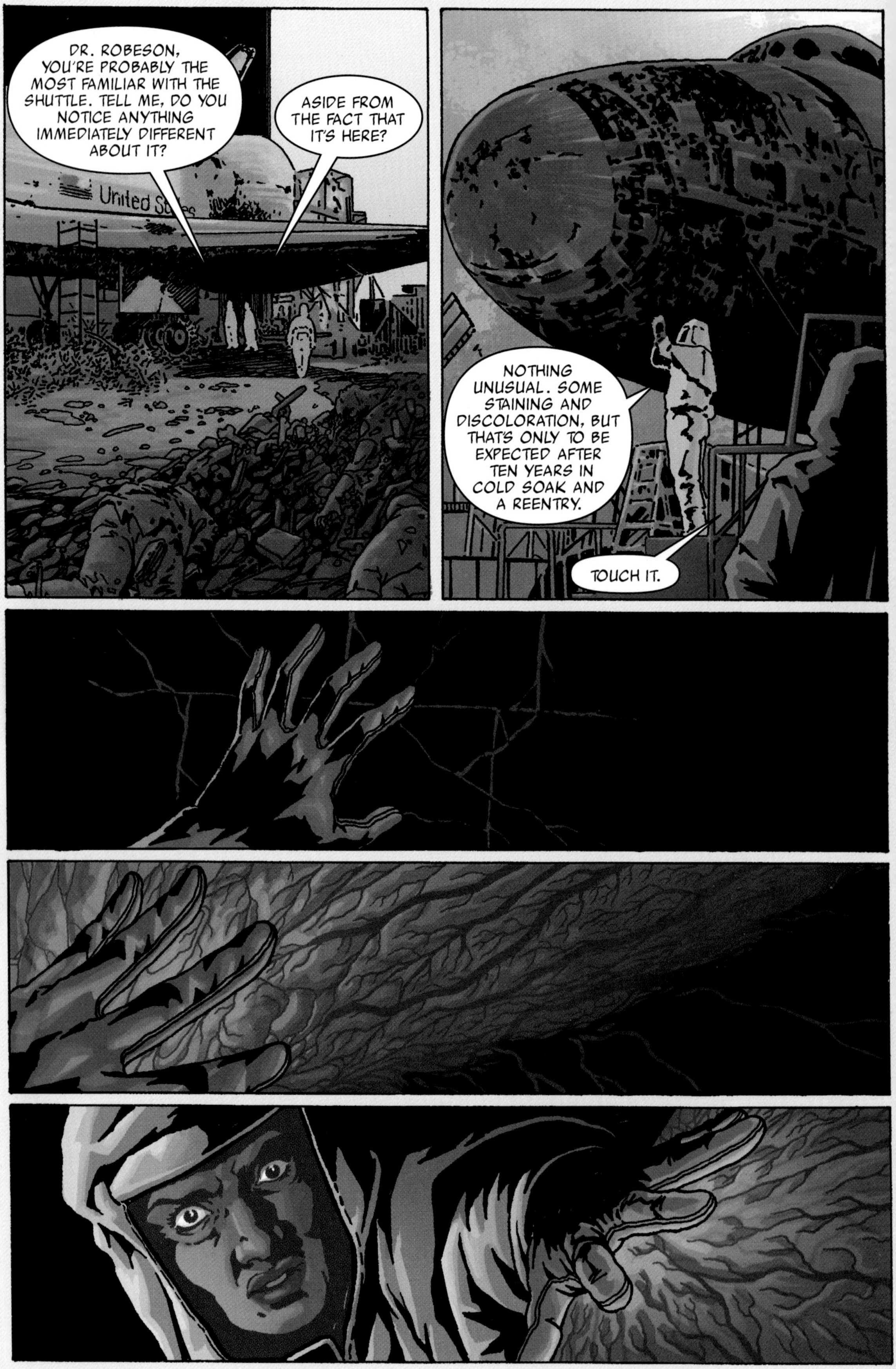
DR. ROBESON, YOU'RE PROBABLY THE MOST FAMILIAR WITH THE SHUTTLE. TELL ME, DO YOU NOTICE ANYTHING IMMEDIATELY DIFFERENT ABOUT IT?
ASIDE FROM THE FACT THAT IT'S HERE?
NOTHING UNUSUAL. SOME STAINING AND DISCOLORATION, BUT THAT'S ONLY TO BE EXPECTED AFTER TEN YEARS IN COLD SOAK AND A REENTRY.
TOUCH IT.

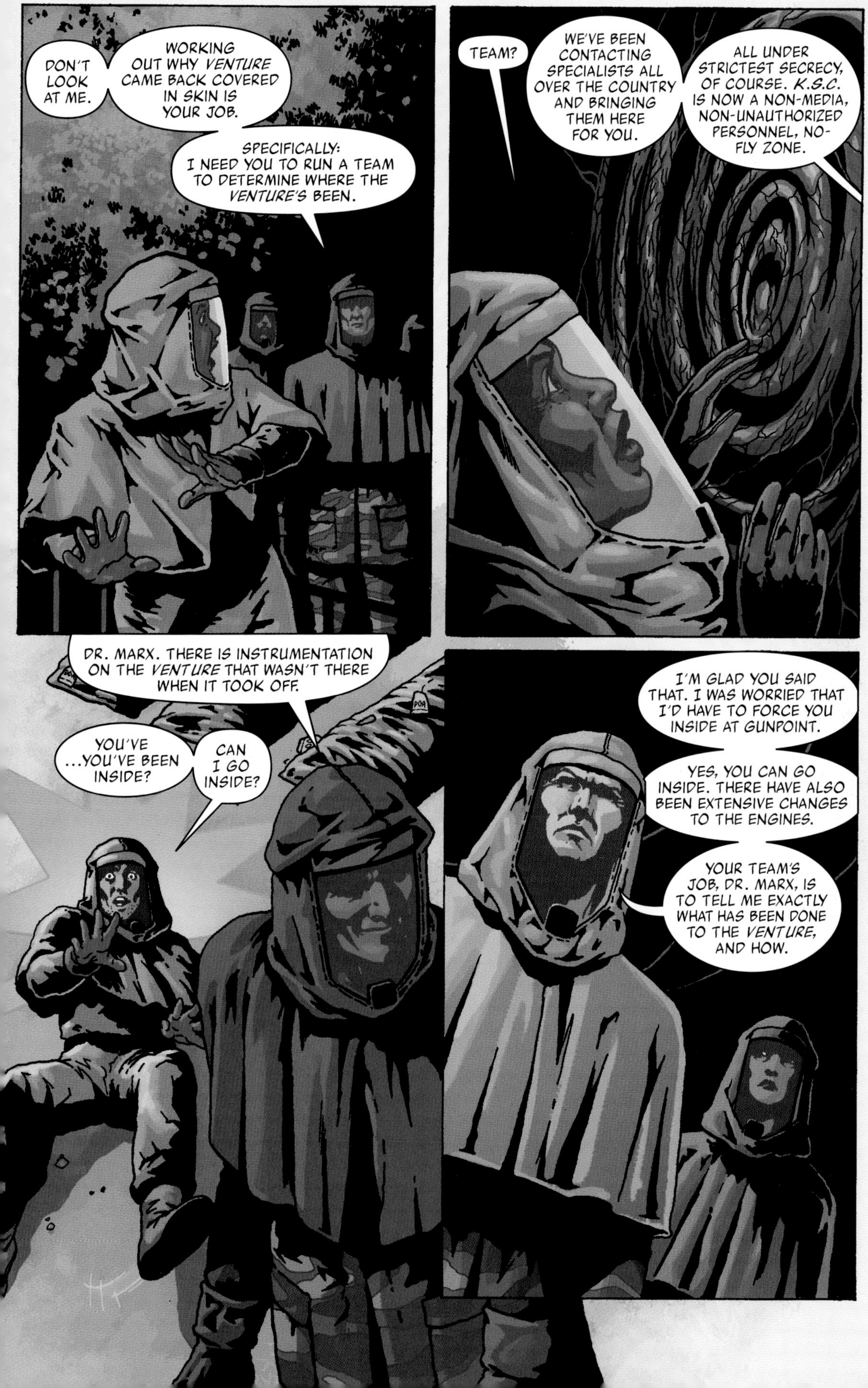
DON'T LOOK AT ME.
WORKING OUT WHY VENTURE CAME BACK COVERED IN SKIN IS YOUR JOB.
SPECIFICALLY: I NEED YOU TO RUN A TEAM TO DETERMINE WHERE THE VENTURE'S BEEN.
TEAM?
WE'VE BEEN CONTACTING SPECIALISTS ALL OVER THE COUNTRY AND BRINGING THEM HERE FOR YOU.
ALL UNDER STRICTEST SECRECY, OF COURSE. K.S.C. IS NOW A NON-MEDIA, NON-UNAUTHORIZED PERSONNEL, NO-FLY ZONE.
DR. MARX. THERE IS INSTRUMENTATION ON THE VENTURE THAT WASN'T THERE WHEN IT TOOK OFF.
YOU'VE ...YOU'VE BEEN INSIDE?
CAN I GO INSIDE?
I'M GLAD YOU SAID THAT. I WAS WORRIED THAT I'D HAVE TO FORCE YOU INSIDE AT GUNPOINT.
YES, YOU CAN GO INSIDE. THERE HAVE ALSO BEEN EXTENSIVE CHANGES TO THE ENGINES.
YOUR TEAM'S JOB, DR. MARX, IS TO TELL ME EXACTLY WHAT HAS BEEN DONE TO THE VENTURE, AND HOW.

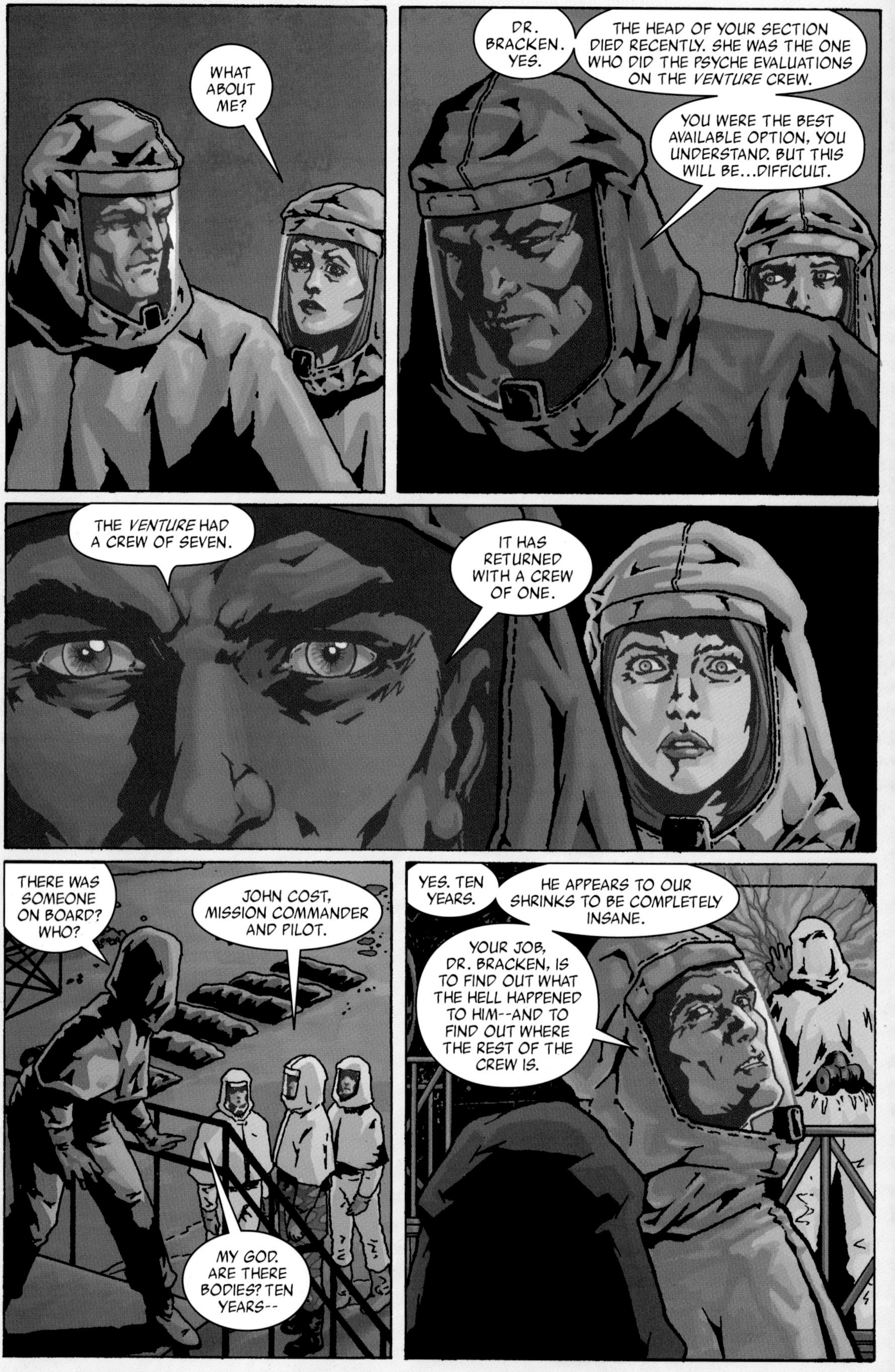
WHAT ABOUT ME?
DR. BRACKEN. YES.
THE HEAD OF YOUR SECTION DIED RECENTLY. SHE WAS THE ONE WHO DID THE PSYCHE EVALUATIONS ON THE *VENTURE* CREW.
YOU WERE THE BEST AVAILABLE OPTION, YOU UNDERSTAND. BUT THIS WILL BE...DIFFICULT.
THE *VENTURE* HAD A CREW OF SEVEN.
IT HAS RETURNED WITH A CREW OF ONE.
THERE WAS SOMEONE ON BOARD? WHO?
JOHN COST, MISSION COMMANDER AND PILOT.
MY GOD. ARE THERE BODIES? TEN YEARS--
YES. TEN YEARS.
HE APPEARS TO OUR SHRINKS TO BE COMPLETELY INSANE.
YOUR JOB, DR. BRACKEN, IS TO FIND OUT WHAT THE HELL HAPPENED TO HIM--AND TO FIND OUT WHERE THE REST OF THE CREW IS.

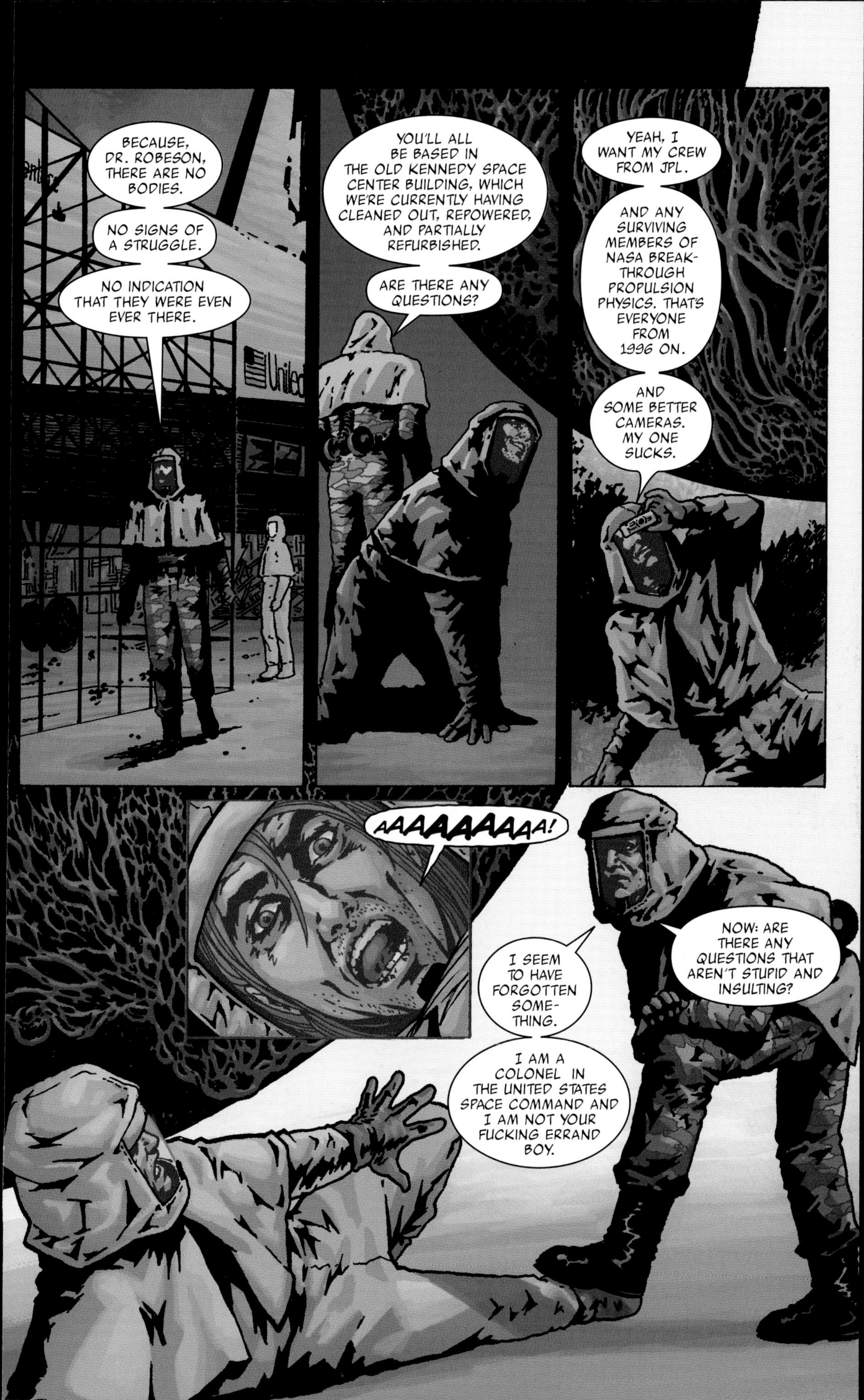
BECAUSE, DR. ROBESON, THERE ARE NO BODIES.
NO SIGNS OF A STRUGGLE.
NO INDICATION THAT THEY WERE EVEN EVER THERE.
YOU'LL ALL BE BASED IN THE OLD KENNEDY SPACE CENTER BUILDING, WHICH WE'RE CURRENTLY HAVING CLEANED OUT, REPOWERED, AND PARTIALLY REFURBISHED.
ARE THERE ANY QUESTIONS?
YEAH, I WANT MY CREW FROM JPL.
AND ANY SURVIVING MEMBERS OF NASA BREAK-THROUGH PROPULSION PHYSICS. THAT'S EVERYONE FROM 1996 ON.
AND SOME BETTER CAMERAS. MY ONE SUCKS.
AAAAAAAAA!
I SEEM TO HAVE FORGOTTEN SOME-THING.
I AM A COLONEL IN THE UNITED STATES SPACE COMMAND AND I AM NOT YOUR FUCKING ERRAND BOY.
NOW: ARE THERE ANY QUESTIONS THAT AREN'T STUPID AND INSULTING?

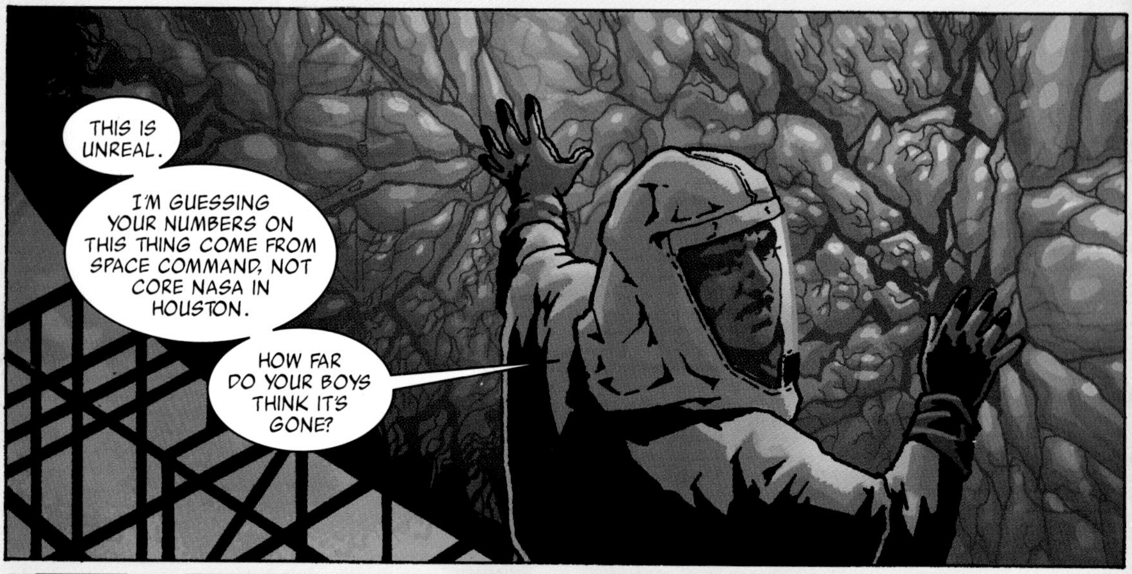
THIS IS UNREAL.
I'M GUESSING YOUR NUMBERS ON THIS THING COME FROM SPACE COMMAND, NOT CORE NASA IN HOUSTON.
HOW FAR DO YOUR BOYS THINK IT'S GONE?

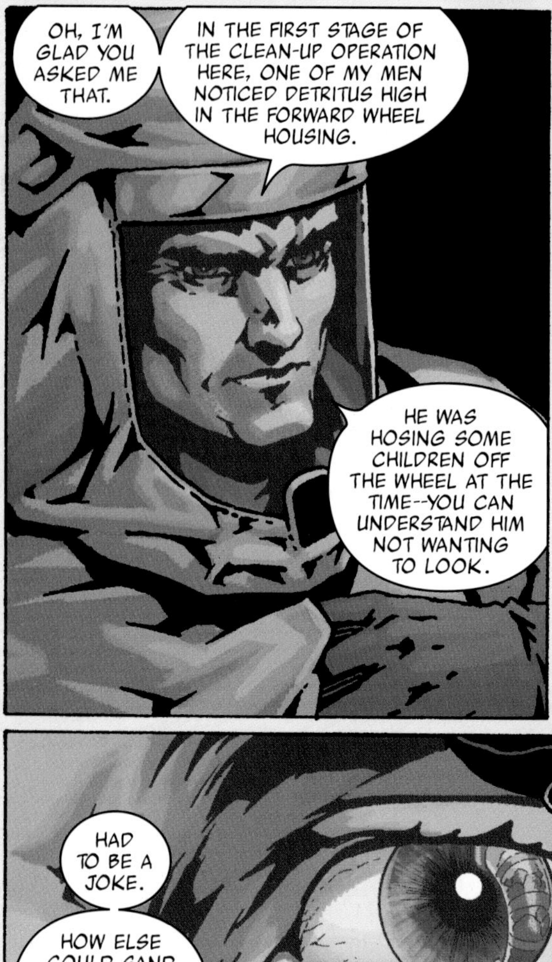
OH, I'M GLAD YOU ASKED ME THAT.
IN THE FIRST STAGE OF THE CLEAN-UP OPERATION HERE, ONE OF MY MEN NOTICED DETRITUS HIGH IN THE FORWARD WHEEL HOUSING.
HE WAS HOSING SOME CHILDREN OFF THE WHEEL AT THE TIME--YOU CAN UNDERSTAND HIM NOT WANTING TO LOOK.

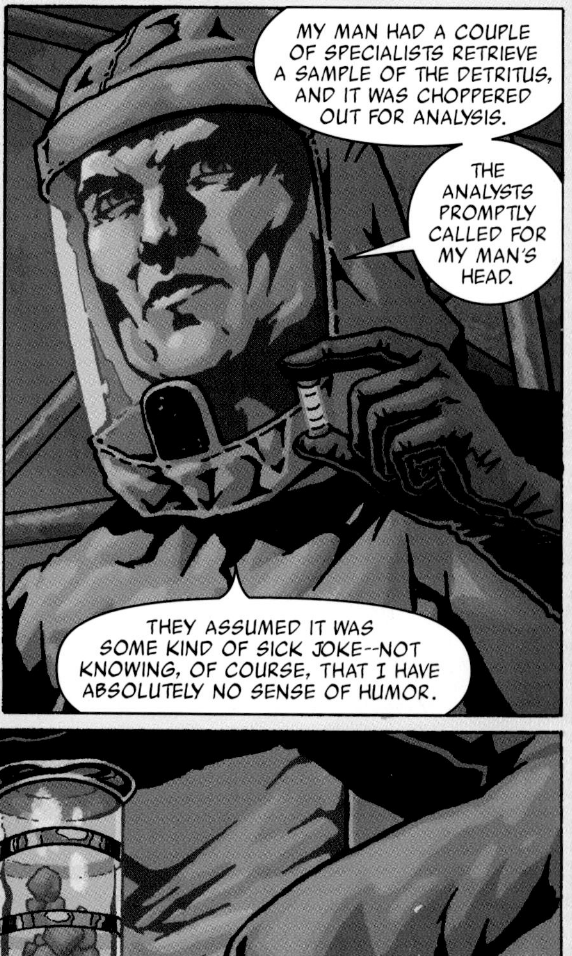
MY MAN HAD A COUPLE OF SPECIALISTS RETRIEVE A SAMPLE OF THE DETRITUS, AND IT WAS CHOPPERED OUT FOR ANALYSIS.
THE ANALYSTS PROMPTLY CALLED FOR MY MAN'S HEAD.
THEY ASSUMED IT WAS SOME KIND OF SICK JOKE--NOT KNOWING, OF COURSE, THAT I HAVE ABSOLUTELY NO SENSE OF HUMOR.

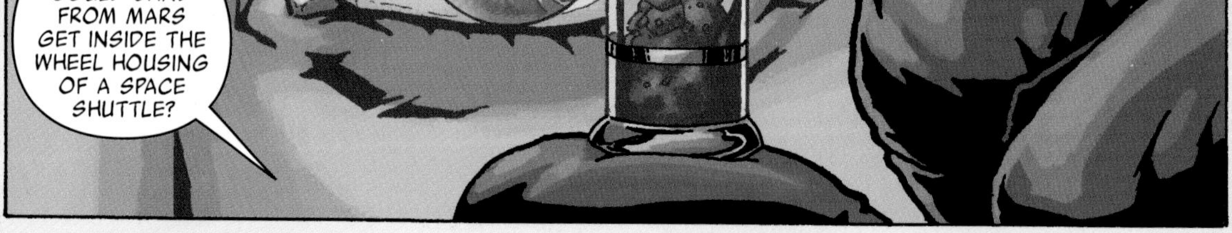
HAD TO BE A JOKE.
HOW ELSE COULD SAND FROM MARS GET INSIDE THE WHEEL HOUSING OF A SPACE SHUTTLE?

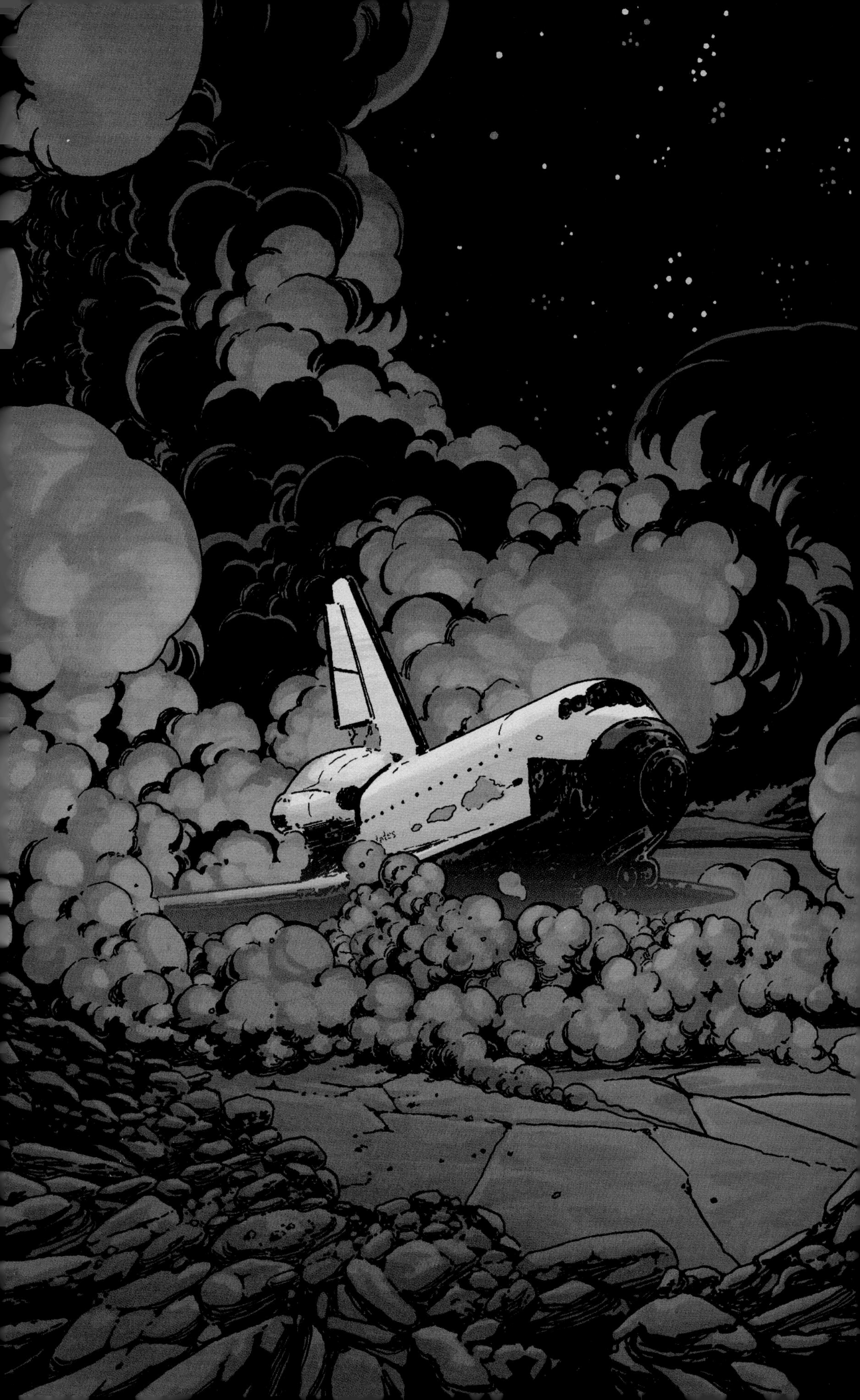

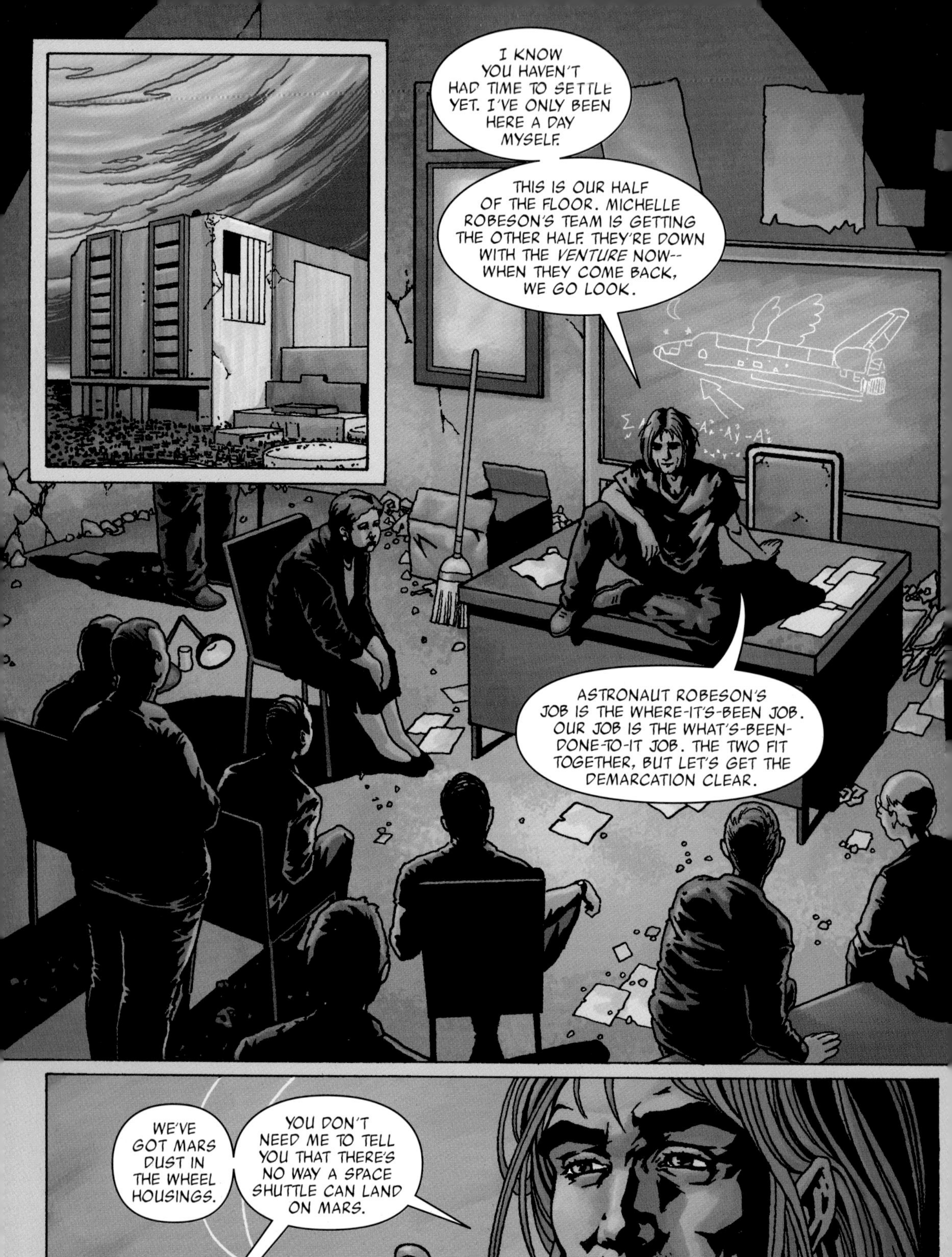
I KNOW YOU HAVEN'T HAD TIME TO SETTLE YET. I'VE ONLY BEEN HERE A DAY MYSELF.
THIS IS OUR HALF OF THE FLOOR. MICHELLE ROBESON'S TEAM IS GETTING THE OTHER HALF. THEY'RE DOWN WITH THE *VENTURE* NOW-- WHEN THEY COME BACK, WE GO LOOK.
ASTRONAUT ROBESON'S JOB IS THE WHERE-IT'S-BEEN JOB. OUR JOB IS THE WHAT'S-BEEN-DONE-TO-IT JOB. THE TWO FIT TOGETHER, BUT LET'S GET THE DEMARCATION CLEAR.

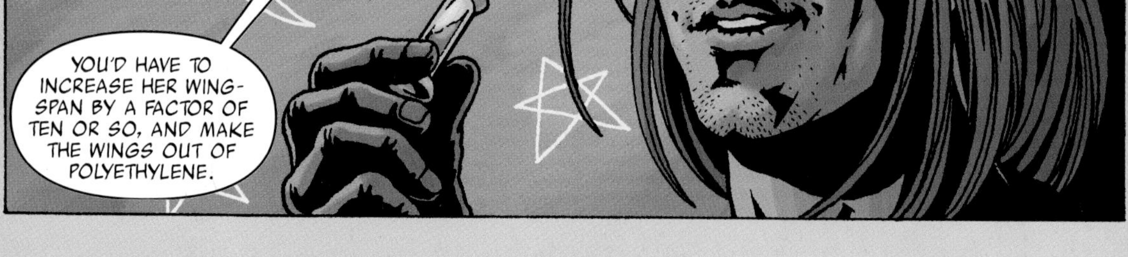
WE'VE GOT MARS DUST IN THE WHEEL HOUSINGS.
YOU DON'T NEED ME TO TELL YOU THAT THERE'S NO WAY A SPACE SHUTTLE CAN LAND ON MARS.
YOU'D HAVE TO INCREASE HER WING-SPAN BY A FACTOR OF TEN OR SO, AND MAKE THE WINGS OUT OF POLYETHYLENE.

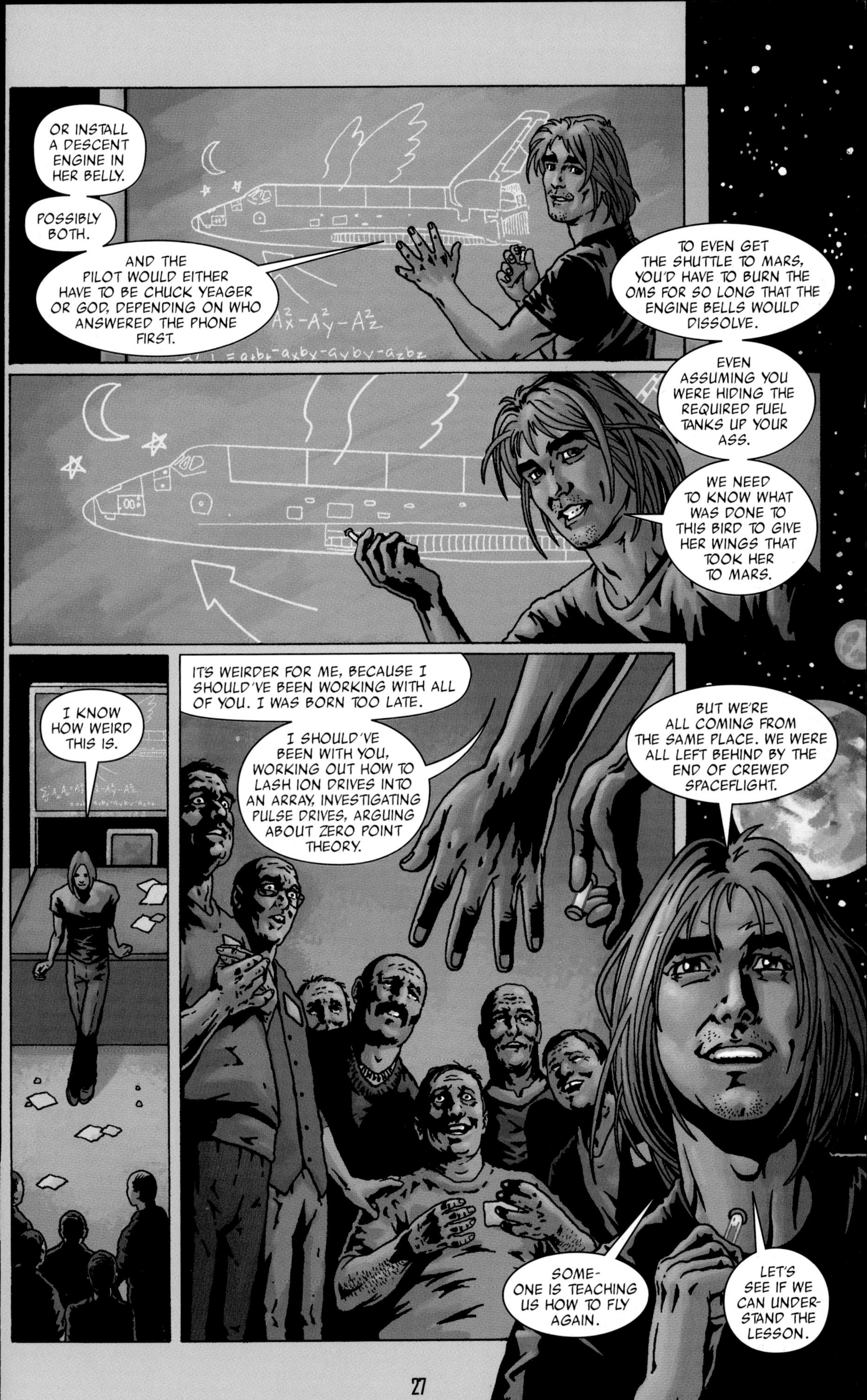
OR INSTALL A DESCENT ENGINE IN HER BELLY.
POSSIBLY BOTH.
AND THE PILOT WOULD EITHER HAVE TO BE CHUCK YEAGER OR GOD, DEPENDING ON WHO ANSWERED THE PHONE FIRST.
TO EVEN GET THE SHUTTLE TO MARS, YOU'D HAVE TO BURN THE OMS FOR SO LONG THAT THE ENGINE BELLS WOULD DISSOLVE.
EVEN ASSUMING YOU WERE HIDING THE REQUIRED FUEL TANKS UP YOUR ASS.
WE NEED TO KNOW WHAT WAS DONE TO THIS BIRD TO GIVE HER WINGS THAT TOOK HER TO MARS.
I KNOW HOW WEIRD THIS IS.
IT'S WEIRDER FOR ME, BECAUSE I SHOULD'VE BEEN WORKING WITH ALL OF YOU. I WAS BORN TOO LATE.
I SHOULD'VE BEEN WITH YOU, WORKING OUT HOW TO LASH ION DRIVES INTO AN ARRAY, INVESTIGATING PULSE DRIVES, ARGUING ABOUT ZERO POINT THEORY.
BUT WE'RE ALL COMING FROM THE SAME PLACE. WE WERE ALL LEFT BEHIND BY THE END OF CREWED SPACEFLIGHT.
SOME-ONE IS TEACHING US HOW TO FLY AGAIN.
LET'S SEE IF WE CAN UNDER-STAND THE LESSON.

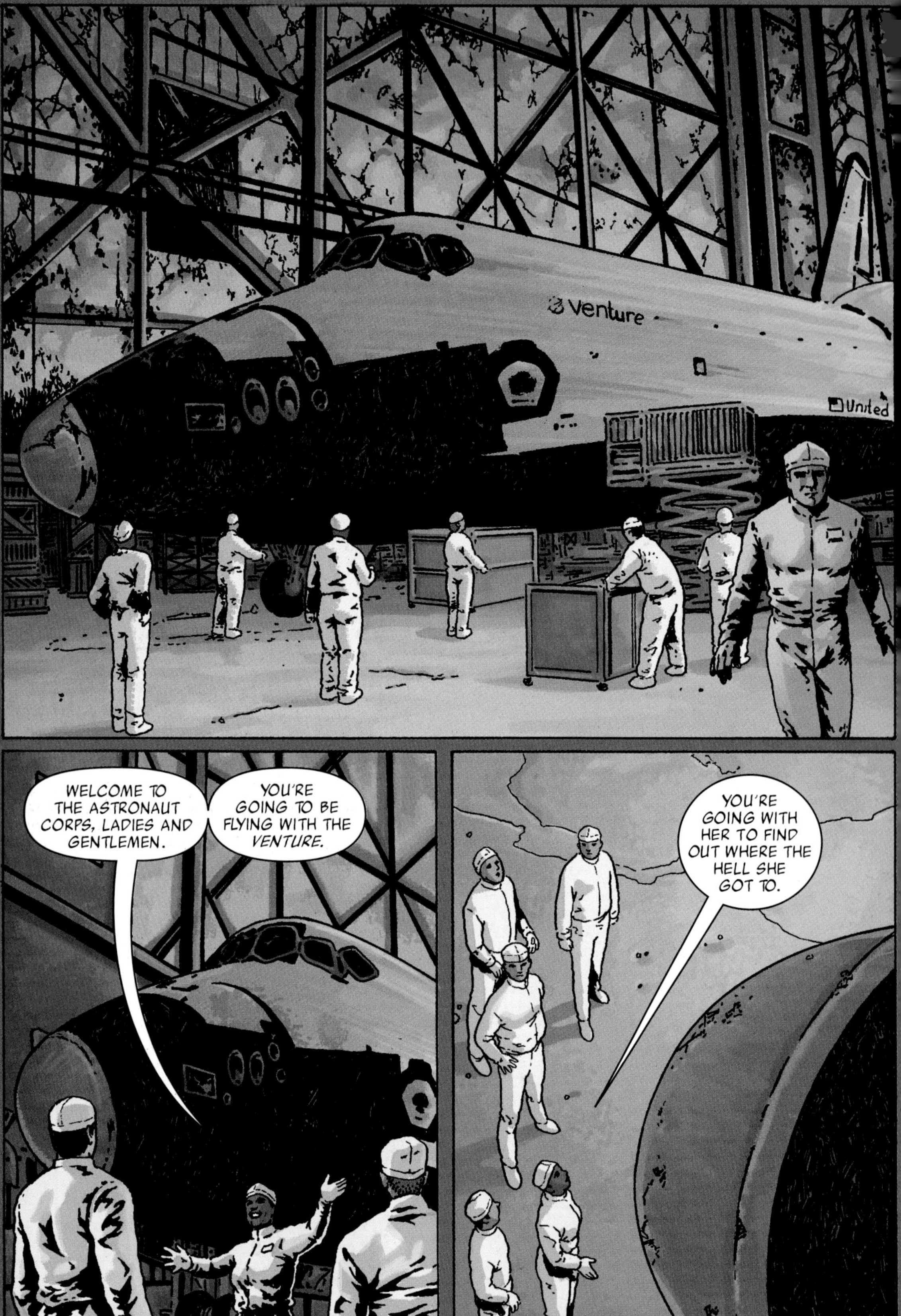
Venture
United
WELCOME TO THE ASTRONAUT CORPS, LADIES AND GENTLEMEN.
YOU'RE GOING TO BE FLYING WITH THE *VENTURE*.
YOU'RE GOING WITH HER TO FIND OUT WHERE THE HELL SHE GOT TO.

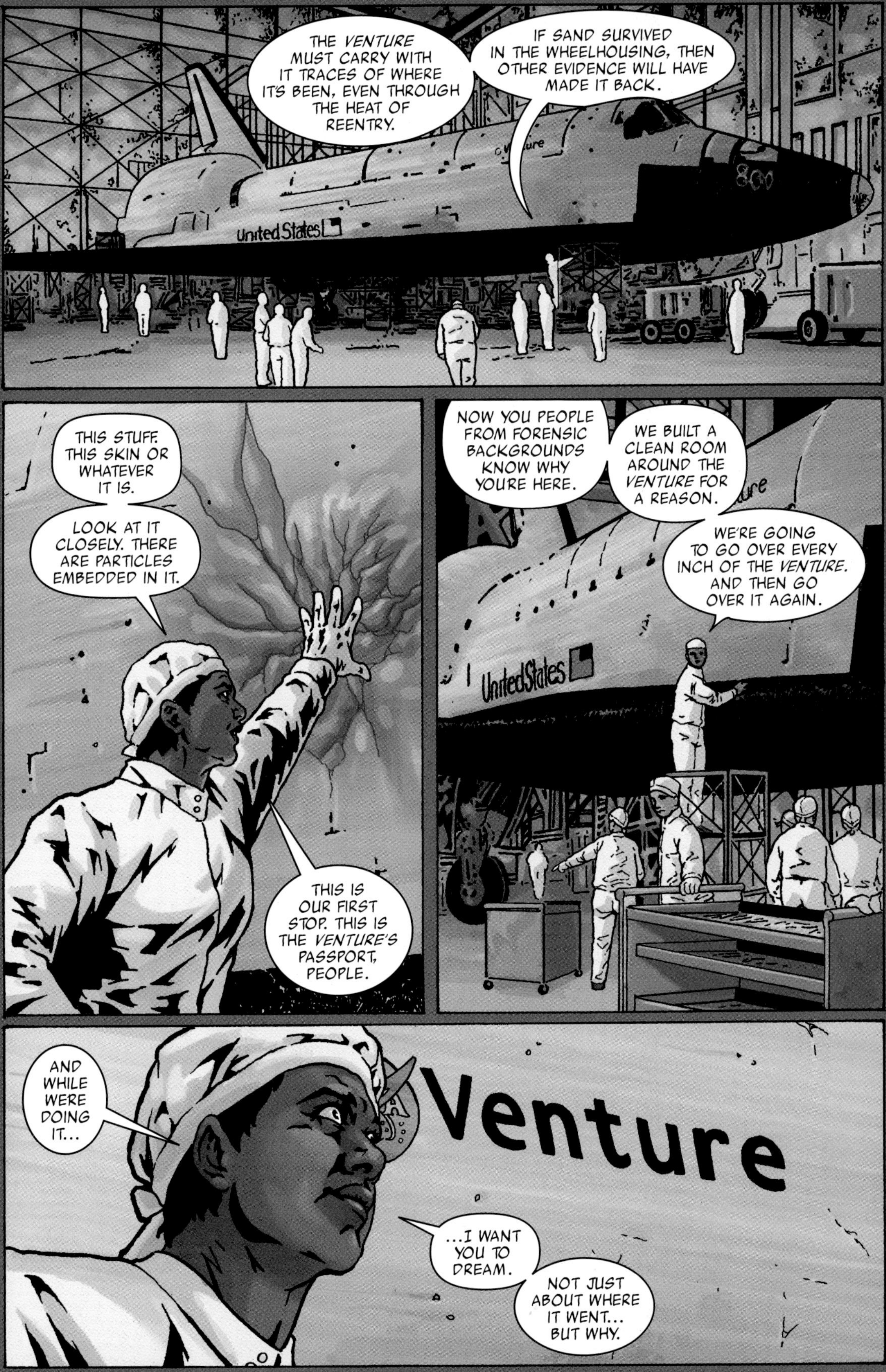
THE VENTURE MUST CARRY WITH IT TRACES OF WHERE IT'S BEEN, EVEN THROUGH THE HEAT OF REENTRY.
IF SAND SURVIVED IN THE WHEELHOUSING, THEN OTHER EVIDENCE WILL HAVE MADE IT BACK.
United States
THIS STUFF. THIS SKIN OR WHATEVER IT IS.
LOOK AT IT CLOSELY. THERE ARE PARTICLES EMBEDDED IN IT.
THIS IS OUR FIRST STOP. THIS IS THE VENTURE'S PASSPORT, PEOPLE.
NOW YOU PEOPLE FROM FORENSIC BACKGROUNDS KNOW WHY YOU'RE HERE.
WE BUILT A CLEAN ROOM AROUND THE VENTURE FOR A REASON.
WE'RE GOING TO GO OVER EVERY INCH OF THE VENTURE. AND THEN GO OVER IT AGAIN.
United States
AND WHILE WERE DOING IT...
Venture
...I WANT YOU TO DREAM.
NOT JUST ABOUT WHERE IT WENT... BUT WHY.

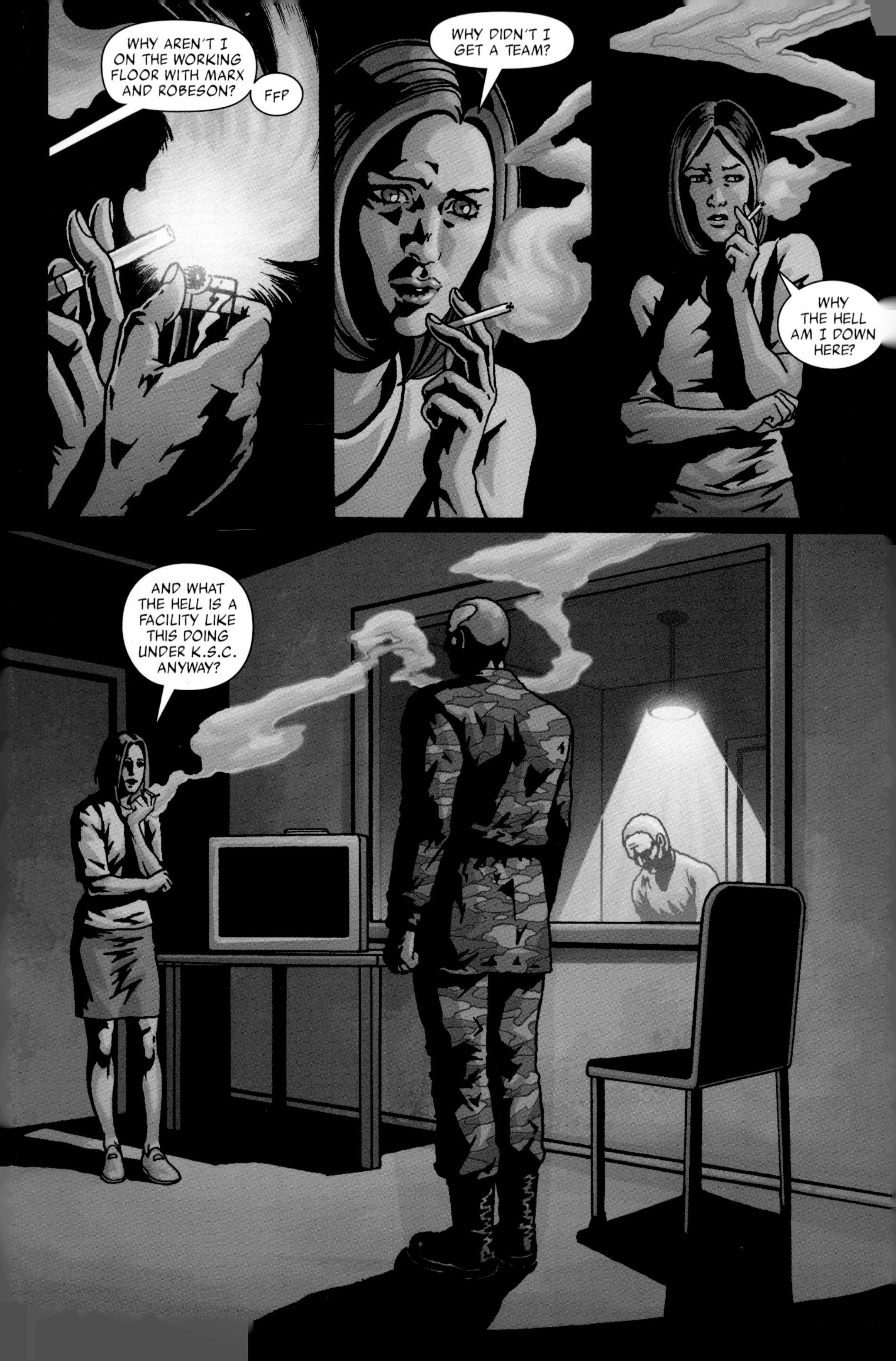
WHY AREN'T I ON THE WORKING FLOOR WITH MARX AND ROBESON?
FFP
WHY DIDN'T I GET A TEAM?
WHY THE HELL AM I DOWN HERE?
AND WHAT THE HELL IS A FACILITY LIKE THIS DOING UNDER K.S.C. ANYWAY?

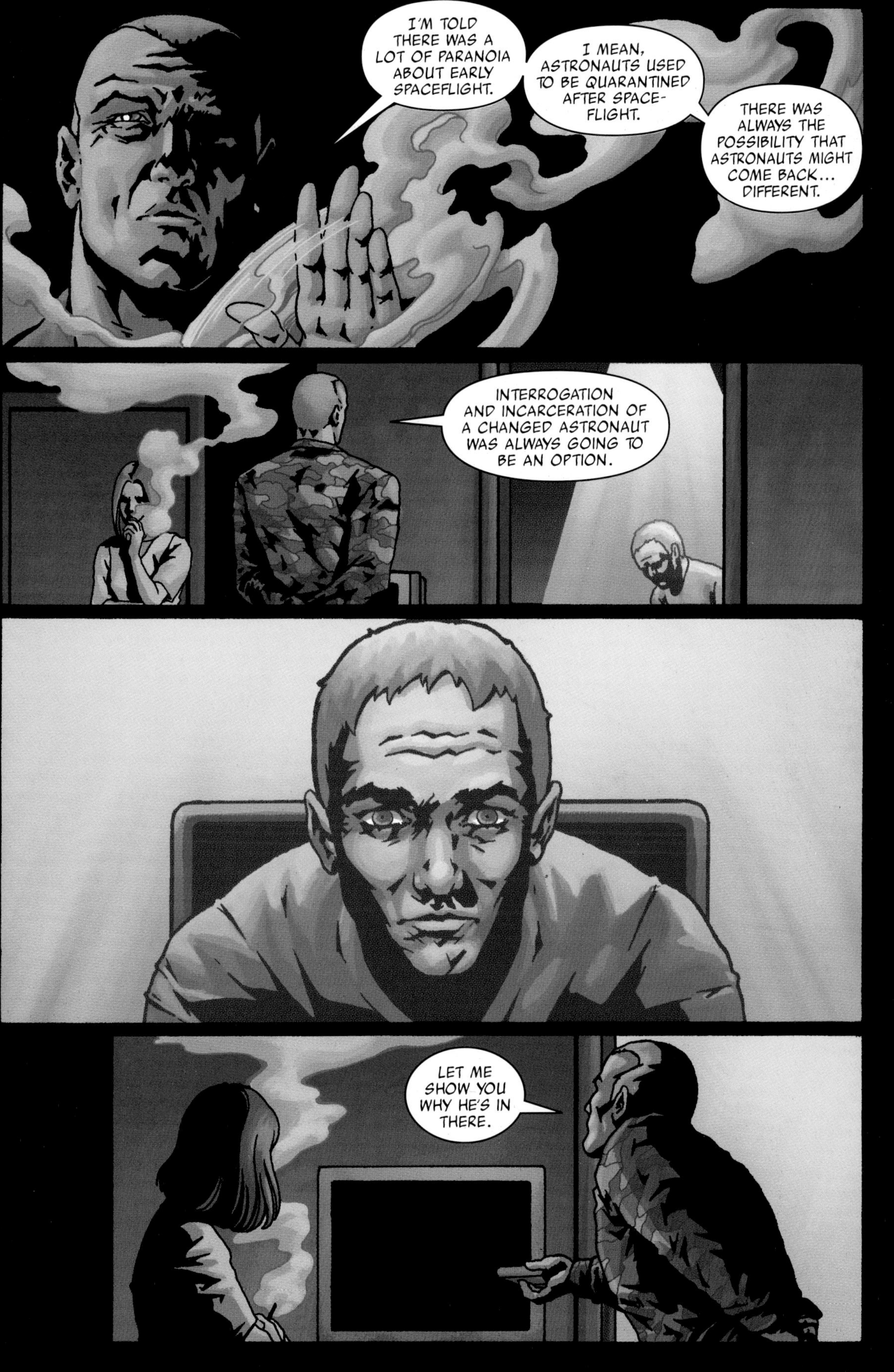
I'M TOLD THERE WAS A LOT OF PARANOIA ABOUT EARLY SPACEFLIGHT.
I MEAN, ASTRONAUTS USED TO BE QUARANTINED AFTER SPACE-FLIGHT.
THERE WAS ALWAYS THE POSSIBILITY THAT ASTRONAUTS MIGHT COME BACK... DIFFERENT.
INTERROGATION AND INCARCERATION OF A CHANGED ASTRONAUT WAS ALWAYS GOING TO BE AN OPTION.
LET ME SHOW YOU WHY HE'S IN THERE.

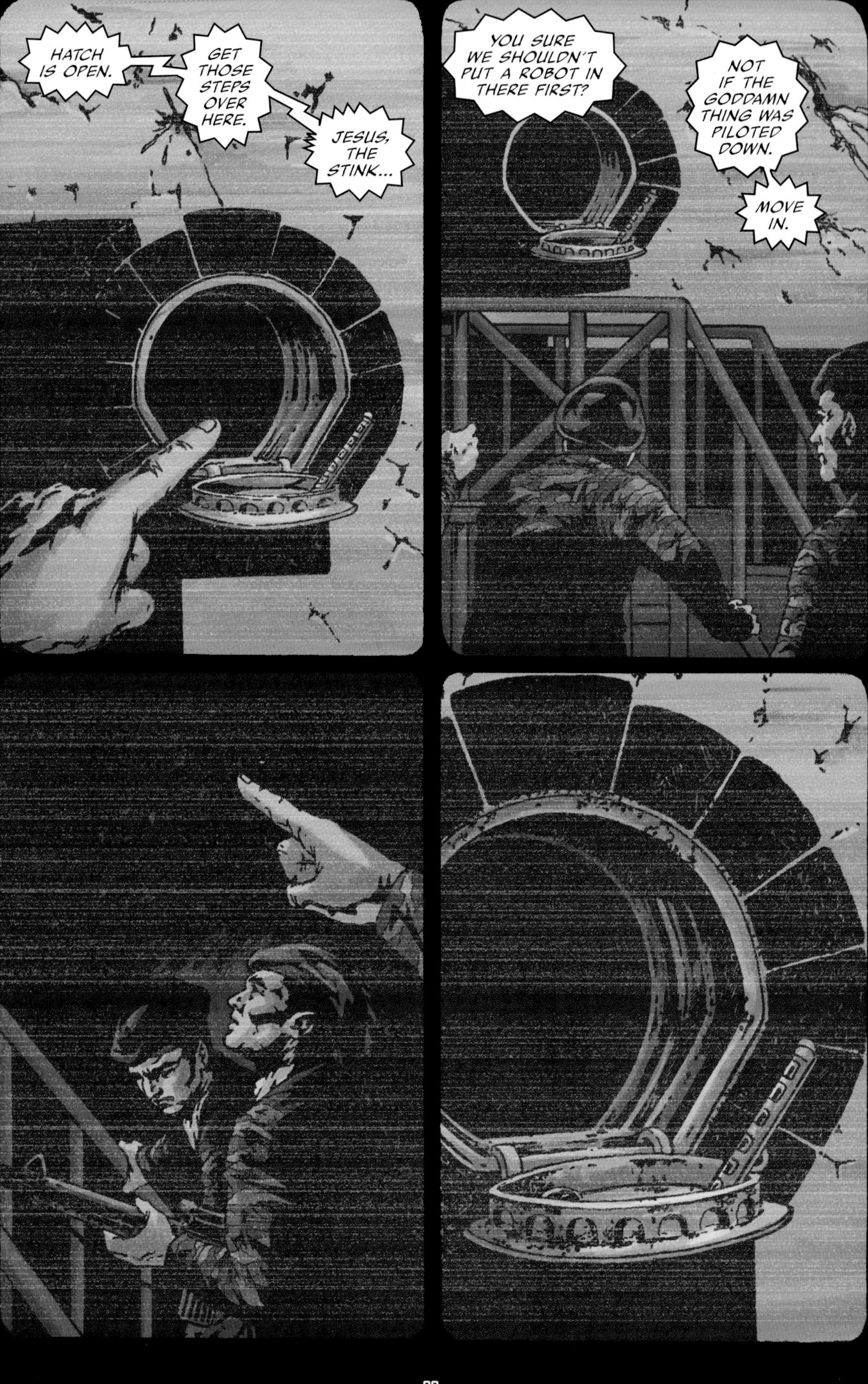
HATCH IS OPEN.
GET THOSE STEPS OVER HERE.
JESUS, THE STINK...
YOU SURE WE SHOULDN'T PUT A ROBOT IN THERE FIRST?
NOT IF THE GODDAMN THING WAS PILOTED DOWN.
MOVE IN.

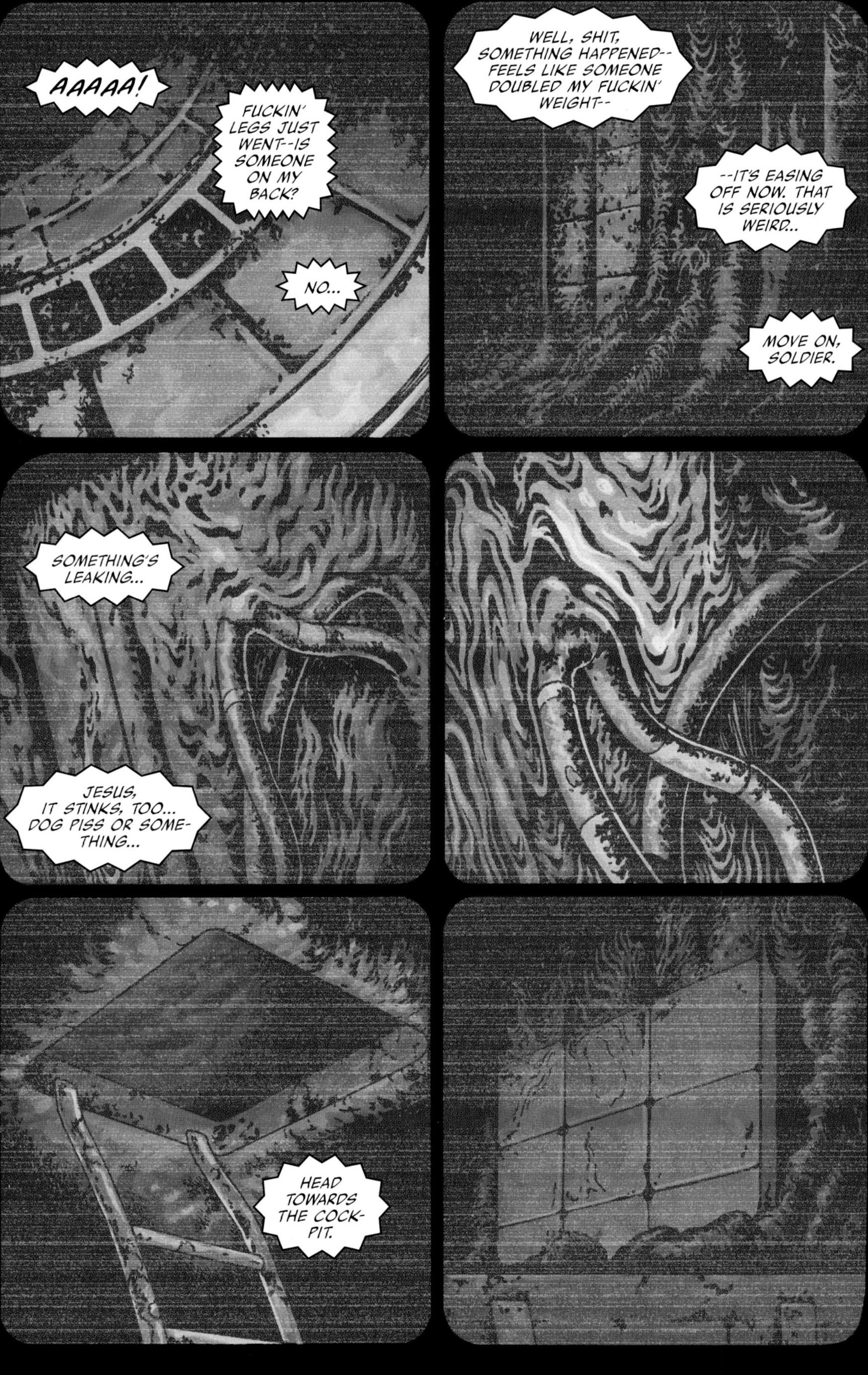
AAAAA!
FUCKIN' LEGS JUST WENT--IS SOMEONE ON MY BACK?
NO...
WELL, SHIT, SOMETHING HAPPENED--FEELS LIKE SOMEONE DOUBLED MY FUCKIN' WEIGHT--
--IT'S EASING OFF NOW. THAT IS SERIOUSLY WEIRD...
MOVE ON, SOLDIER.
SOMETHING'S LEAKING...
JESUS, IT STINKS, TOO... DOG PISS OR SOME-THING...
HEAD TOWARDS THE COCK-PIT.

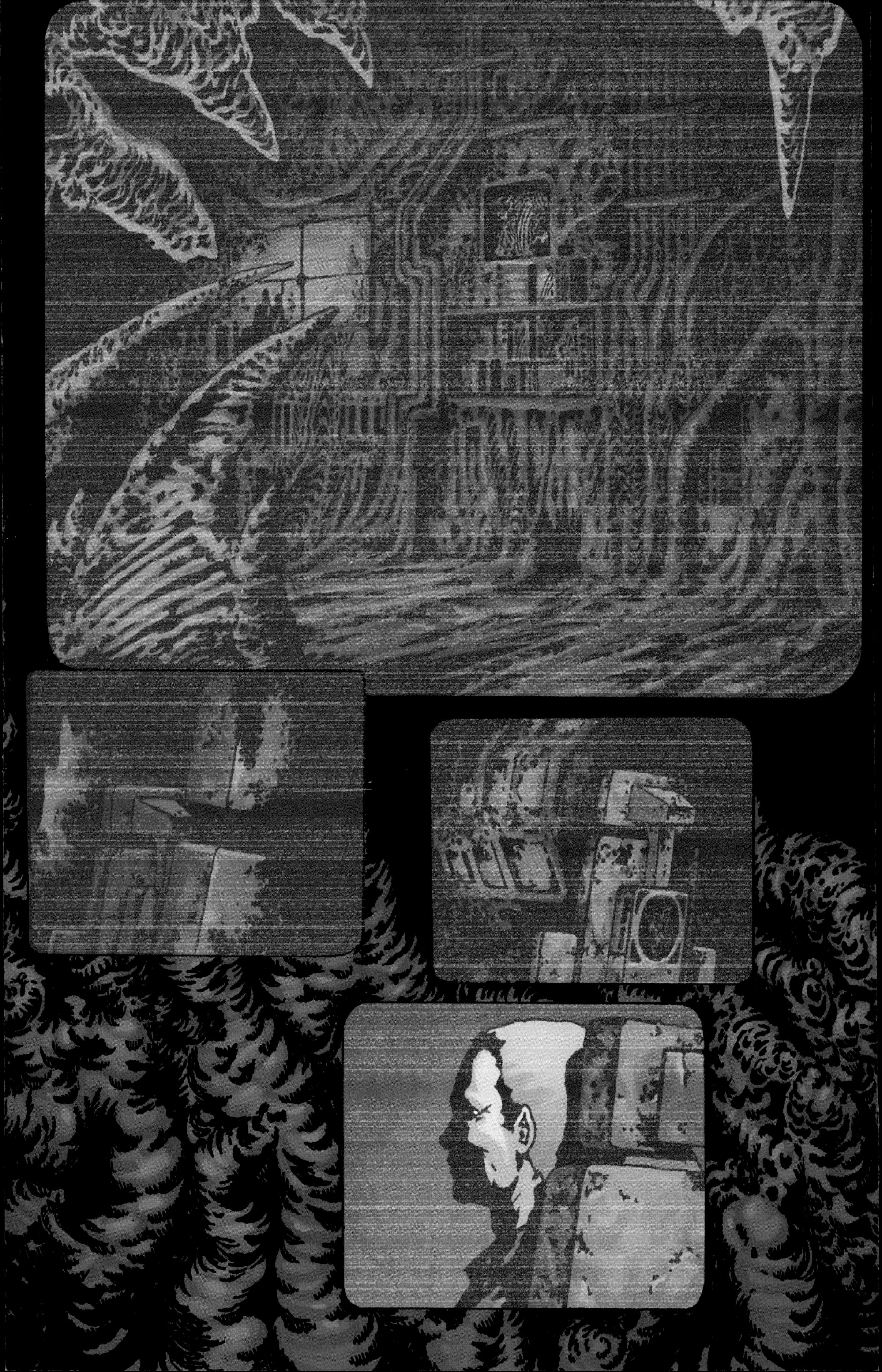

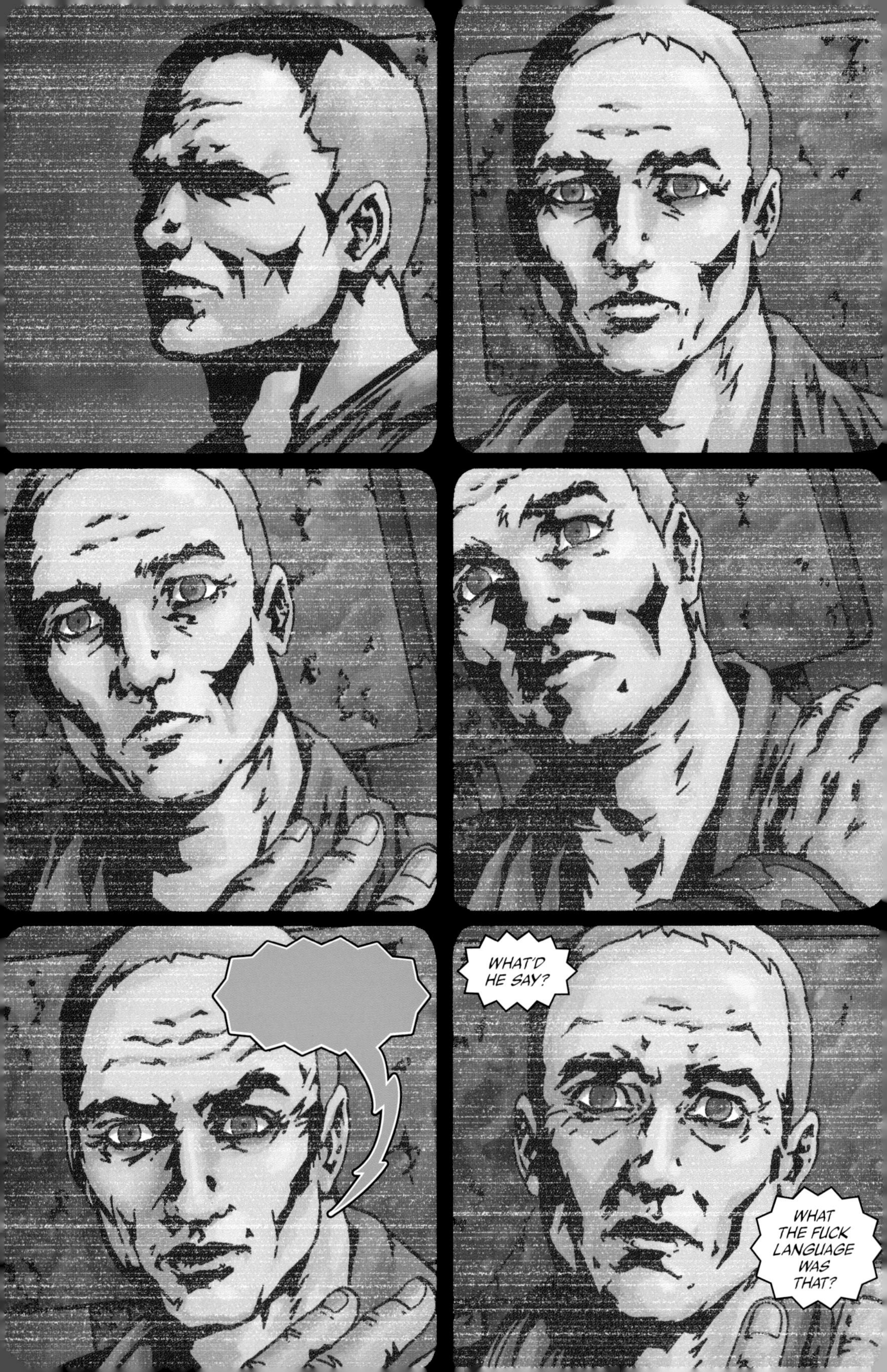
WHAT'D HE SAY?
WHAT THE FUCK LANGUAGE WAS THAT?

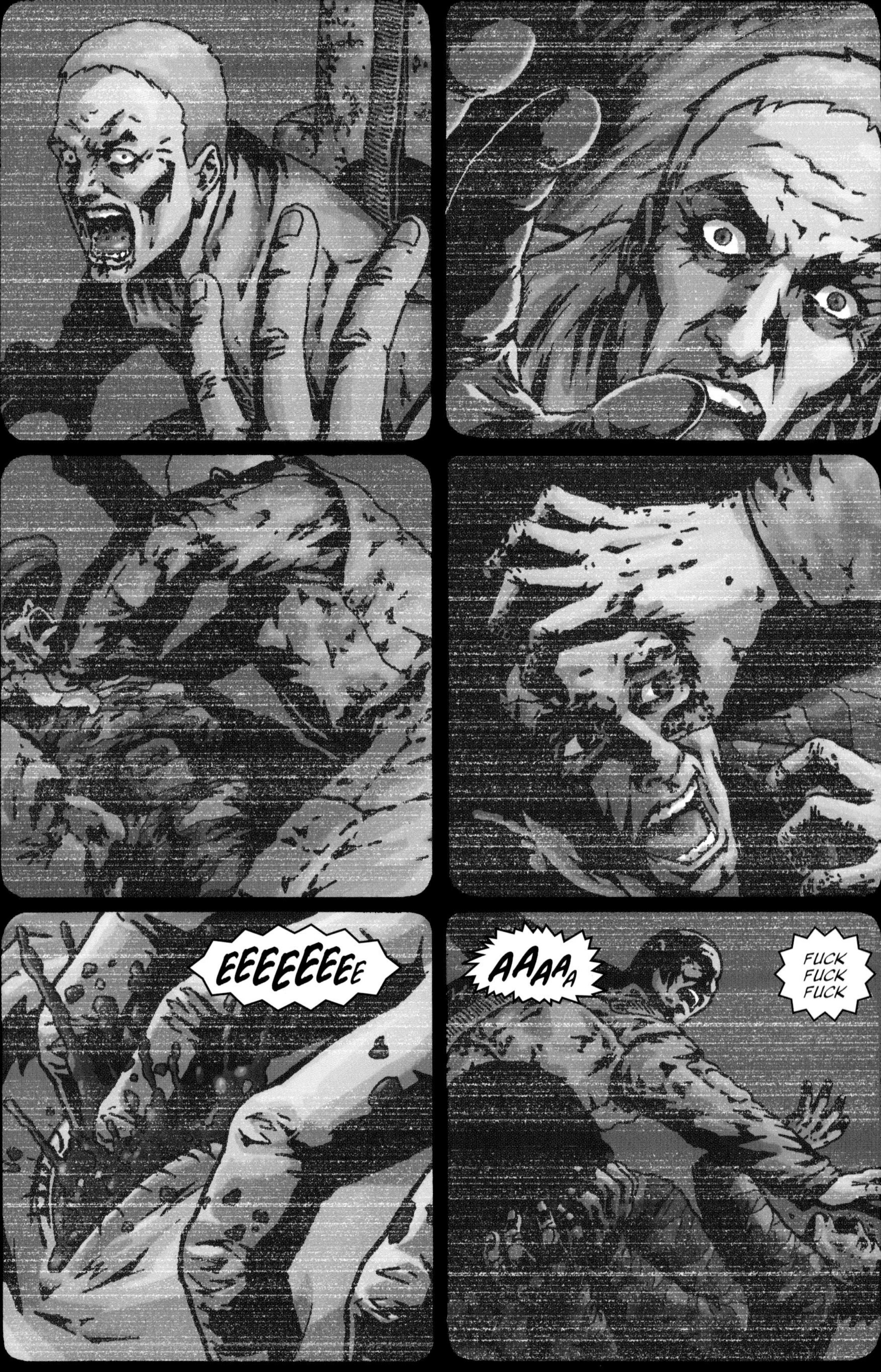
EEEEEEEEE
AAAAA
FUCK
FUCK
FUCK

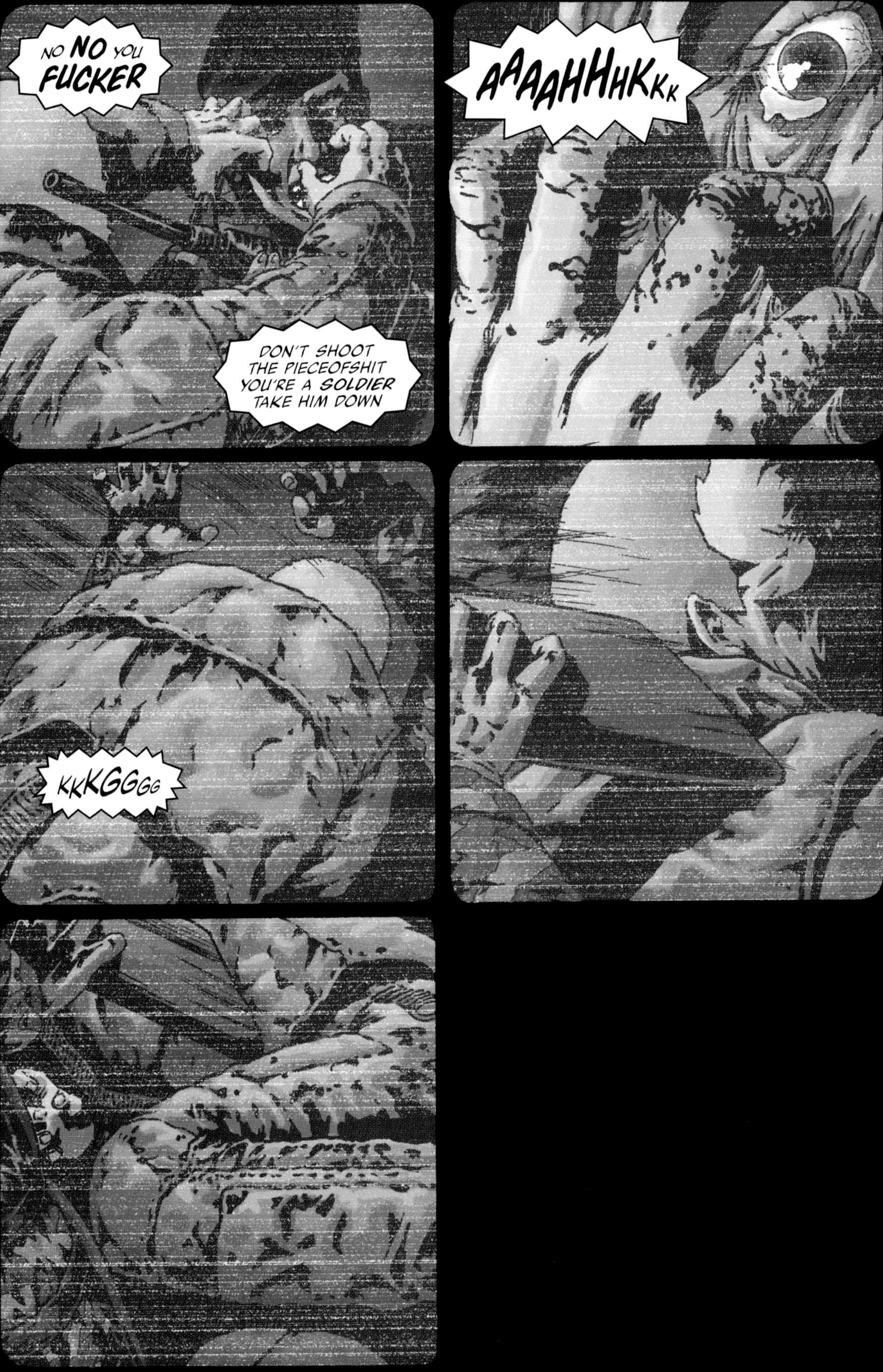
NO NO YOU FUCKER
DON'T SHOOT THE PIECEOFSHIT YOU'RE A SOLDIER TAKE HIM DOWN
AAAAHHHKKK
KKKGGGG

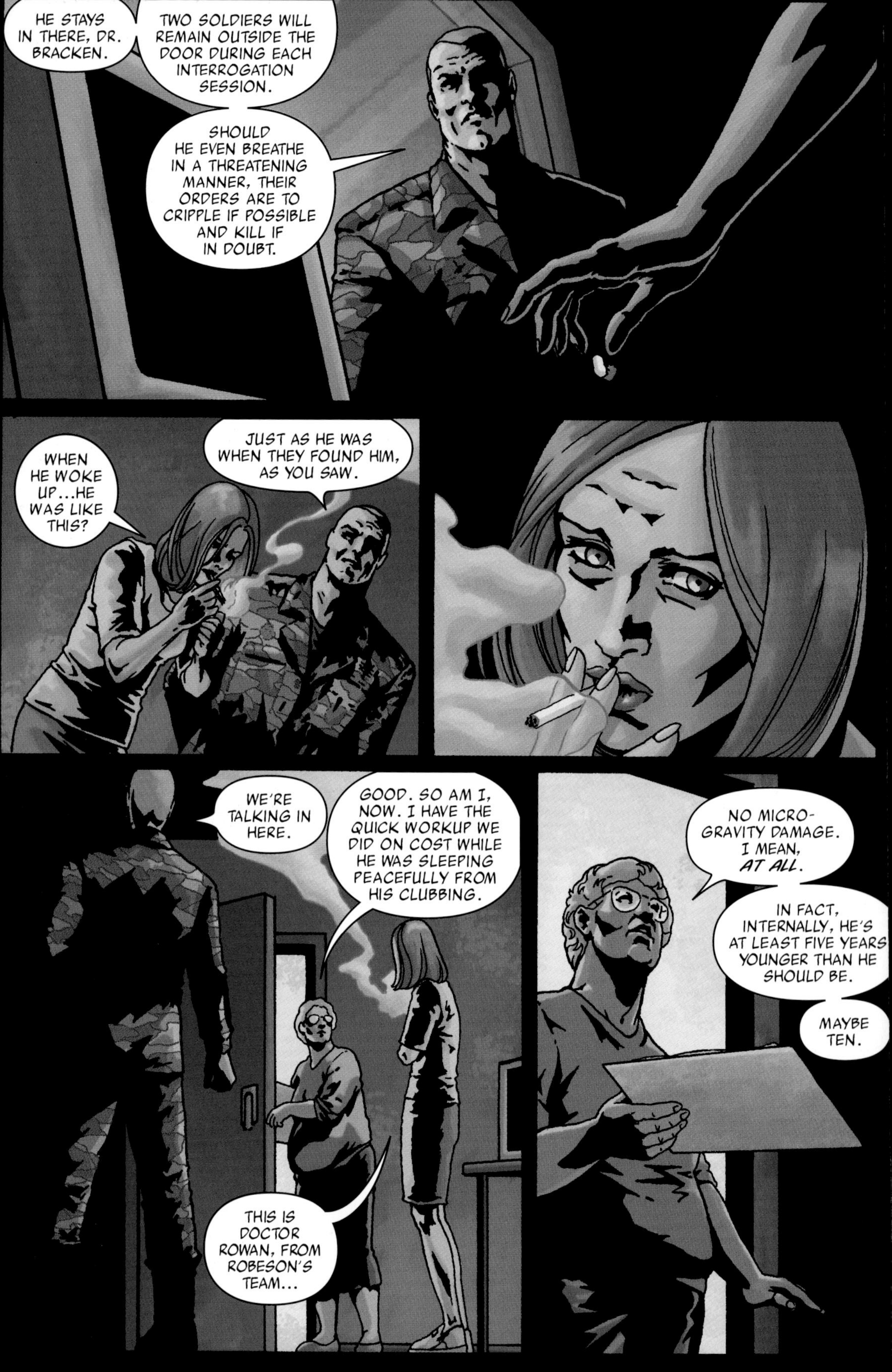
HE STAYS IN THERE, DR. BRACKEN.
TWO SOLDIERS WILL REMAIN OUTSIDE THE DOOR DURING EACH INTERROGATION SESSION.
SHOULD HE EVEN BREATHE IN A THREATENING MANNER, THEIR ORDERS ARE TO CRIPPLE IF POSSIBLE AND KILL IF IN DOUBT.
WHEN HE WOKE UP...HE WAS LIKE THIS?
JUST AS HE WAS WHEN THEY FOUND HIM, AS YOU SAW.
WE'RE TALKING IN HERE.
GOOD. SO AM I, NOW. I HAVE THE QUICK WORKUP WE DID ON COST WHILE HE WAS SLEEPING PEACEFULLY FROM HIS CLUBBING.
THIS IS DOCTOR ROWAN, FROM ROBESON'S TEAM...
NO MICRO-GRAVITY DAMAGE. I MEAN, *AT ALL*.
IN FACT, INTERNALLY, HE'S AT LEAST FIVE YEARS YOUNGER THAN HE SHOULD BE.
MAYBE TEN.

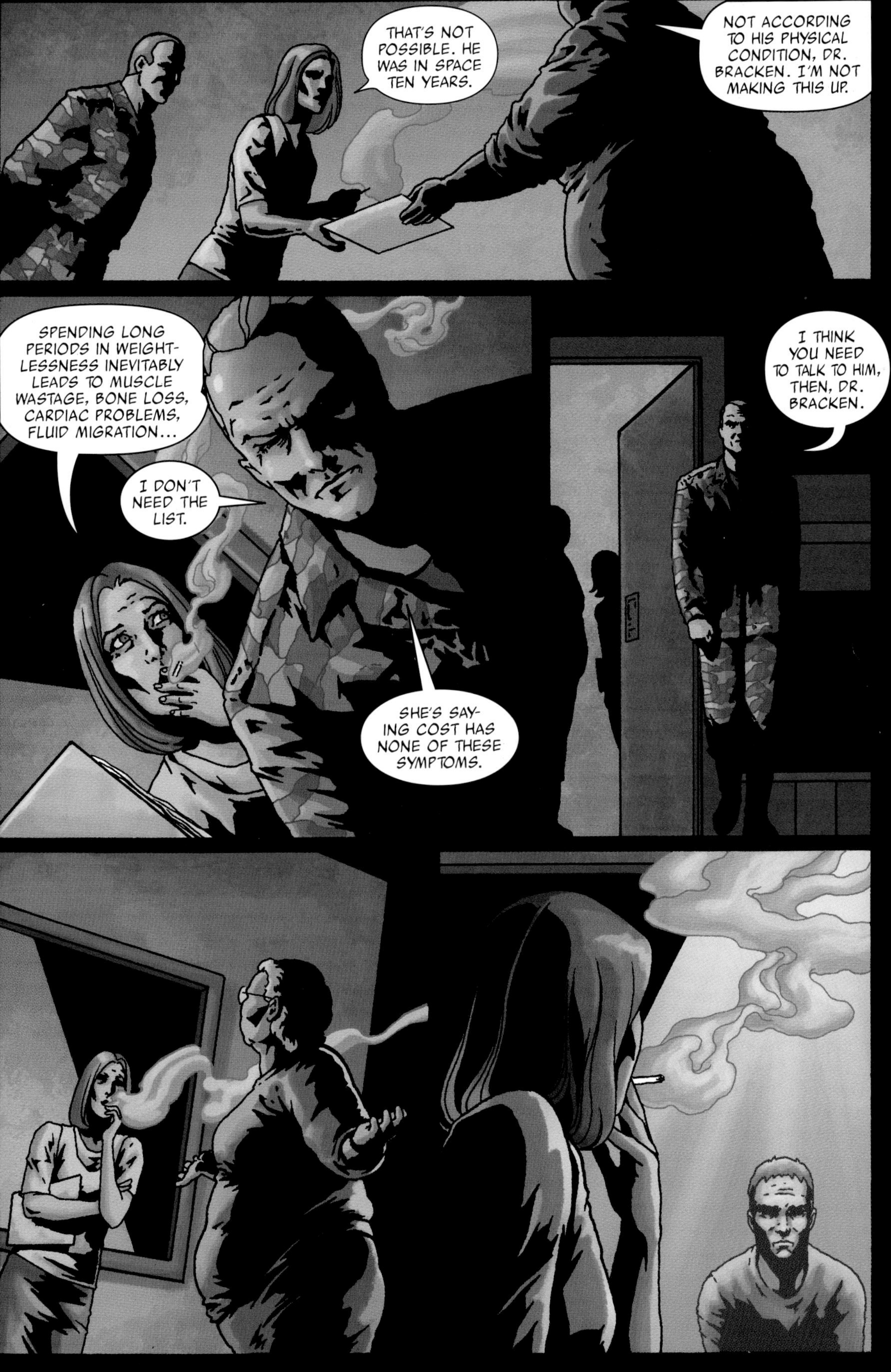
THAT'S NOT POSSIBLE. HE WAS IN SPACE TEN YEARS.
NOT ACCORDING TO HIS PHYSICAL CONDITION, DR. BRACKEN. I'M NOT MAKING THIS UP.
SPENDING LONG PERIODS IN WEIGHT-LESSNESS INEVITABLY LEADS TO MUSCLE WASTAGE, BONE LOSS, CARDIAC PROBLEMS, FLUID MIGRATION...
I DON'T NEED THE LIST.
SHE'S SAY-ING COST HAS NONE OF THESE SYMPTOMS.
I THINK YOU NEED TO TALK TO HIM, THEN, DR. BRACKEN.

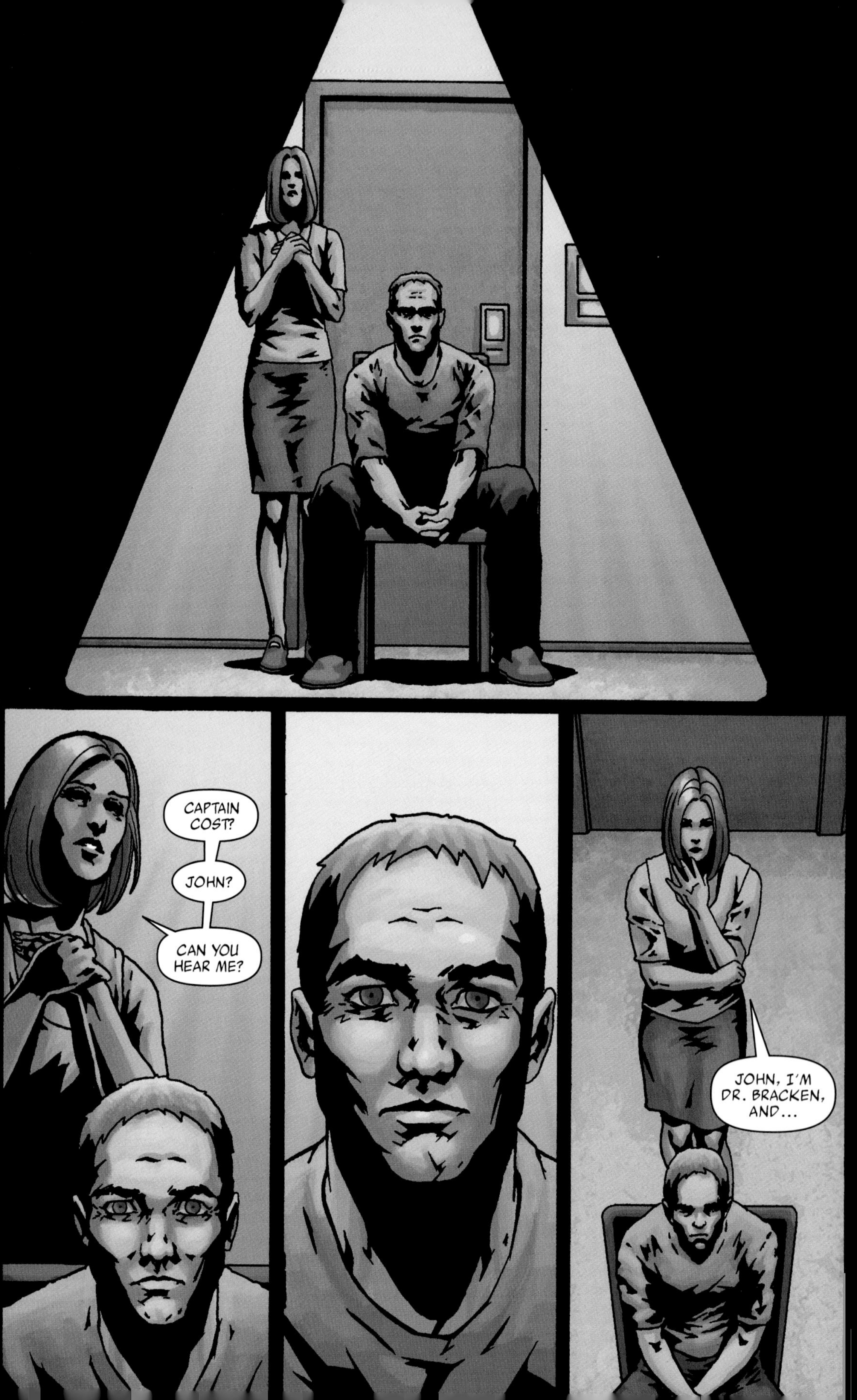

CAPTAIN COST?
JOHN?
CAN YOU HEAR ME?
JOHN, I'M DR. BRACKEN, AND...

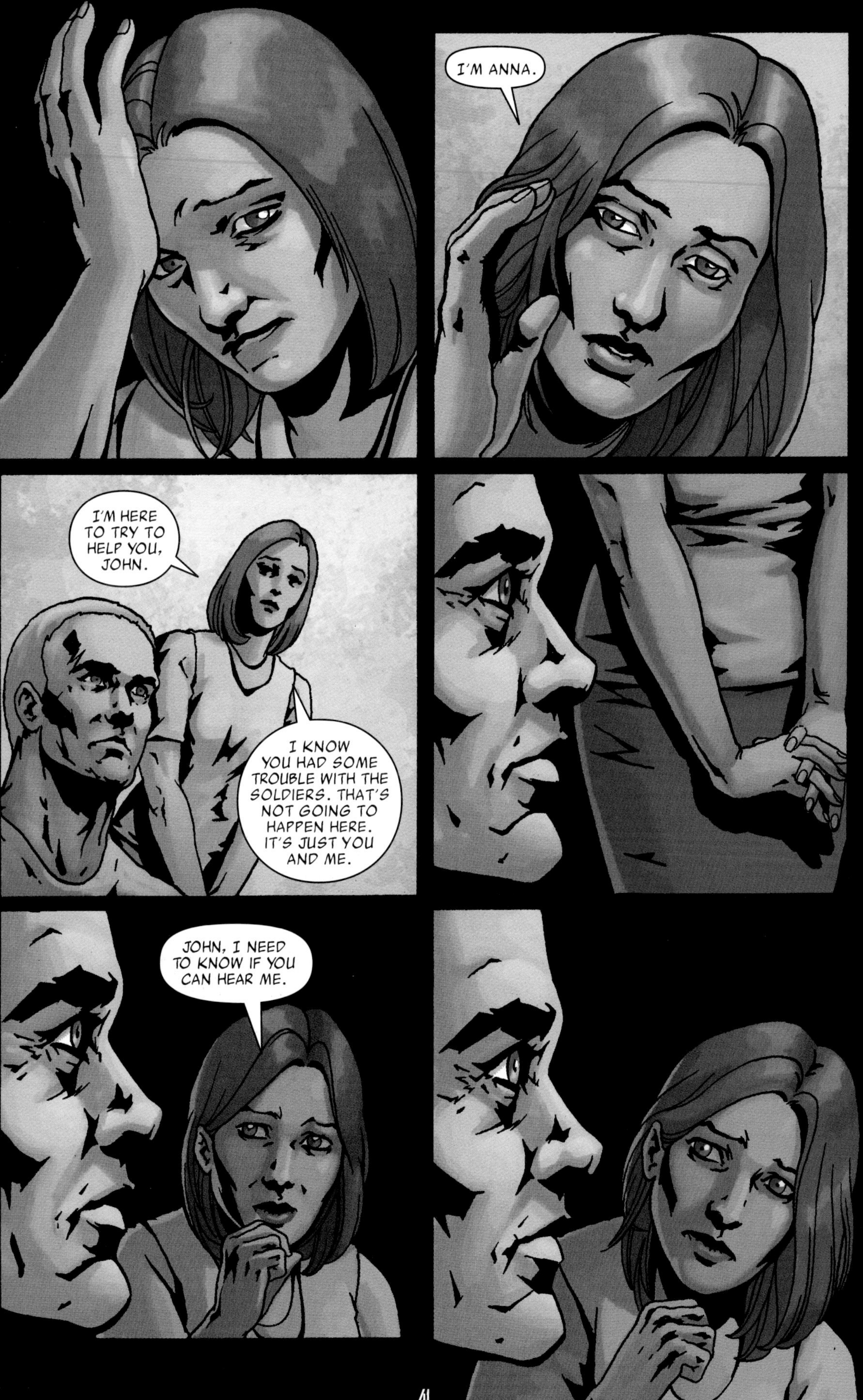
I'M ANNA.
I'M HERE TO TRY TO HELP YOU, JOHN.
I KNOW YOU HAD SOME TROUBLE WITH THE SOLDIERS. THAT'S NOT GOING TO HAPPEN HERE. IT'S JUST YOU AND ME.
JOHN, I NEED TO KNOW IF YOU CAN HEAR ME.

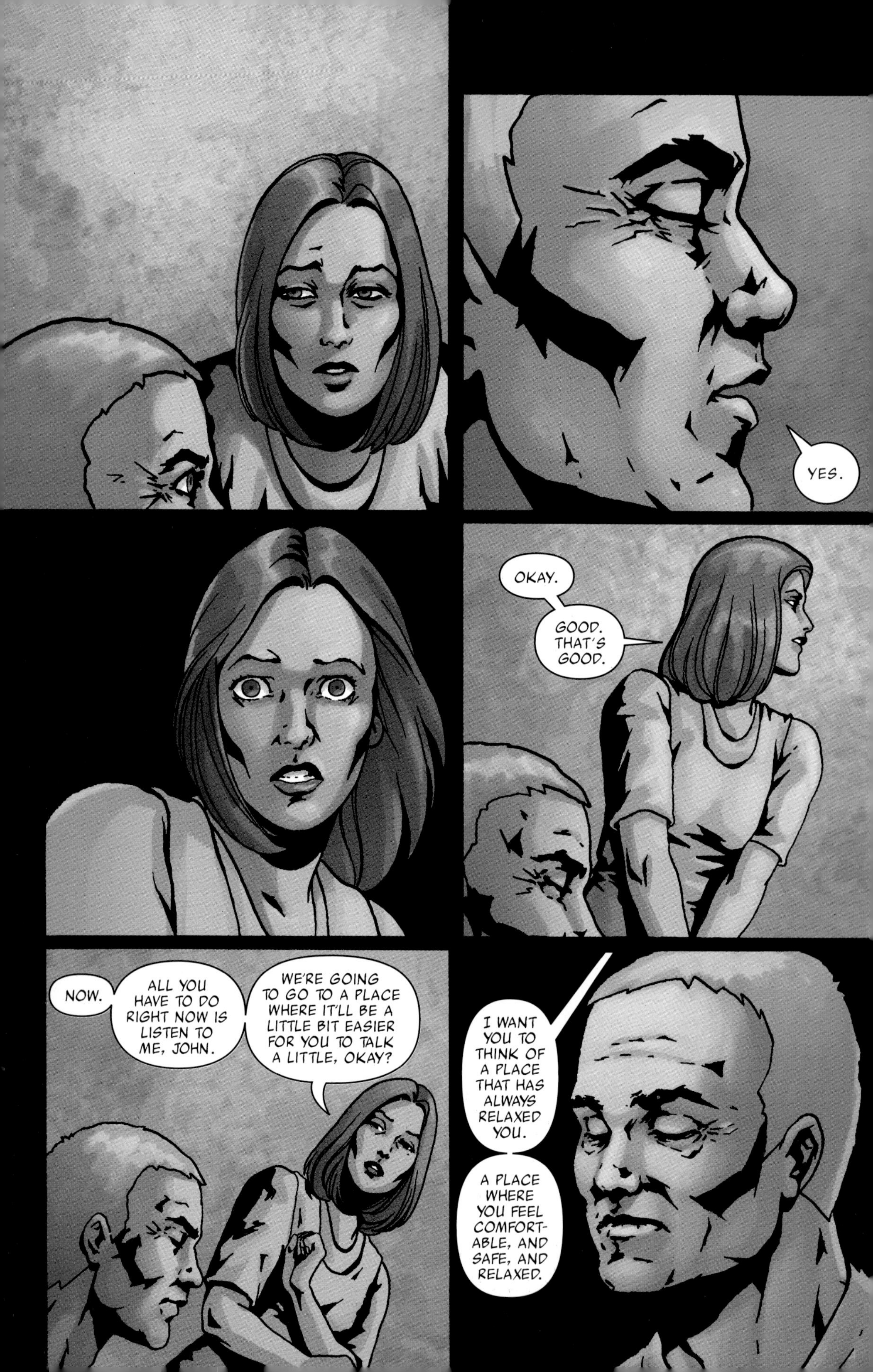
YES.
OKAY.
GOOD. THAT'S GOOD.
NOW.
ALL YOU HAVE TO DO RIGHT NOW IS LISTEN TO ME, JOHN.
WE'RE GOING TO GO TO A PLACE WHERE IT'LL BE A LITTLE BIT EASIER FOR YOU TO TALK A LITTLE, OKAY?
I WANT YOU TO THINK OF A PLACE THAT HAS ALWAYS RELAXED YOU.
A PLACE WHERE YOU FEEL COMFORT-ABLE, AND SAFE, AND RELAXED.

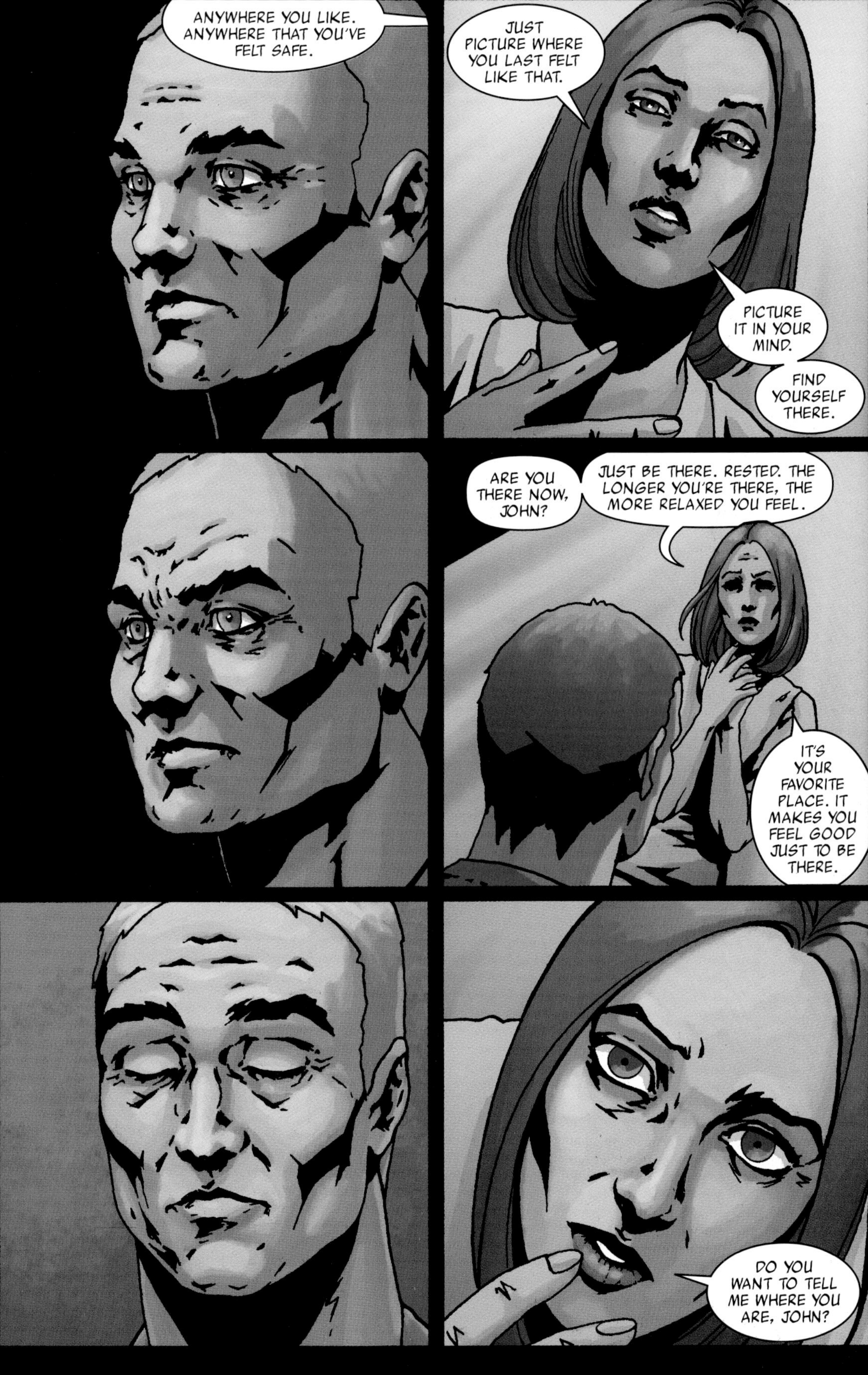
ANYWHERE YOU LIKE. ANYWHERE THAT YOU'VE FELT SAFE.
JUST PICTURE WHERE YOU LAST FELT LIKE THAT.
PICTURE IT IN YOUR MIND.
FIND YOURSELF THERE.
JUST BE THERE. RESTED. THE LONGER YOU'RE THERE, THE MORE RELAXED YOU FEEL.
IT'S YOUR FAVORITE PLACE. IT MAKES YOU FEEL GOOD JUST TO BE THERE.
ARE YOU THERE NOW, JOHN?
DO YOU WANT TO TELL ME WHERE YOU ARE, JOHN?

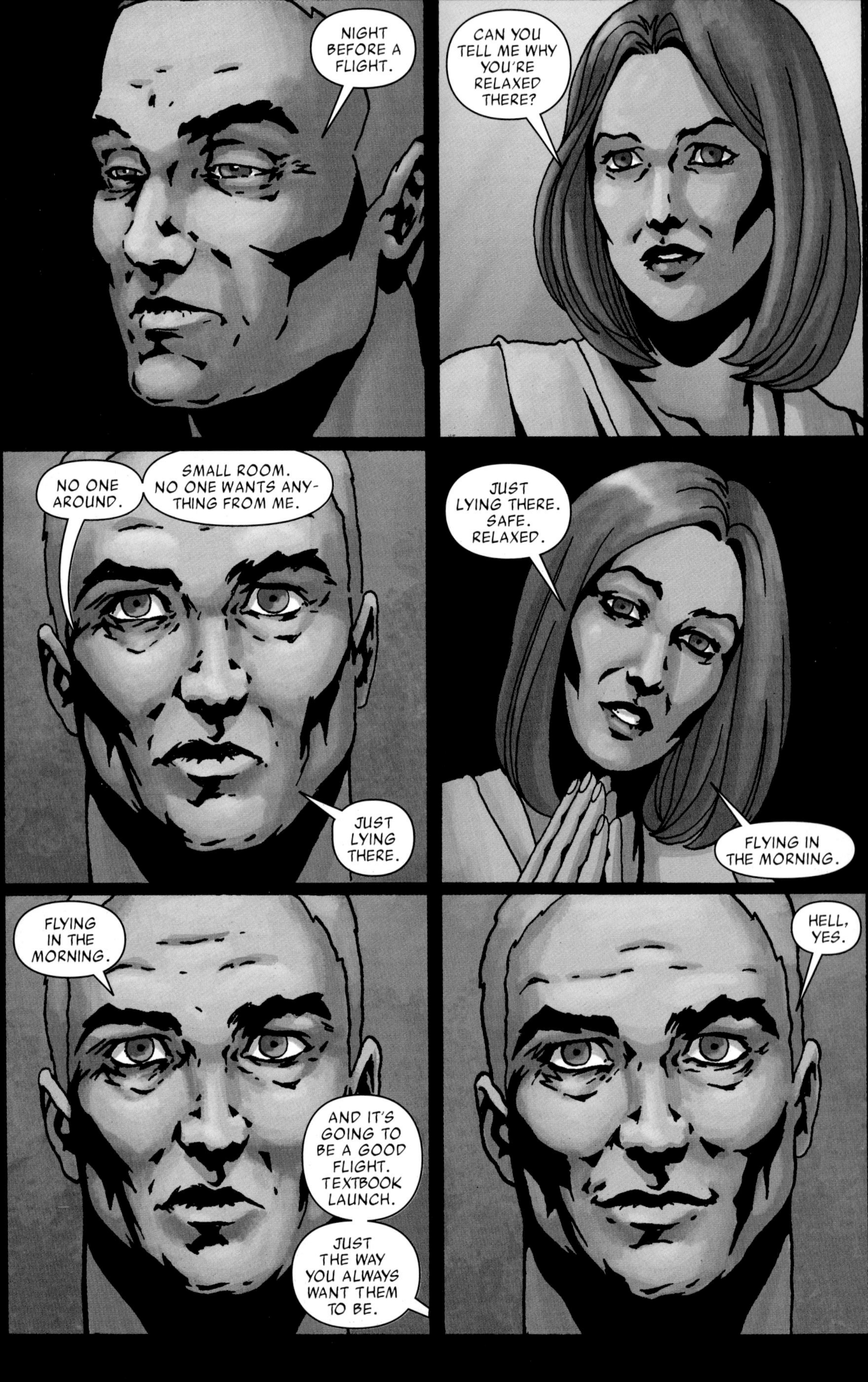
NIGHT BEFORE A FLIGHT.
CAN YOU TELL ME WHY YOU'RE RELAXED THERE?
NO ONE AROUND.
SMALL ROOM. NO ONE WANTS ANY-THING FROM ME.
JUST LYING THERE.
JUST LYING THERE. SAFE. RELAXED.
FLYING IN THE MORNING.
FLYING IN THE MORNING.
AND IT'S GOING TO BE A GOOD FLIGHT. TEXTBOOK LAUNCH.
JUST THE WAY YOU ALWAYS WANT THEM TO BE.
HELL, YES.

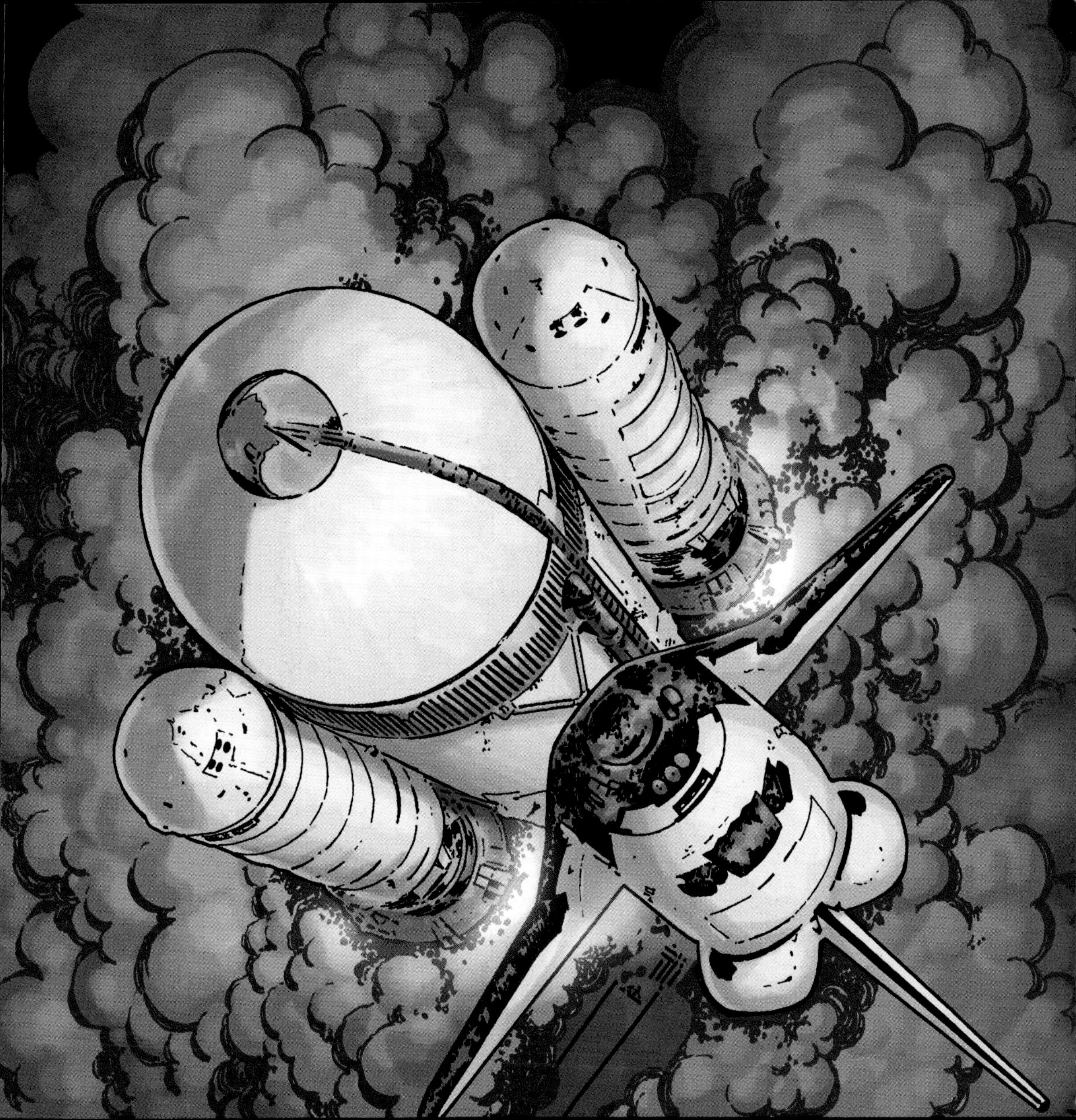

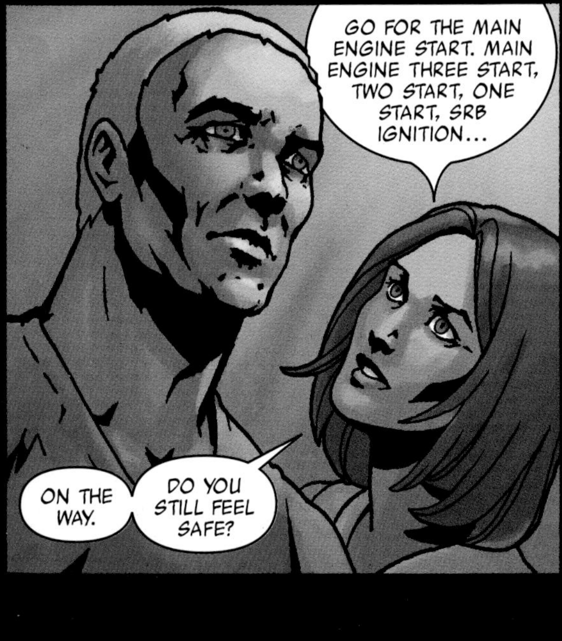
GO FOR THE MAIN ENGINE START. MAIN ENGINE THREE START, TWO START, ONE START, SRB IGNITION...
ON THE WAY.
DO YOU STILL FEEL SAFE?

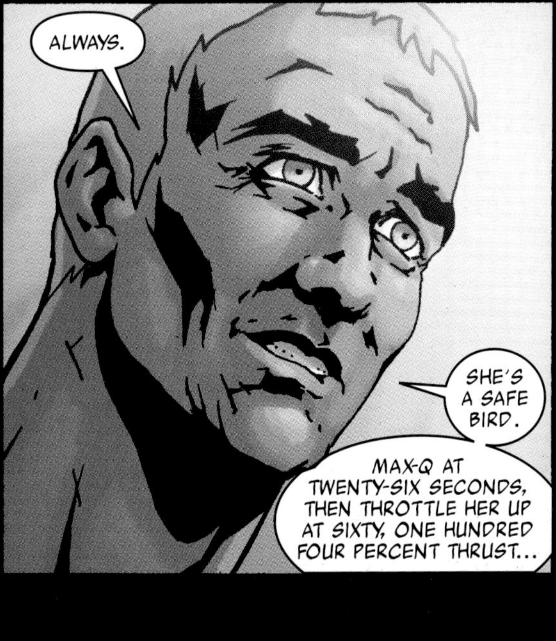
ALWAYS.
SHE'S A SAFE BIRD.
MAX-Q AT TWENTY-SIX SECONDS, THEN THROTTLE HER UP AT SIXTY, ONE HUNDRED FOUR PERCENT THRUST...

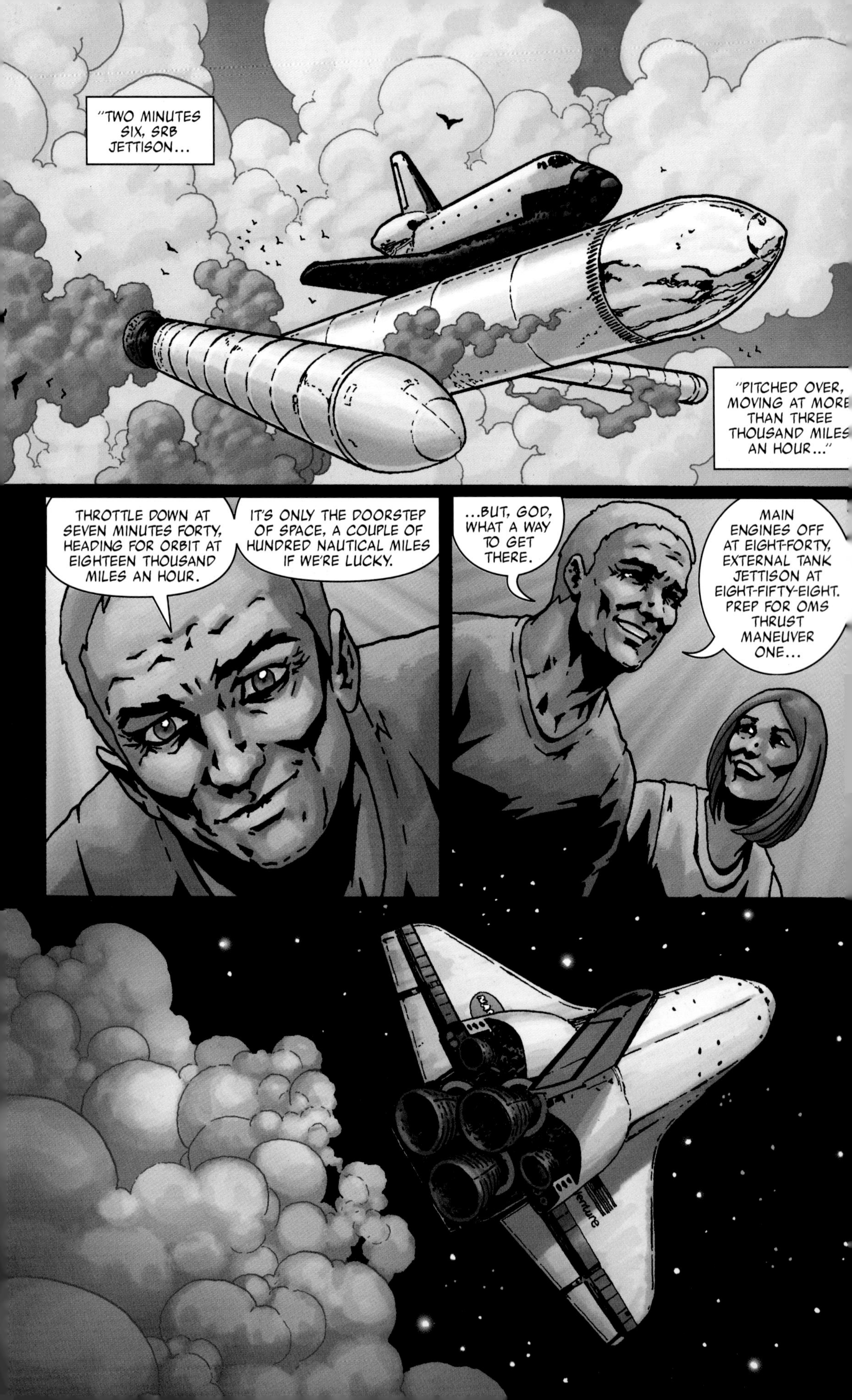
"TWO MINUTES SIX, SRB JETTISON...
"PITCHED OVER, MOVING AT MORE THAN THREE THOUSAND MILES AN HOUR..."
THROTTLE DOWN AT SEVEN MINUTES FORTY, HEADING FOR ORBIT AT EIGHTEEN THOUSAND MILES AN HOUR.
IT'S ONLY THE DOORSTEP OF SPACE, A COUPLE OF HUNDRED NAUTICAL MILES IF WE'RE LUCKY.
...BUT, GOD, WHAT A WAY TO GET THERE.
MAIN ENGINES OFF AT EIGHT-FORTY, EXTERNAL TANK JETTISON AT EIGHT-FIFTY-EIGHT. PREP FOR OMS THRUST MANEUVER ONE...

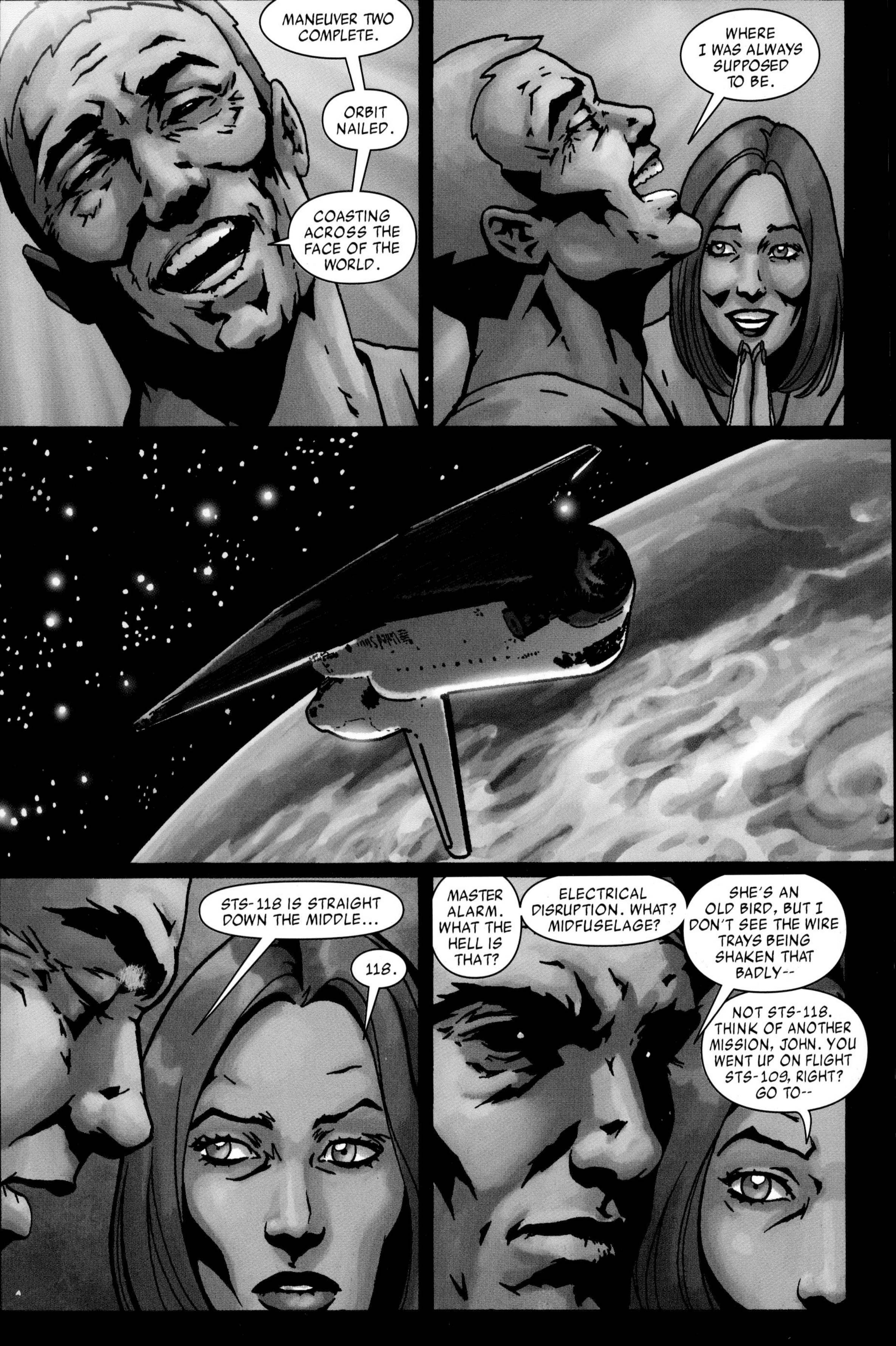
MANEUVER TWO COMPLETE.
ORBIT NAILED.
COASTING ACROSS THE FACE OF THE WORLD.
WHERE I WAS ALWAYS SUPPOSED TO BE.
STS-118 IS STRAIGHT DOWN THE MIDDLE...
118.
MASTER ALARM. WHAT THE HELL IS THAT?
ELECTRICAL DISRUPTION. WHAT? MIDFUSELAGE?
SHE'S AN OLD BIRD, BUT I DON'T SEE THE WIRE TRAYS BEING SHAKEN THAT BADLY--
NOT STS-118. THINK OF ANOTHER MISSION, JOHN. YOU WENT UP ON FLIGHT STS-109, RIGHT? GO TO--

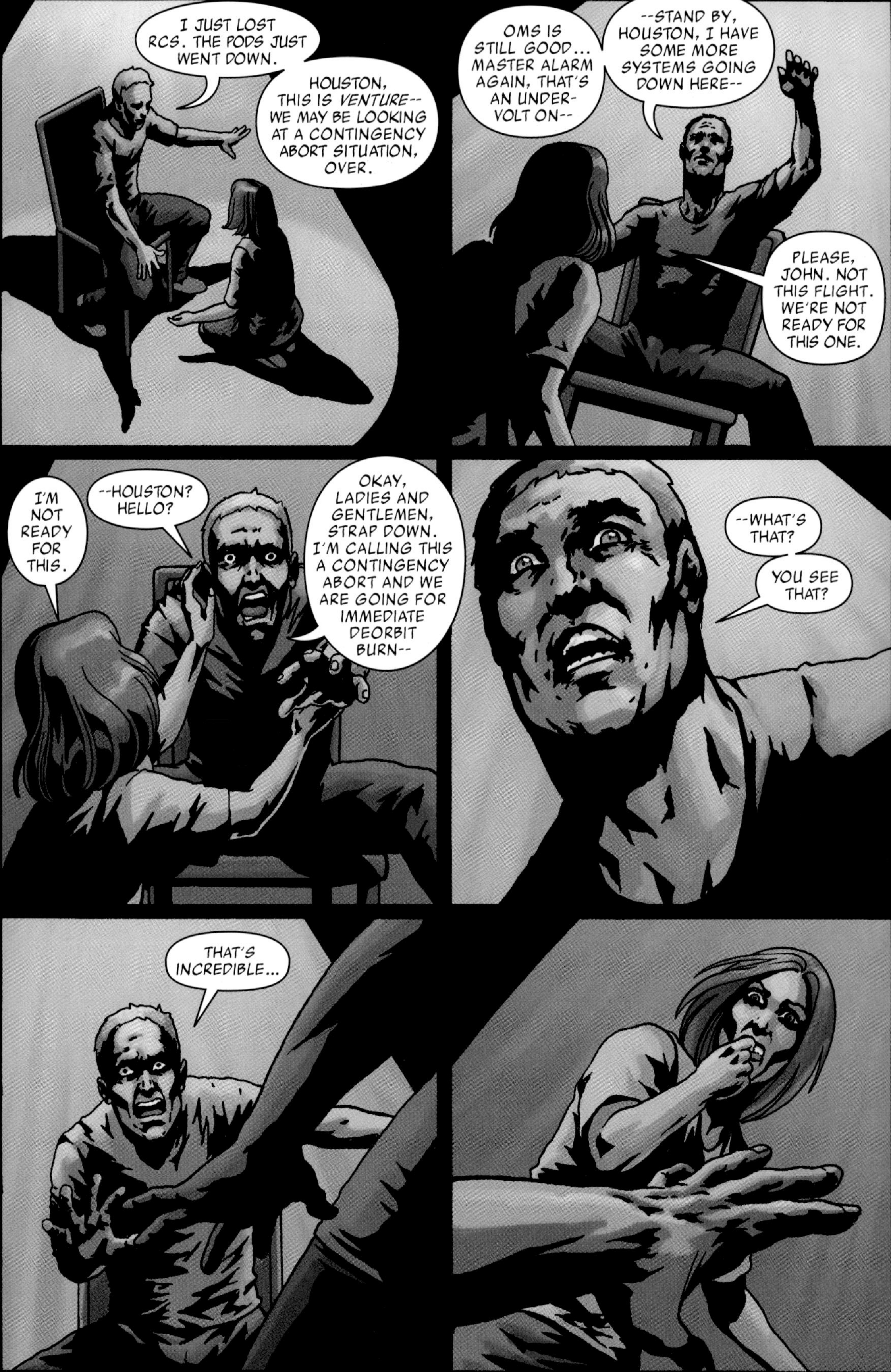
I JUST LOST RCS. THE PODS JUST WENT DOWN.
HOUSTON, THIS IS VENTURE-- WE MAY BE LOOKING AT A CONTINGENCY ABORT SITUATION, OVER.
OMS IS STILL GOOD... MASTER ALARM AGAIN, THAT'S AN UNDER-VOLT ON--
--STAND BY, HOUSTON, I HAVE SOME MORE SYSTEMS GOING DOWN HERE--
PLEASE, JOHN. NOT THIS FLIGHT. WE'RE NOT READY FOR THIS ONE.
I'M NOT READY FOR THIS.
--HOUSTON? HELLO?
OKAY, LADIES AND GENTLEMEN, STRAP DOWN. I'M CALLING THIS A CONTINGENCY ABORT AND WE ARE GOING FOR IMMEDIATE DEORBIT BURN--
--WHAT'S THAT?
YOU SEE THAT?
THAT'S INCREDIBLE...

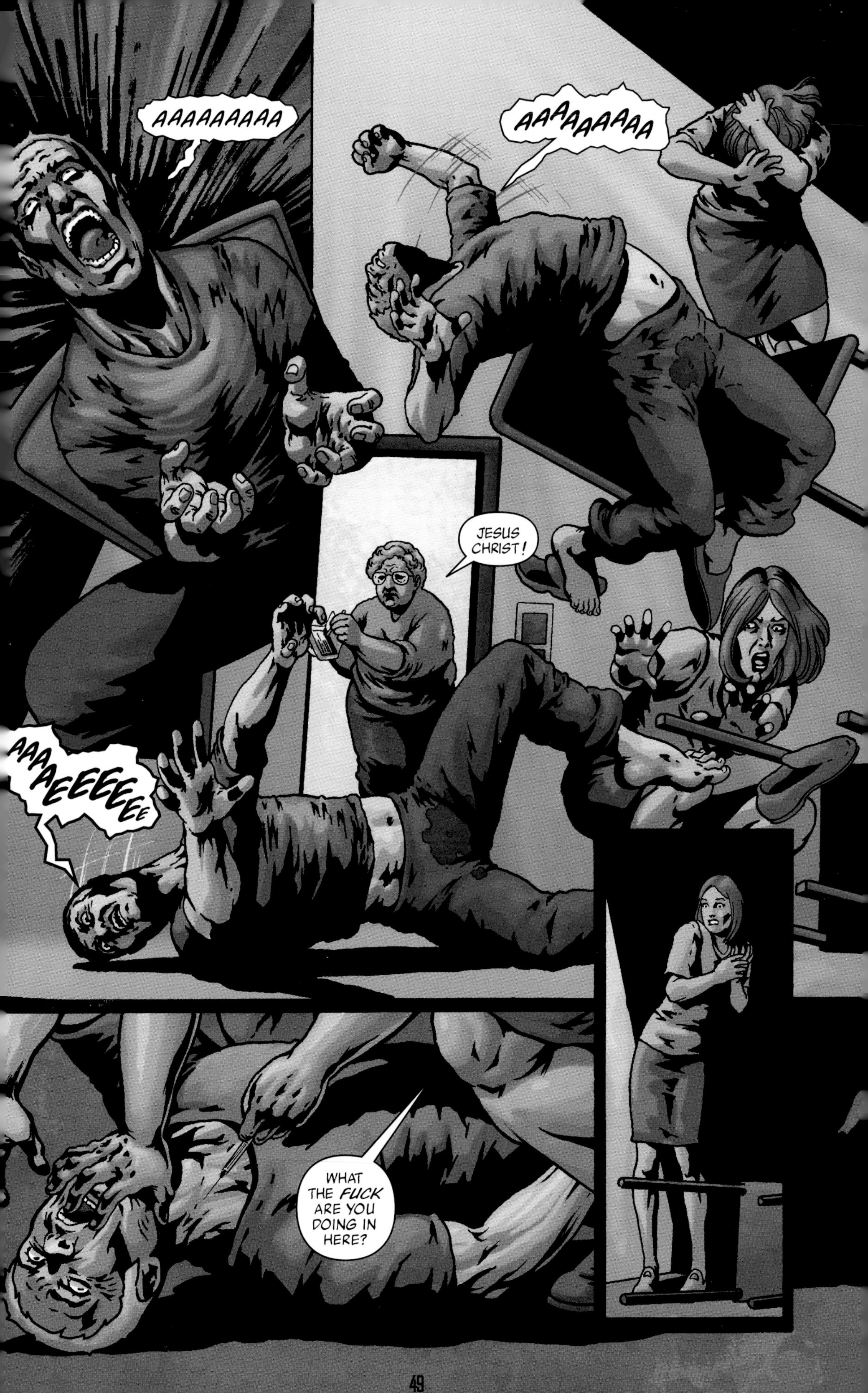
AAAAAAAAA
AAAAAAAA
JESUS CHRIST!
AAAEEEEEEE
WHAT THE FUCK ARE YOU DOING IN HERE?

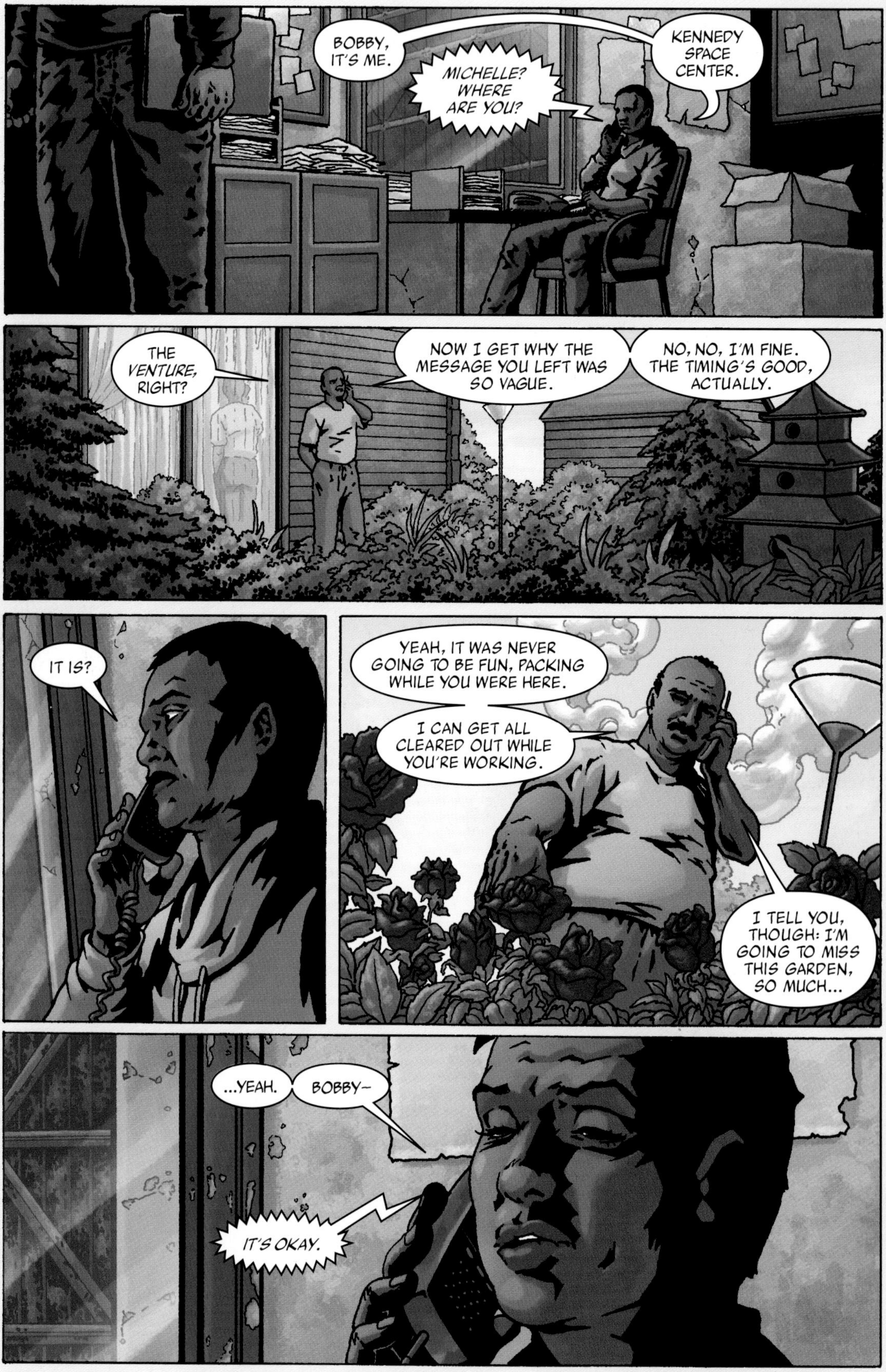
BOBBY, IT'S ME.
MICHELLE? WHERE ARE YOU?
KENNEDY SPACE CENTER.
THE VENTURE, RIGHT?
NOW I GET WHY THE MESSAGE YOU LEFT WAS SO VAGUE.
NO, NO, I'M FINE. THE TIMING'S GOOD, ACTUALLY.
IT IS?
YEAH, IT WAS NEVER GOING TO BE FUN, PACKING WHILE YOU WERE HERE.
I CAN GET ALL CLEARED OUT WHILE YOU'RE WORKING.
I TELL YOU, THOUGH: I'M GOING TO MISS THIS GARDEN, SO MUCH...
...YEAH.
BOBBY–
IT'S OKAY.

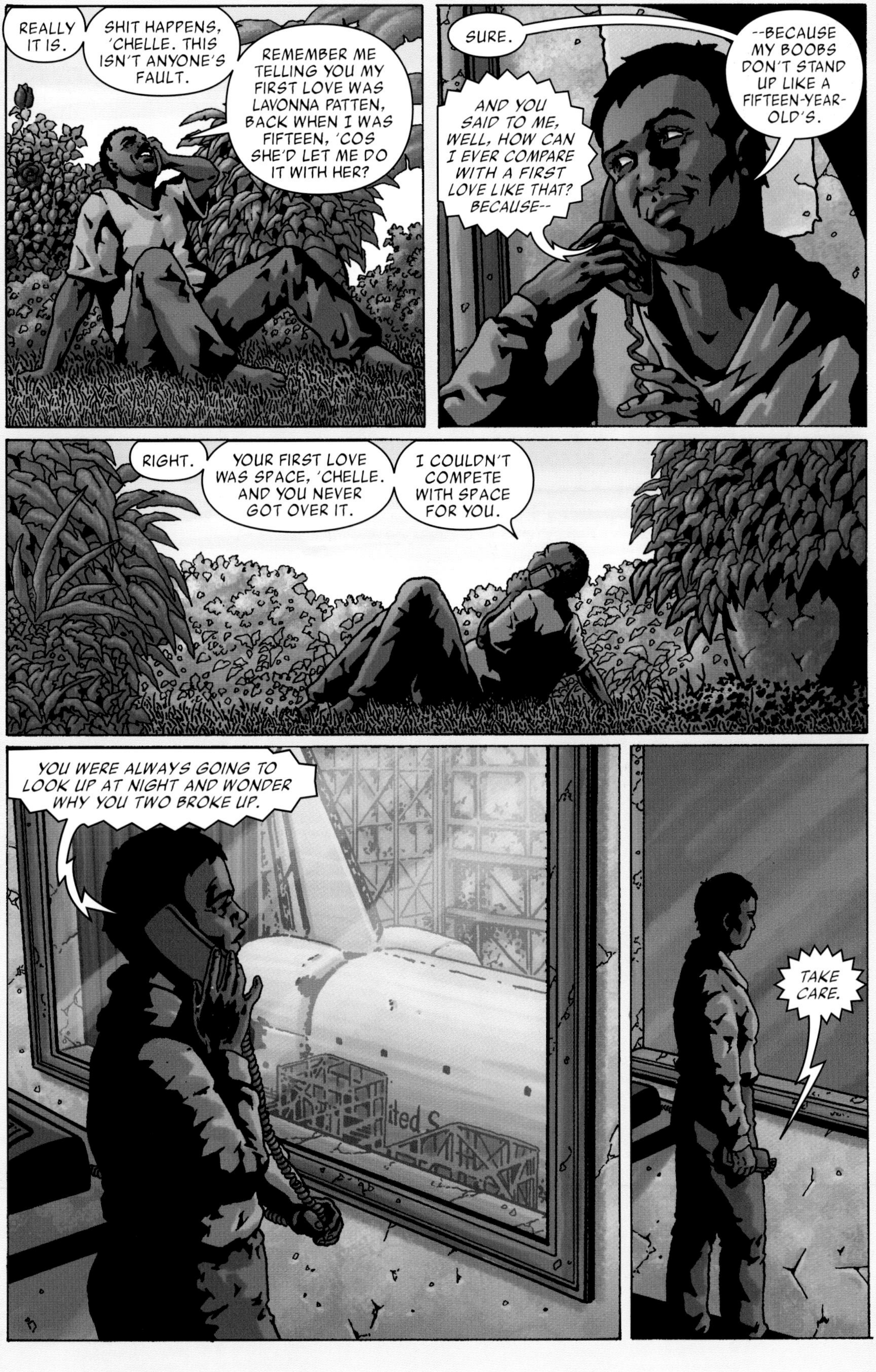
REALLY IT IS.
SHIT HAPPENS, 'CHELLE. THIS ISN'T ANYONE'S FAULT.
REMEMBER ME TELLING YOU MY FIRST LOVE WAS LAVONNA PATTEN, BACK WHEN I WAS FIFTEEN, 'COS SHE'D LET ME DO IT WITH HER?
SURE.
AND YOU SAID TO ME, WELL, HOW CAN I EVER COMPARE WITH A FIRST LOVE LIKE THAT? BECAUSE--
--BECAUSE MY BOOBS DON'T STAND UP LIKE A FIFTEEN-YEAR-OLD'S.
RIGHT.
YOUR FIRST LOVE WAS SPACE, 'CHELLE. AND YOU NEVER GOT OVER IT.
I COULDN'T COMPETE WITH SPACE FOR YOU.
YOU WERE ALWAYS GOING TO LOOK UP AT NIGHT AND WONDER WHY YOU TWO BROKE UP.
TAKE CARE.

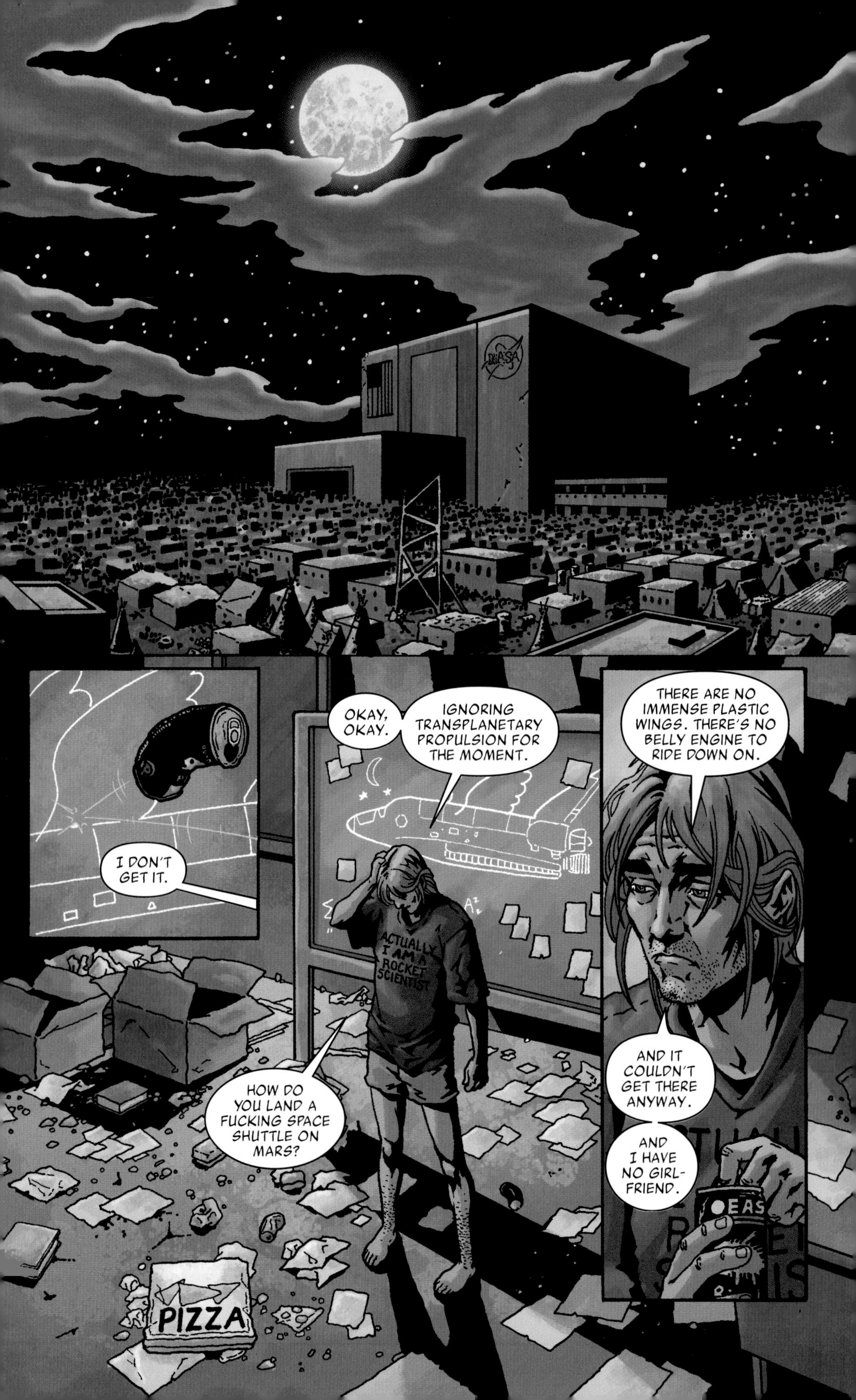

I DON'T GET IT.
OKAY, OKAY.
IGNORING TRANSPLANETARY PROPULSION FOR THE MOMENT.
HOW DO YOU LAND A FUCKING SPACE SHUTTLE ON MARS?
ACTUALLY I AM A ROCKET SCIENTIST
THERE ARE NO IMMENSE PLASTIC WINGS. THERE'S NO BELLY ENGINE TO RIDE DOWN ON.
AND IT COULDN'T GET THERE ANYWAY.
AND I HAVE NO GIRL-FRIEND.
PIZZA

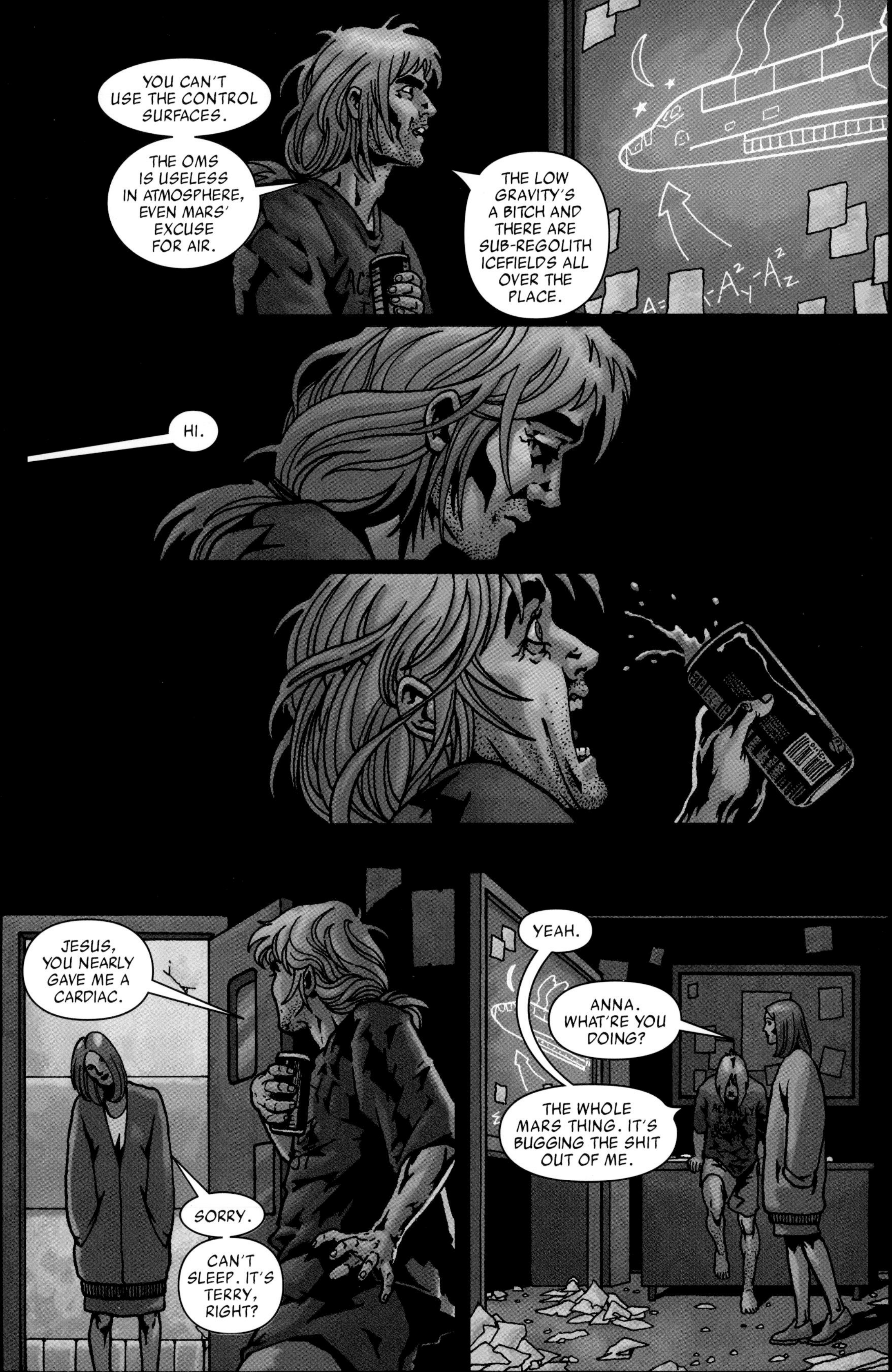
YOU CAN'T USE THE CONTROL SURFACES.
THE OMS IS USELESS IN ATMOSPHERE, EVEN MARS' EXCUSE FOR AIR.
THE LOW GRAVITY'S A BITCH AND THERE ARE SUB-REGOLITH ICEFIELDS ALL OVER THE PLACE.
HI.
JESUS, YOU NEARLY GAVE ME A CARDIAC.
SORRY.
CAN'T SLEEP. IT'S TERRY, RIGHT?
YEAH.
ANNA. WHAT'RE YOU DOING?
THE WHOLE MARS THING. IT'S BUGGING THE SHIT OUT OF ME.

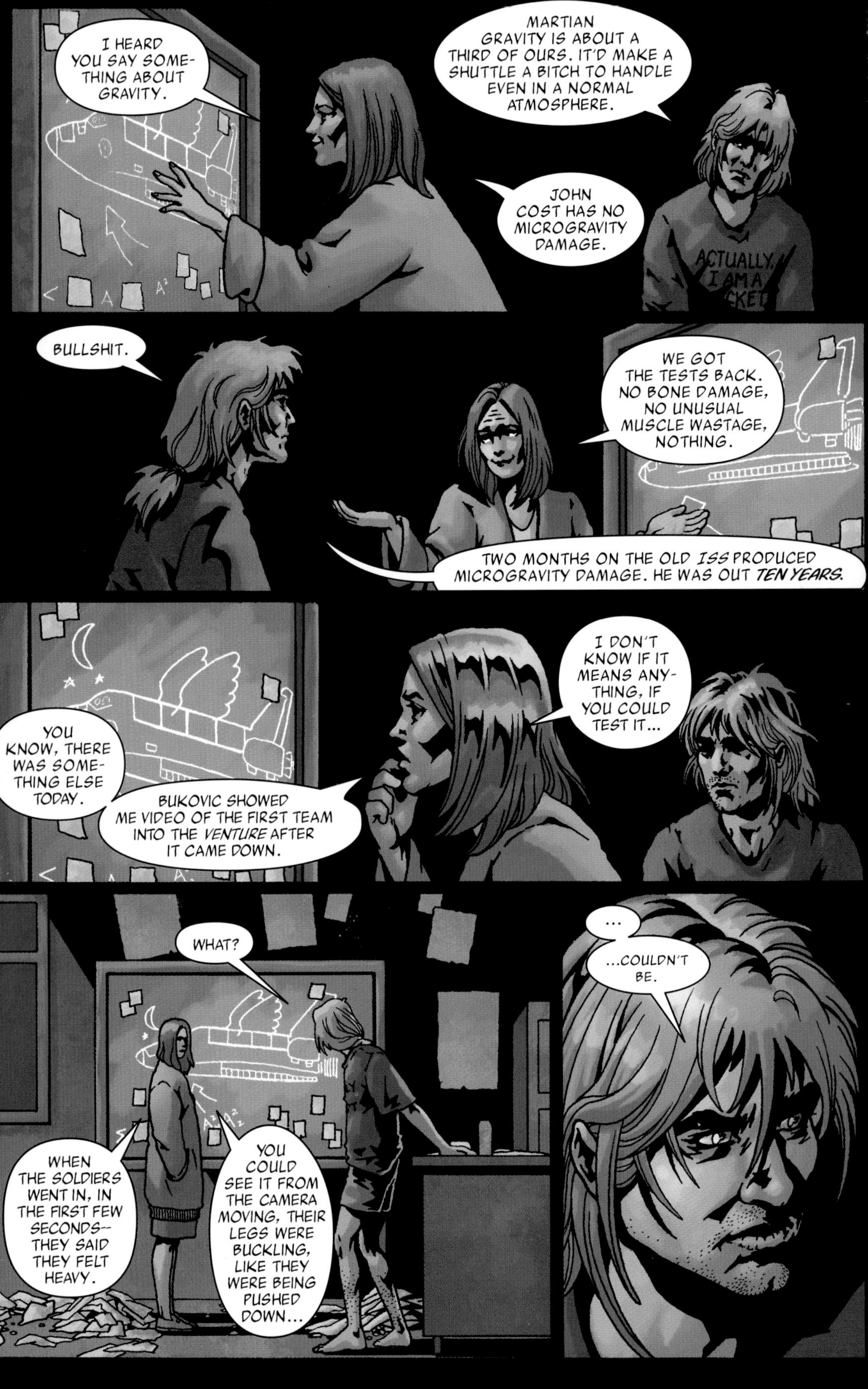
I HEARD YOU SAY SOMETHING ABOUT GRAVITY.
MARTIAN GRAVITY IS ABOUT A THIRD OF OURS. IT'D MAKE A SHUTTLE A BITCH TO HANDLE EVEN IN A NORMAL ATMOSPHERE.
JOHN COST HAS NO MICROGRAVITY DAMAGE.
ACTUALLY, I AM A
BULLSHIT.
WE GOT THE TESTS BACK. NO BONE DAMAGE, NO UNUSUAL MUSCLE WASTAGE, NOTHING.
TWO MONTHS ON THE OLD *ISS* PRODUCED MICROGRAVITY DAMAGE. HE WAS OUT ***TEN YEARS.***
YOU KNOW, THERE WAS SOMETHING ELSE TODAY.
BUKOVIC SHOWED ME VIDEO OF THE FIRST TEAM INTO THE *VENTURE* AFTER IT CAME DOWN.
I DON'T KNOW IF IT MEANS ANYTHING, IF YOU COULD TEST IT...
WHAT?
WHEN THE SOLDIERS WENT IN, IN THE FIRST FEW SECONDS-- THEY SAID THEY FELT HEAVY.
YOU COULD SEE IT FROM THE CAMERA MOVING, THEIR LEGS WERE BUCKLING, LIKE THEY WERE BEING PUSHED DOWN...
...
...COULDN'T BE.

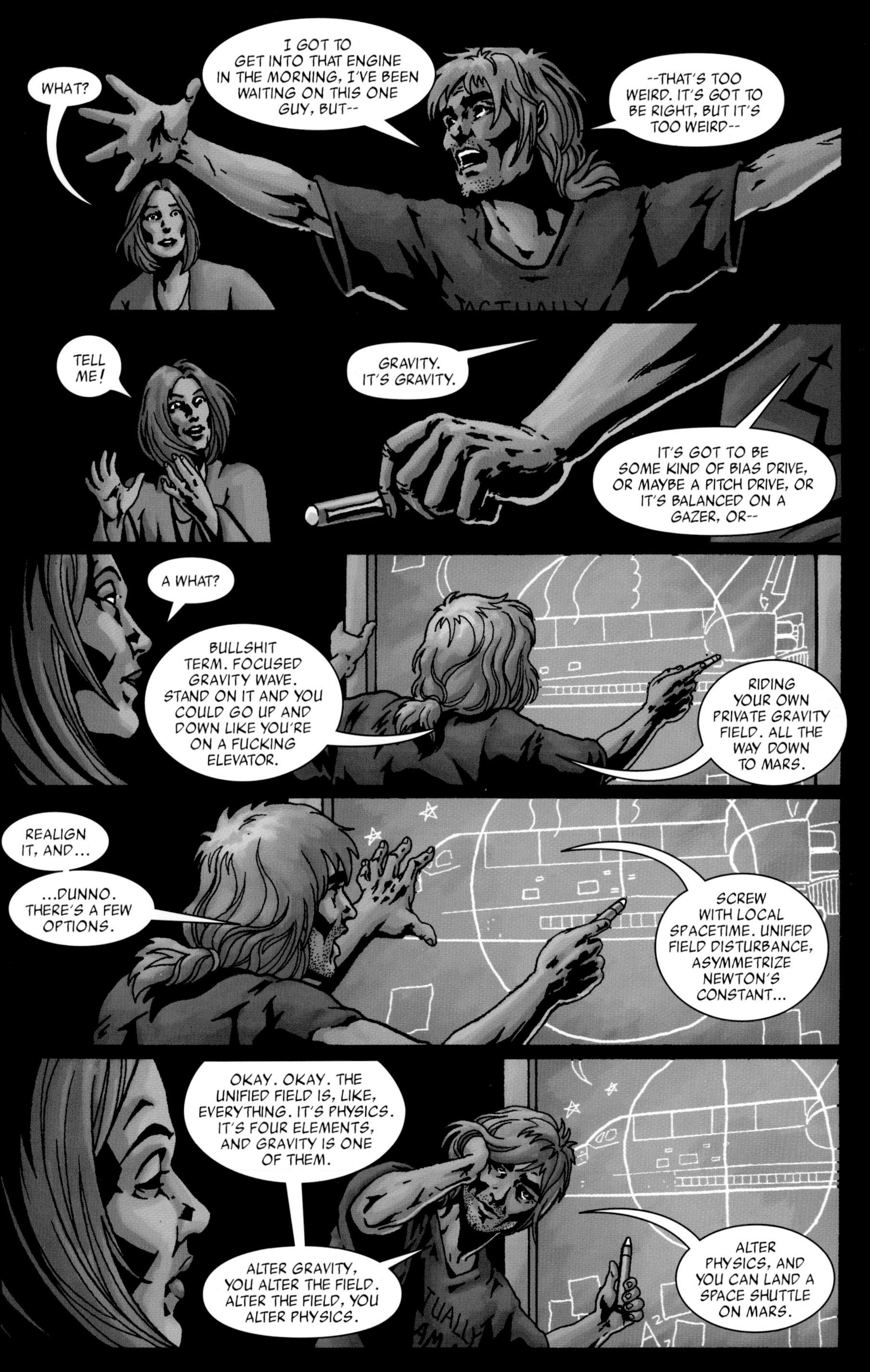
WHAT?
I GOT TO GET INTO THAT ENGINE IN THE MORNING, I'VE BEEN WAITING ON THIS ONE GUY, BUT--
--THAT'S TOO WEIRD. IT'S GOT TO BE RIGHT, BUT IT'S TOO WEIRD--
TELL ME!
GRAVITY. IT'S GRAVITY.
IT'S GOT TO BE SOME KIND OF BIAS DRIVE, OR MAYBE A PITCH DRIVE, OR IT'S BALANCED ON A GAZER, OR--
A WHAT?
BULLSHIT TERM. FOCUSED GRAVITY WAVE. STAND ON IT AND YOU COULD GO UP AND DOWN LIKE YOU'RE ON A FUCKING ELEVATOR.
RIDING YOUR OWN PRIVATE GRAVITY FIELD. ALL THE WAY DOWN TO MARS.
REALIGN IT, AND...
...DUNNO. THERE'S A FEW OPTIONS.
SCREW WITH LOCAL SPACETIME. UNIFIED FIELD DISTURBANCE, ASYMMETRIZE NEWTON'S CONSTANT...
OKAY. OKAY. THE UNIFIED FIELD IS, LIKE, EVERYTHING. IT'S PHYSICS. IT'S FOUR ELEMENTS, AND GRAVITY IS ONE OF THEM.
ALTER GRAVITY, YOU ALTER THE FIELD. ALTER THE FIELD, YOU ALTER PHYSICS.
ALTER PHYSICS, AND YOU CAN LAND A SPACE SHUTTLE ON MARS.

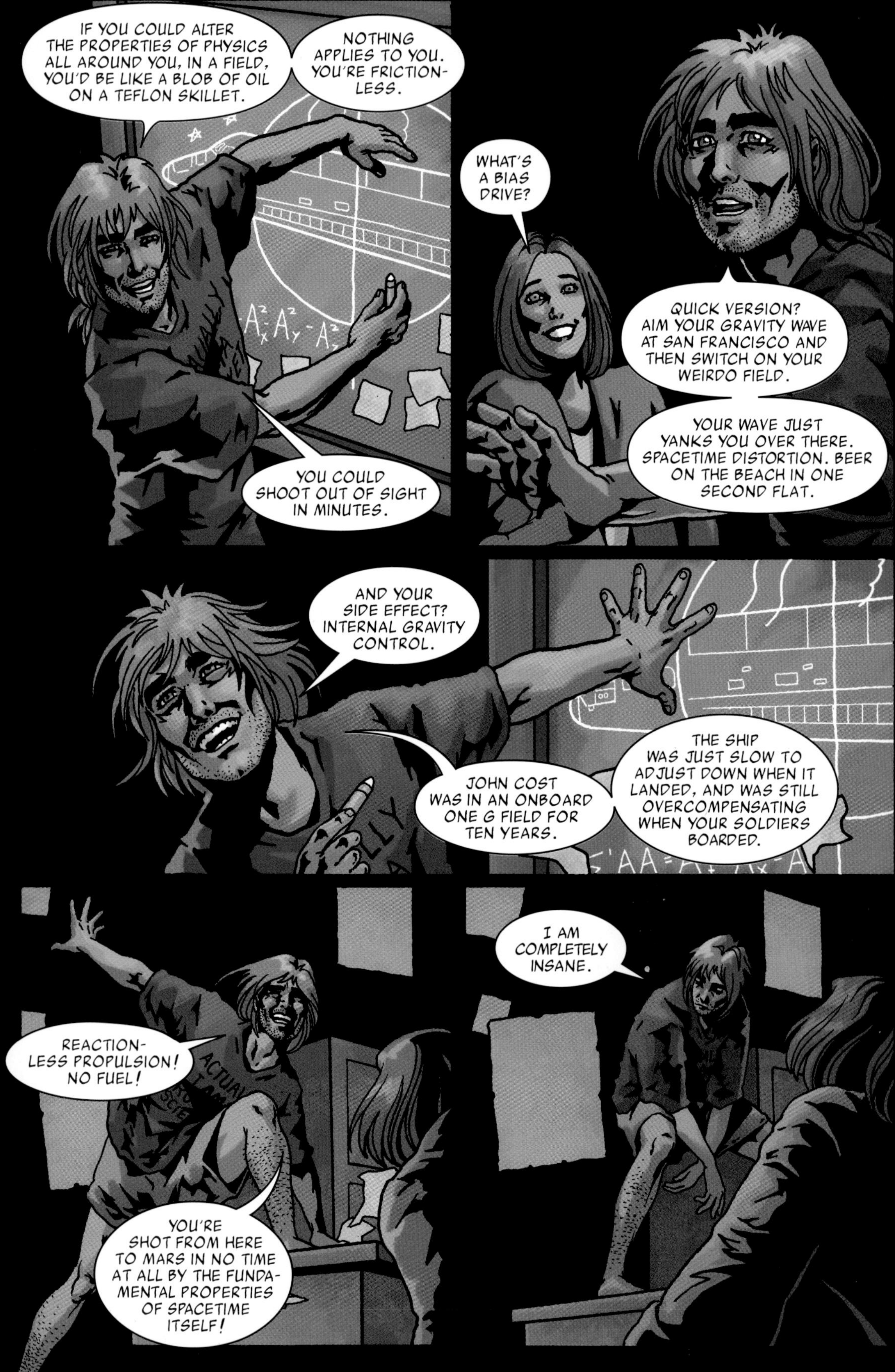
IF YOU COULD ALTER THE PROPERTIES OF PHYSICS ALL AROUND YOU, IN A FIELD, YOU'D BE LIKE A BLOB OF OIL ON A TEFLON SKILLET.
NOTHING APPLIES TO YOU. YOU'RE FRICTION-LESS.
YOU COULD SHOOT OUT OF SIGHT IN MINUTES.
WHAT'S A BIAS DRIVE?
QUICK VERSION? AIM YOUR GRAVITY WAVE AT SAN FRANCISCO AND THEN SWITCH ON YOUR WEIRDO FIELD.
YOUR WAVE JUST YANKS YOU OVER THERE. SPACETIME DISTORTION. BEER ON THE BEACH IN ONE SECOND FLAT.
AND YOUR SIDE EFFECT? INTERNAL GRAVITY CONTROL.
JOHN COST WAS IN AN ONBOARD ONE G FIELD FOR TEN YEARS.
THE SHIP WAS JUST SLOW TO ADJUST DOWN WHEN IT LANDED, AND WAS STILL OVERCOMPENSATING WHEN YOUR SOLDIERS BOARDED.
REACTION-LESS PROPULSION! NO FUEL!
YOU'RE SHOT FROM HERE TO MARS IN NO TIME AT ALL BY THE FUNDA-MENTAL PROPERTIES OF SPACETIME ITSELF!
I AM COMPLETELY INSANE.

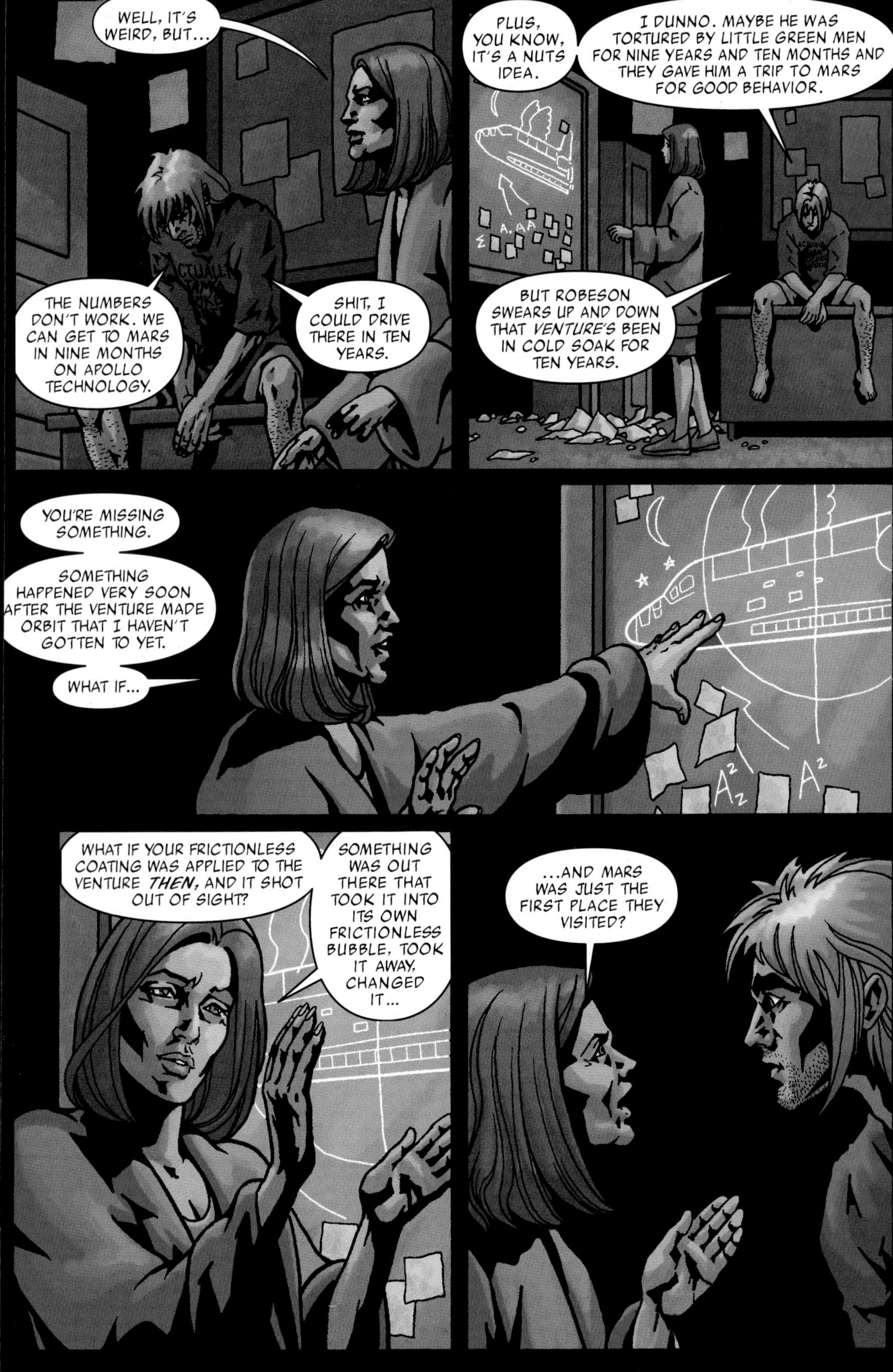
WELL, IT'S WEIRD, BUT...
THE NUMBERS DON'T WORK. WE CAN GET TO MARS IN NINE MONTHS ON APOLLO TECHNOLOGY.
SHIT, I COULD DRIVE THERE IN TEN YEARS.
PLUS, YOU KNOW, IT'S A NUTS IDEA.
I DUNNO. MAYBE HE WAS TORTURED BY LITTLE GREEN MEN FOR NINE YEARS AND TEN MONTHS AND THEY GAVE HIM A TRIP TO MARS FOR GOOD BEHAVIOR.
BUT ROBESON SWEARS UP AND DOWN THAT *VENTURE'S* BEEN IN COLD SOAK FOR TEN YEARS.
YOU'RE MISSING SOMETHING.
SOMETHING HAPPENED VERY SOON AFTER THE VENTURE MADE ORBIT THAT I HAVEN'T GOTTEN TO YET.
WHAT IF...
WHAT IF YOUR FRICTIONLESS COATING WAS APPLIED TO THE VENTURE ***THEN,*** AND IT SHOT OUT OF SIGHT?
SOMETHING WAS OUT THERE THAT TOOK IT INTO ITS OWN FRICTIONLESS BUBBLE, TOOK IT AWAY, CHANGED IT...
...AND MARS WAS JUST THE FIRST PLACE THEY VISITED?

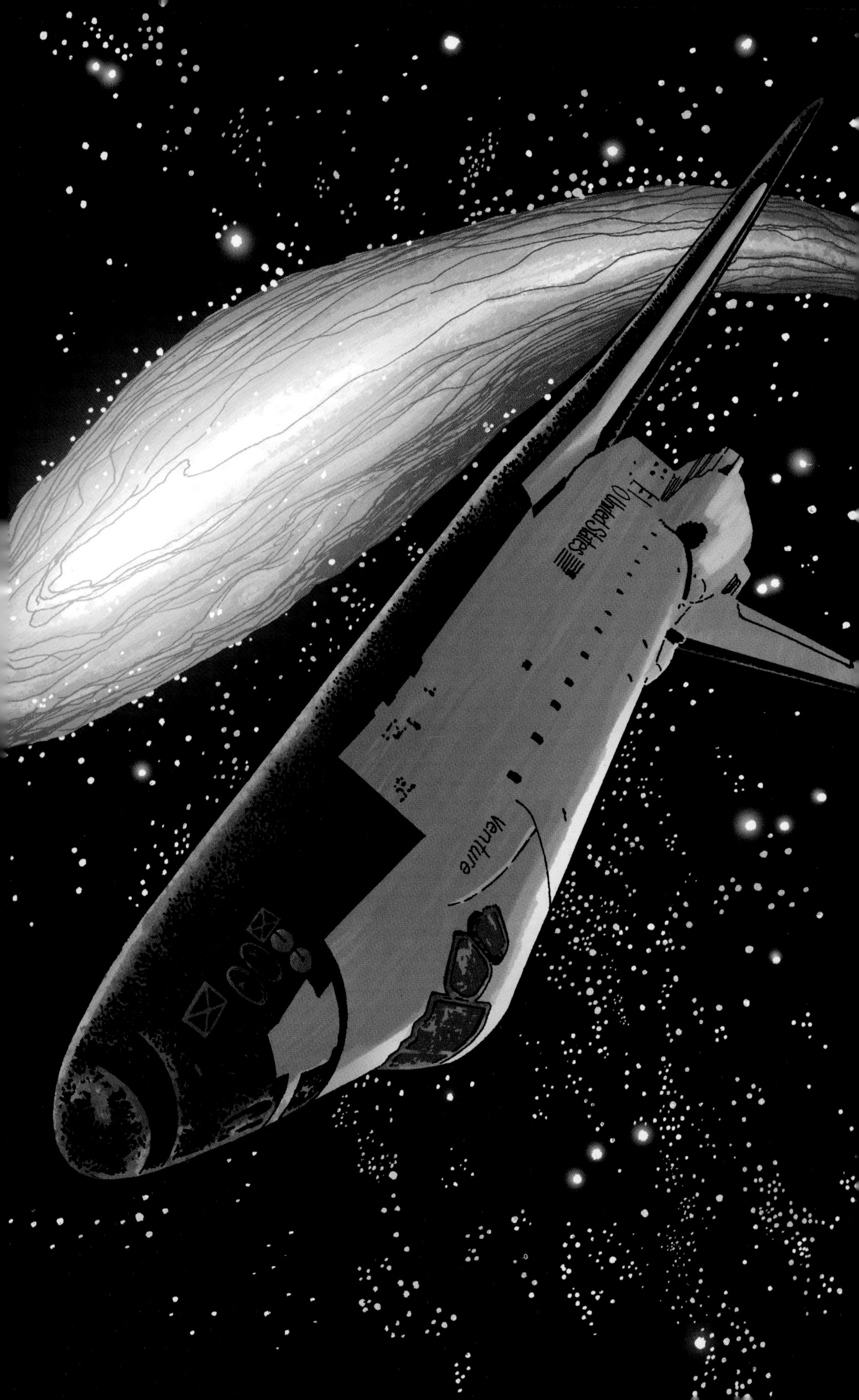

United States
Venture

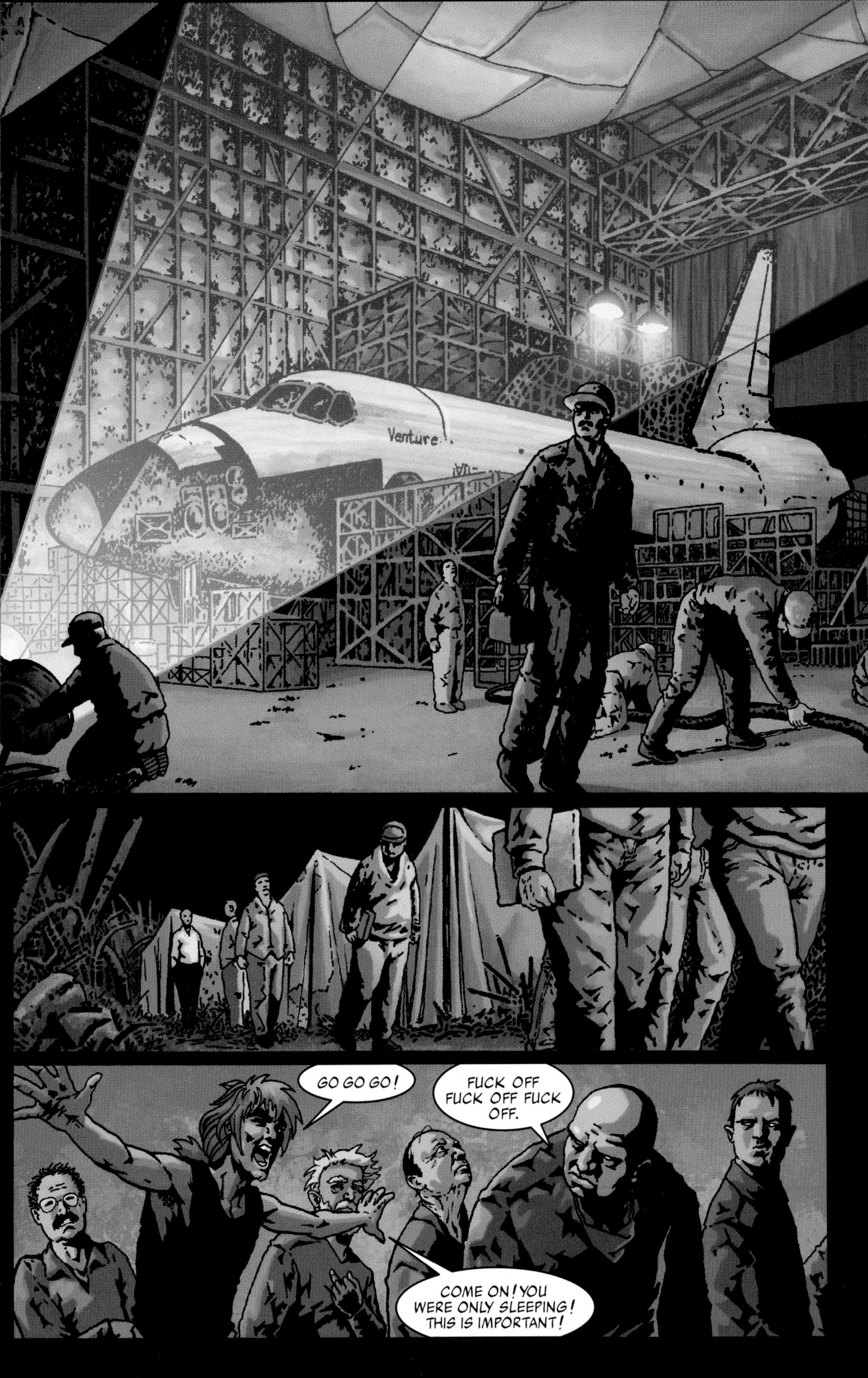
Venture
GO GO GO!
FUCK OFF FUCK OFF FUCK OFF.
COME ON! YOU WERE ONLY SLEEPING! THIS IS IMPORTANT!

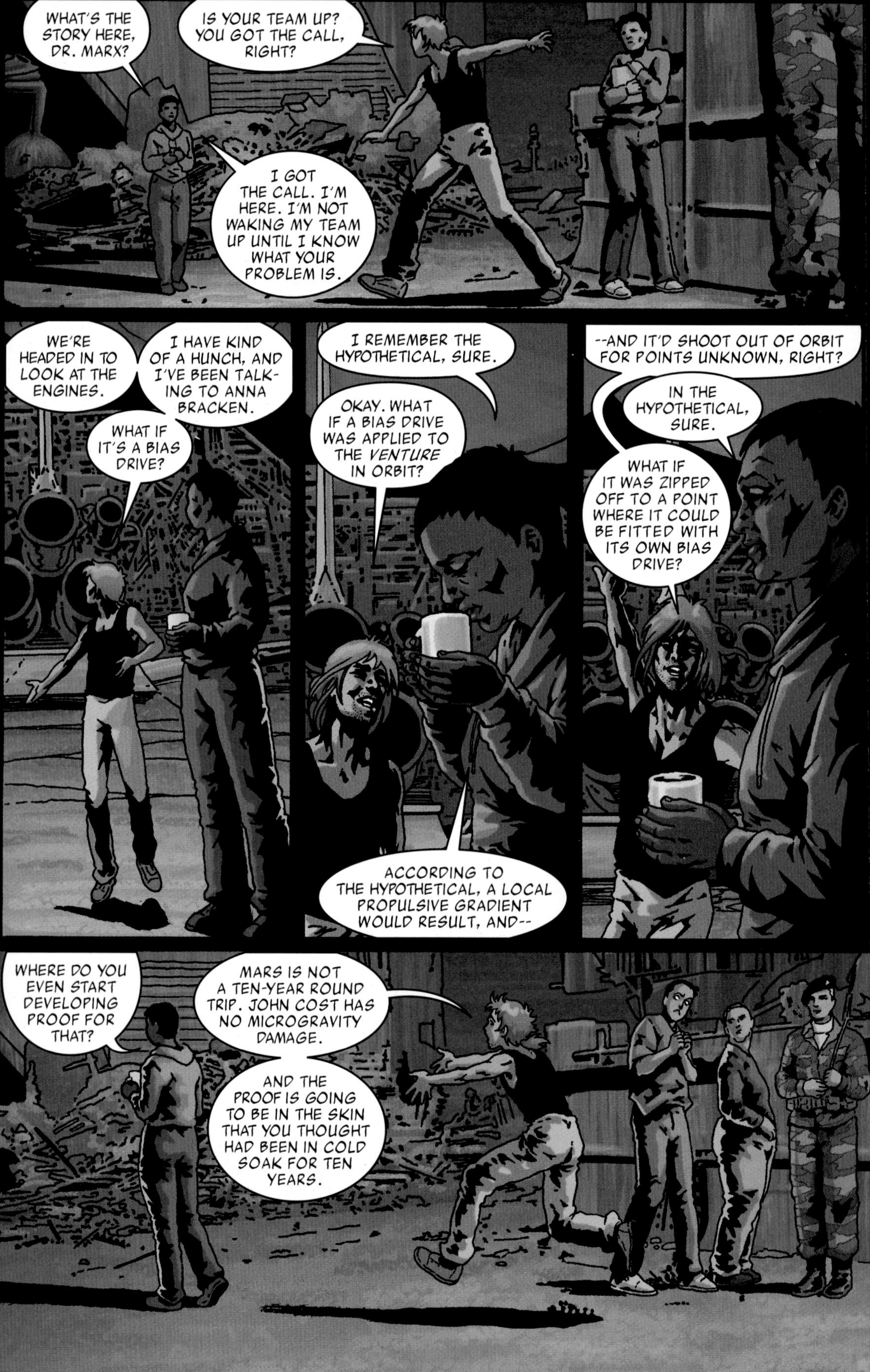
WHAT'S THE STORY HERE, DR. MARX?
IS YOUR TEAM UP? YOU GOT THE CALL, RIGHT?
I GOT THE CALL. I'M HERE. I'M NOT WAKING MY TEAM UP UNTIL I KNOW WHAT YOUR PROBLEM IS.
WE'RE HEADED IN TO LOOK AT THE ENGINES.
I HAVE KIND OF A HUNCH, AND I'VE BEEN TALKING TO ANNA BRACKEN.
WHAT IF IT'S A BIAS DRIVE?
I REMEMBER THE HYPOTHETICAL, SURE.
OKAY. WHAT IF A BIAS DRIVE WAS APPLIED TO THE *VENTURE* IN ORBIT?
ACCORDING TO THE HYPOTHETICAL, A LOCAL PROPULSIVE GRADIENT WOULD RESULT, AND--
--AND IT'D SHOOT OUT OF ORBIT FOR POINTS UNKNOWN, RIGHT?
IN THE HYPOTHETICAL, SURE.
WHAT IF IT WAS ZIPPED OFF TO A POINT WHERE IT COULD BE FITTED WITH ITS OWN BIAS DRIVE?
WHERE DO YOU EVEN START DEVELOPING PROOF FOR THAT?
MARS IS NOT A TEN-YEAR ROUND TRIP. JOHN COST HAS NO MICROGRAVITY DAMAGE.
AND THE PROOF IS GOING TO BE IN THE SKIN THAT YOU THOUGHT HAD BEEN IN COLD SOAK FOR TEN YEARS.

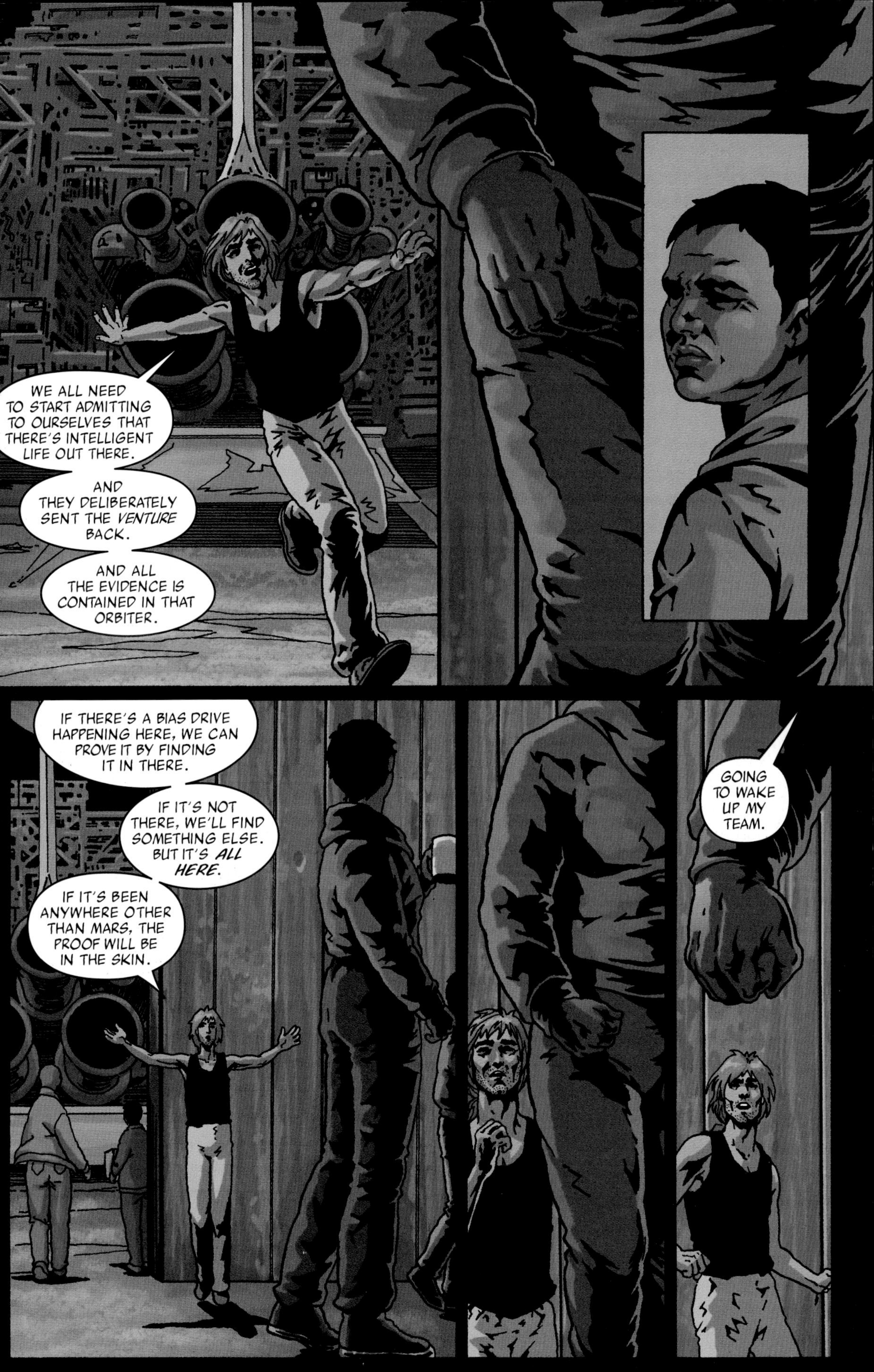
WE ALL NEED TO START ADMITTING TO OURSELVES THAT THERE'S INTELLIGENT LIFE OUT THERE.
AND THEY DELIBERATELY SENT THE *VENTURE* BACK.
AND ALL THE EVIDENCE IS CONTAINED IN THAT ORBITER.
IF THERE'S A BIAS DRIVE HAPPENING HERE, WE CAN PROVE IT BY FINDING IT IN THERE.
IF IT'S NOT THERE, WE'LL FIND SOMETHING ELSE. BUT IT'S ***ALL HERE***.
IF IT'S BEEN ANYWHERE OTHER THAN MARS, THE PROOF WILL BE IN THE SKIN.
GOING TO WAKE UP MY TEAM.

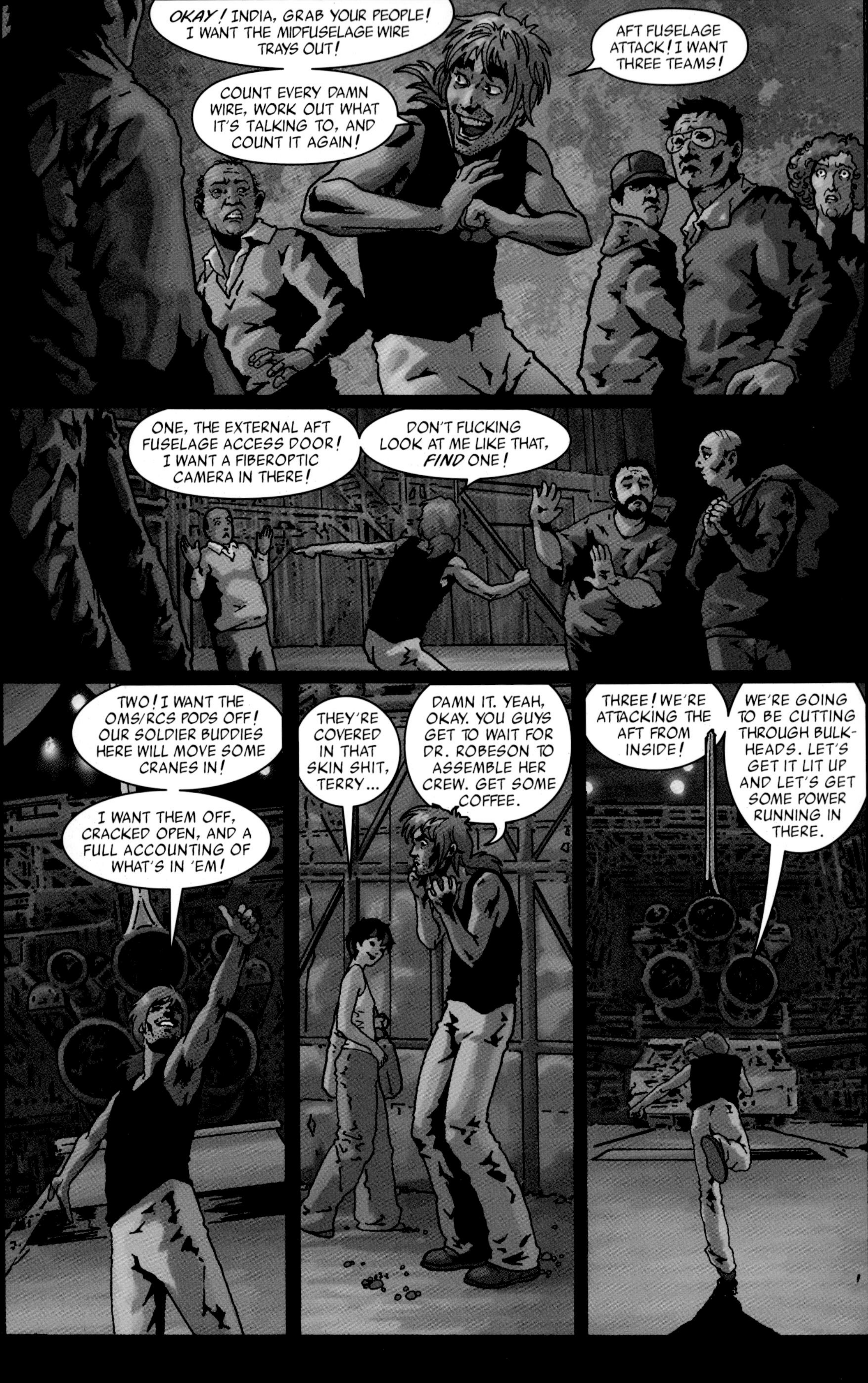
OKAY! INDIA, GRAB YOUR PEOPLE! I WANT THE MIDFUSELAGE WIRE TRAYS OUT!
COUNT EVERY DAMN WIRE, WORK OUT WHAT IT'S TALKING TO, AND COUNT IT AGAIN!
AFT FUSELAGE ATTACK! I WANT THREE TEAMS!
ONE, THE EXTERNAL AFT FUSELAGE ACCESS DOOR! I WANT A FIBEROPTIC CAMERA IN THERE!
DON'T FUCKING LOOK AT ME LIKE THAT, FIND ONE!
TWO! I WANT THE OMS/RCS PODS OFF! OUR SOLDIER BUDDIES HERE WILL MOVE SOME CRANES IN!
I WANT THEM OFF, CRACKED OPEN, AND A FULL ACCOUNTING OF WHAT'S IN 'EM!
THEY'RE COVERED IN THAT SKIN SHIT, TERRY...
DAMN IT. YEAH, OKAY. YOU GUYS GET TO WAIT FOR DR. ROBESON TO ASSEMBLE HER CREW. GET SOME COFFEE.
THREE! WE'RE ATTACKING THE AFT FROM INSIDE!
WE'RE GOING TO BE CUTTING THROUGH BULKHEADS. LET'S GET IT LIT UP AND LET'S GET SOME POWER RUNNING IN THERE.

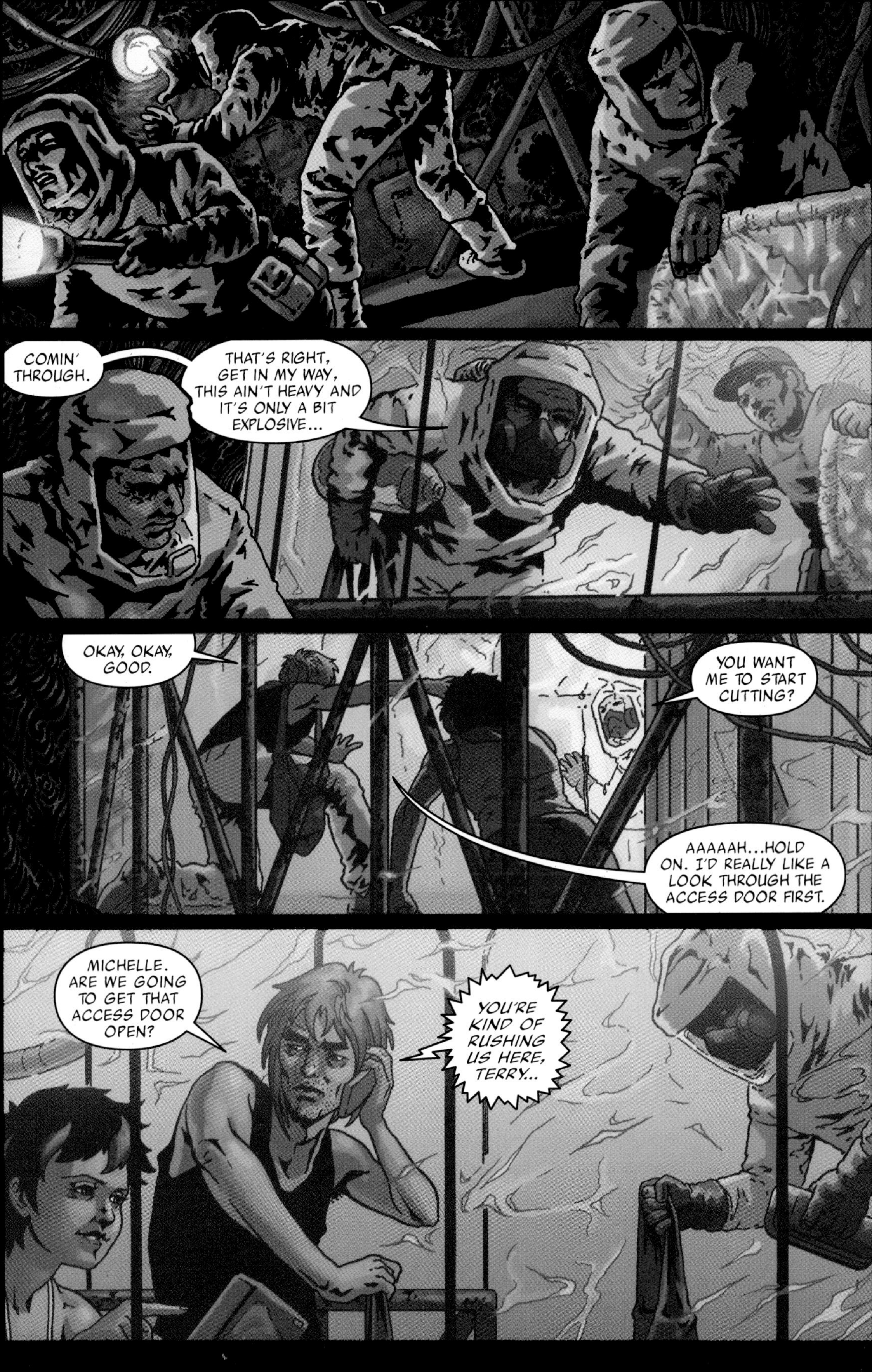
COMIN' THROUGH.
THAT'S RIGHT, GET IN MY WAY, THIS AIN'T HEAVY AND IT'S ONLY A BIT EXPLOSIVE...
OKAY, OKAY, GOOD.
YOU WANT ME TO START CUTTING?
AAAAAH...HOLD ON. I'D REALLY LIKE A LOOK THROUGH THE ACCESS DOOR FIRST.
MICHELLE. ARE WE GOING TO GET THAT ACCESS DOOR OPEN?
YOU'RE KIND OF RUSHING US HERE, TERRY...

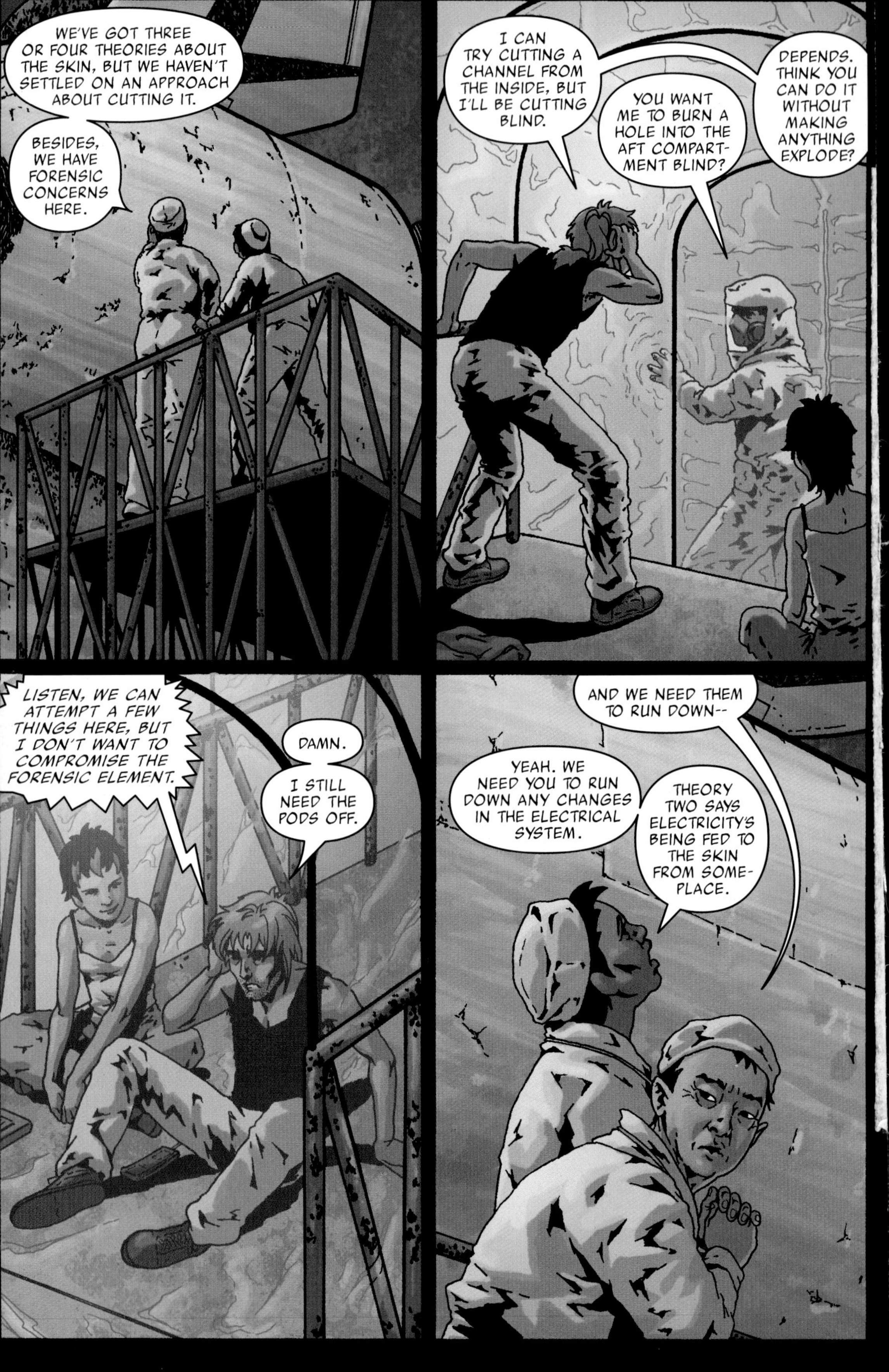
WE'VE GOT THREE OR FOUR THEORIES ABOUT THE SKIN, BUT WE HAVEN'T SETTLED ON AN APPROACH ABOUT CUTTING IT.
BESIDES, WE HAVE FORENSIC CONCERNS HERE.
I CAN TRY CUTTING A CHANNEL FROM THE INSIDE, BUT I'LL BE CUTTING BLIND.
YOU WANT ME TO BURN A HOLE INTO THE AFT COMPARTMENT BLIND?
DEPENDS. THINK YOU CAN DO IT WITHOUT MAKING ANYTHING EXPLODE?
LISTEN, WE CAN ATTEMPT A FEW THINGS HERE, BUT I DON'T WANT TO COMPROMISE THE FORENSIC ELEMENT.
DAMN.
I STILL NEED THE PODS OFF.
AND WE NEED THEM TO RUN DOWN--
YEAH. WE NEED YOU TO RUN DOWN ANY CHANGES IN THE ELECTRICAL SYSTEM.
THEORY TWO SAYS ELECTRICITY'S BEING FED TO THE SKIN FROM SOMEPLACE.

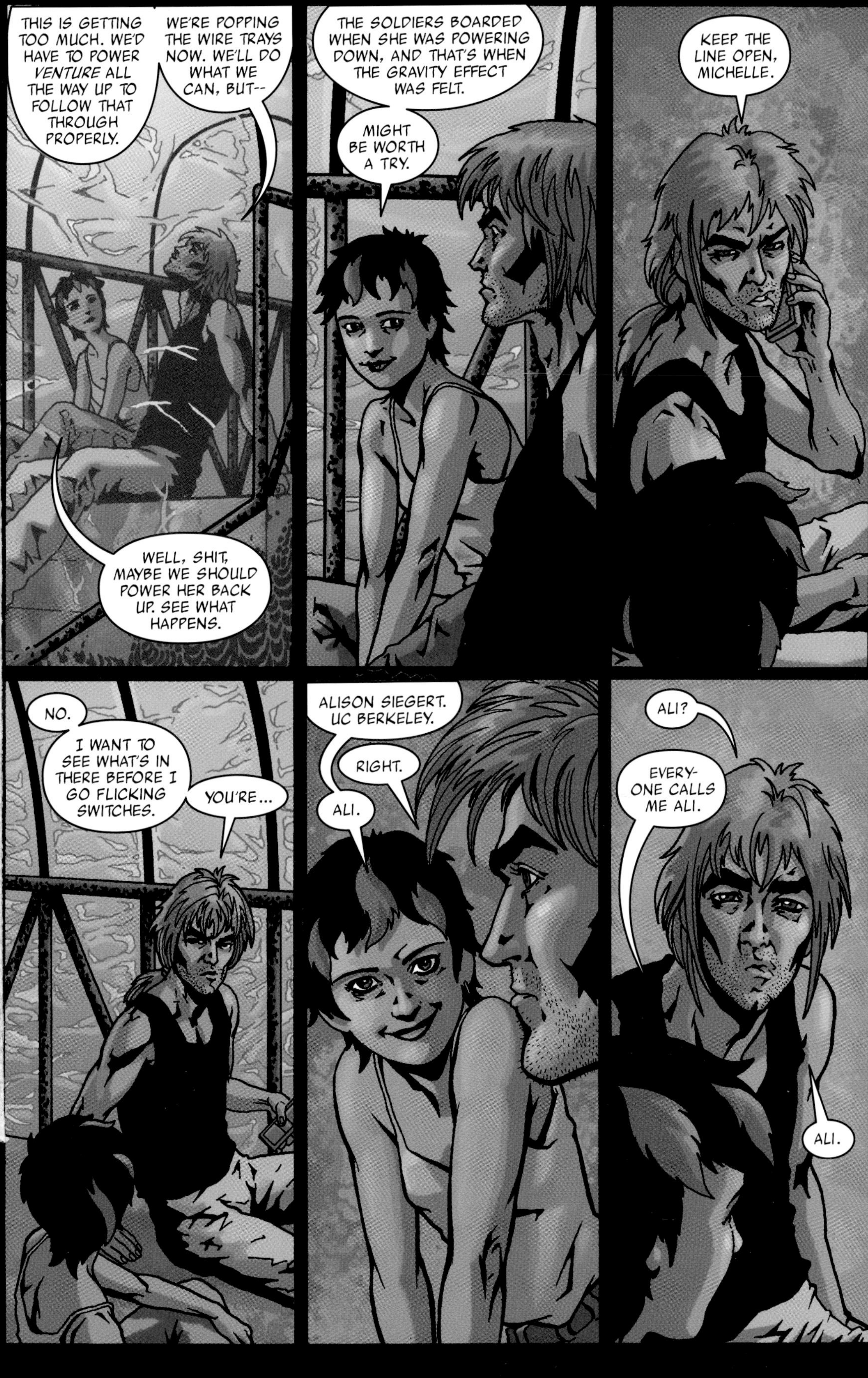
THIS IS GETTING TOO MUCH. WE'D HAVE TO POWER *VENTURE* ALL THE WAY UP TO FOLLOW THAT THROUGH PROPERLY.
WE'RE POPPING THE WIRE TRAYS NOW. WE'LL DO WHAT WE CAN, BUT--
WELL, SHIT, MAYBE WE SHOULD POWER HER BACK UP. SEE WHAT HAPPENS.
THE SOLDIERS BOARDED WHEN SHE WAS POWERING DOWN, AND THAT'S WHEN THE GRAVITY EFFECT WAS FELT.
MIGHT BE WORTH A TRY.
KEEP THE LINE OPEN, MICHELLE.
NO.
I WANT TO SEE WHAT'S IN THERE BEFORE I GO FLICKING SWITCHES.
YOU'RE...
ALISON SIEGERT. UC BERKELEY.
RIGHT.
ALI.
ALI?
EVERY-ONE CALLS ME ALI.
ALI.

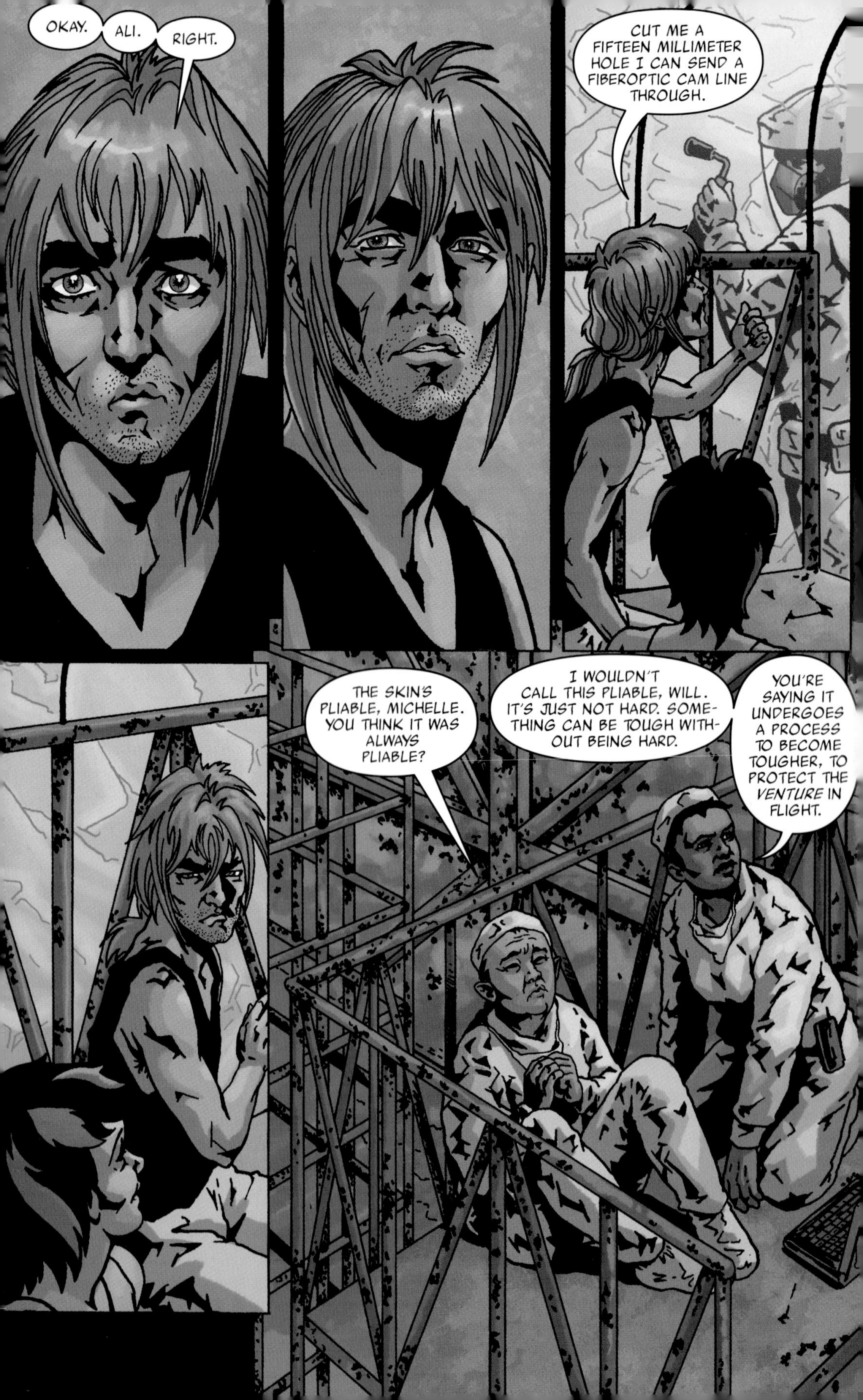
OKAY.
ALI.
RIGHT.
CUT ME A FIFTEEN MILLIMETER HOLE I CAN SEND A FIBEROPTIC CAM LINE THROUGH.
THE SKIN'S PLIABLE, MICHELLE. YOU THINK IT WAS ALWAYS PLIABLE?
I WOULDN'T CALL THIS PLIABLE, WILL. IT'S JUST NOT HARD. SOMETHING CAN BE TOUGH WITHOUT BEING HARD.
YOU'RE SAYING IT UNDERGOES A PROCESS TO BECOME TOUGHER, TO PROTECT THE *VENTURE* IN FLIGHT.

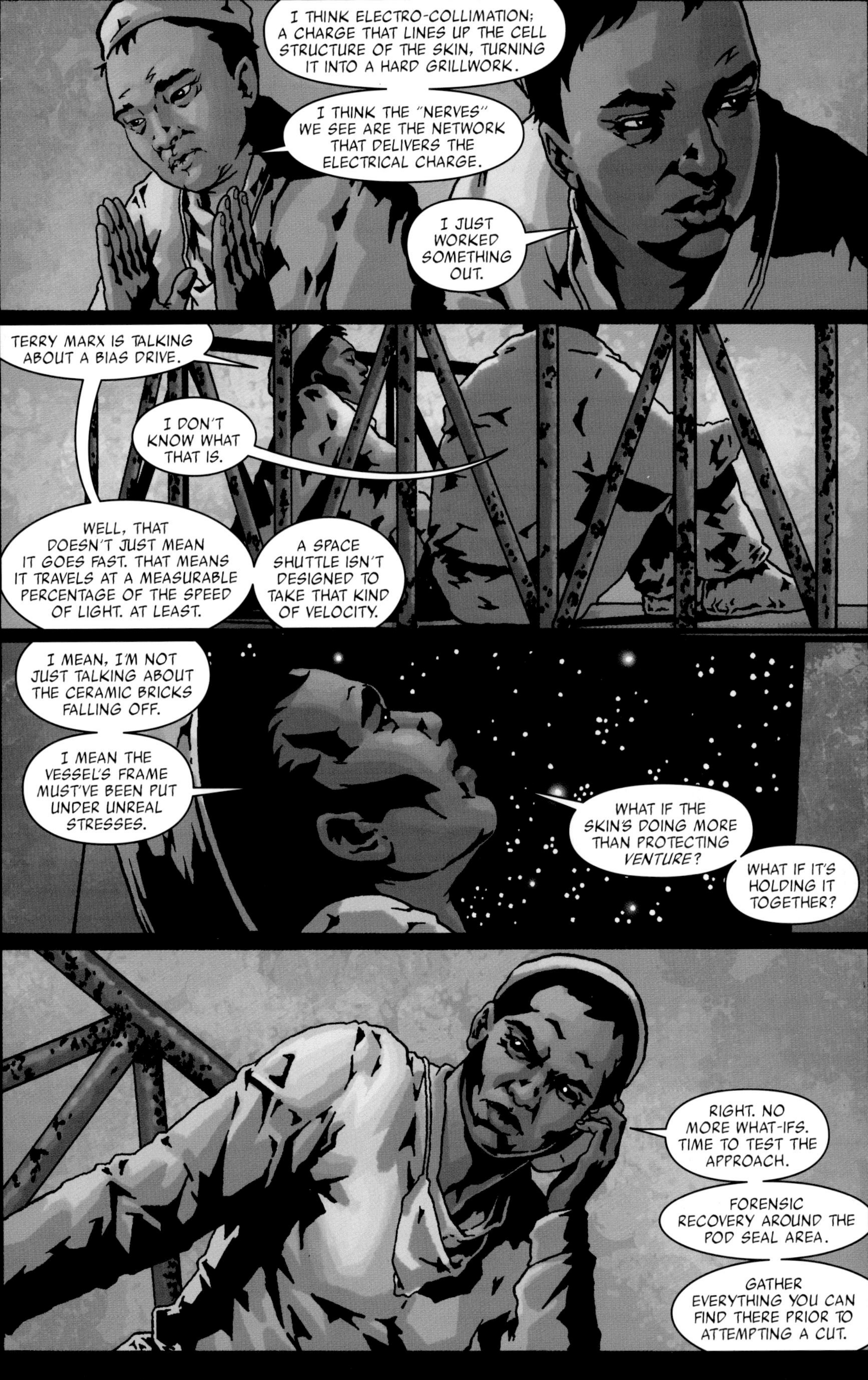
I THINK ELECTRO-COLLIMATION; A CHARGE THAT LINES UP THE CELL STRUCTURE OF THE SKIN, TURNING IT INTO A HARD GRILLWORK.
I THINK THE "NERVES" WE SEE ARE THE NETWORK THAT DELIVERS THE ELECTRICAL CHARGE.
I JUST WORKED SOMETHING OUT.
TERRY MARX IS TALKING ABOUT A BIAS DRIVE.
I DON'T KNOW WHAT THAT IS.
WELL, THAT DOESN'T JUST MEAN IT GOES FAST. THAT MEANS IT TRAVELS AT A MEASURABLE PERCENTAGE OF THE SPEED OF LIGHT. AT LEAST.
A SPACE SHUTTLE ISN'T DESIGNED TO TAKE THAT KIND OF VELOCITY.
I MEAN, I'M NOT JUST TALKING ABOUT THE CERAMIC BRICKS FALLING OFF.
I MEAN THE VESSEL'S FRAME MUST'VE BEEN PUT UNDER UNREAL STRESSES.
WHAT IF THE SKIN'S DOING MORE THAN PROTECTING *VENTURE*?
WHAT IF IT'S HOLDING IT TOGETHER?
RIGHT. NO MORE WHAT-IFS. TIME TO TEST THE APPROACH.
FORENSIC RECOVERY AROUND THE POD SEAL AREA.
GATHER EVERYTHING YOU CAN FIND THERE PRIOR TO ATTEMPTING A CUT.

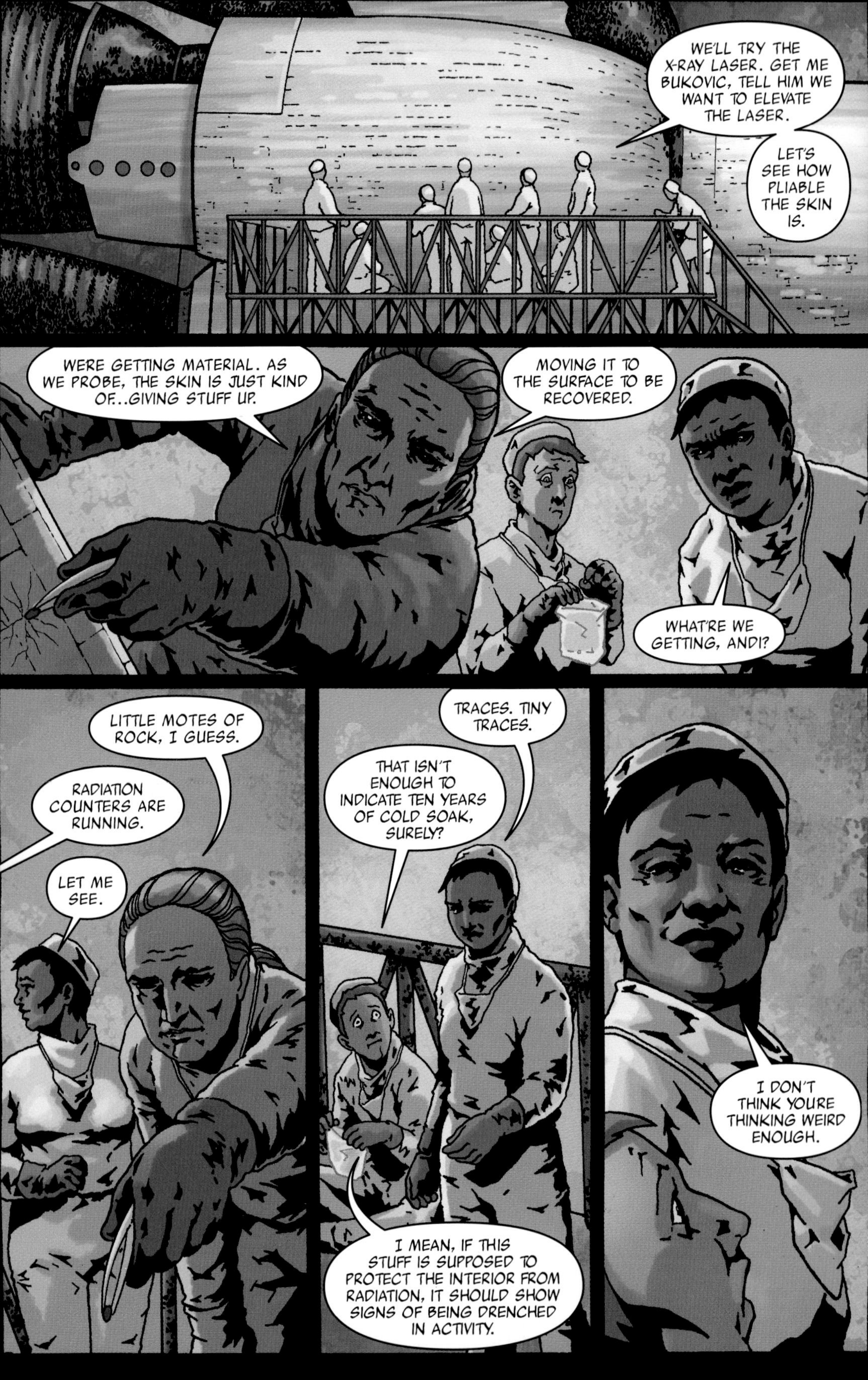
WE'LL TRY THE X-RAY LASER. GET ME BUKOVIC, TELL HIM WE WANT TO ELEVATE THE LASER.
LET'S SEE HOW PLIABLE THE SKIN IS.
WERE GETTING MATERIAL. AS WE PROBE, THE SKIN IS JUST KIND OF...GIVING STUFF UP.
MOVING IT TO THE SURFACE TO BE RECOVERED.
WHAT'RE WE GETTING, ANDI?
LITTLE MOTES OF ROCK, I GUESS.
RADIATION COUNTERS ARE RUNNING.
LET ME SEE.
TRACES. TINY TRACES.
THAT ISN'T ENOUGH TO INDICATE TEN YEARS OF COLD SOAK, SURELY?
I MEAN, IF THIS STUFF IS SUPPOSED TO PROTECT THE INTERIOR FROM RADIATION, IT SHOULD SHOW SIGNS OF BEING DRENCHED IN ACTIVITY.
I DON'T THINK YOURE THINKING WEIRD ENOUGH.

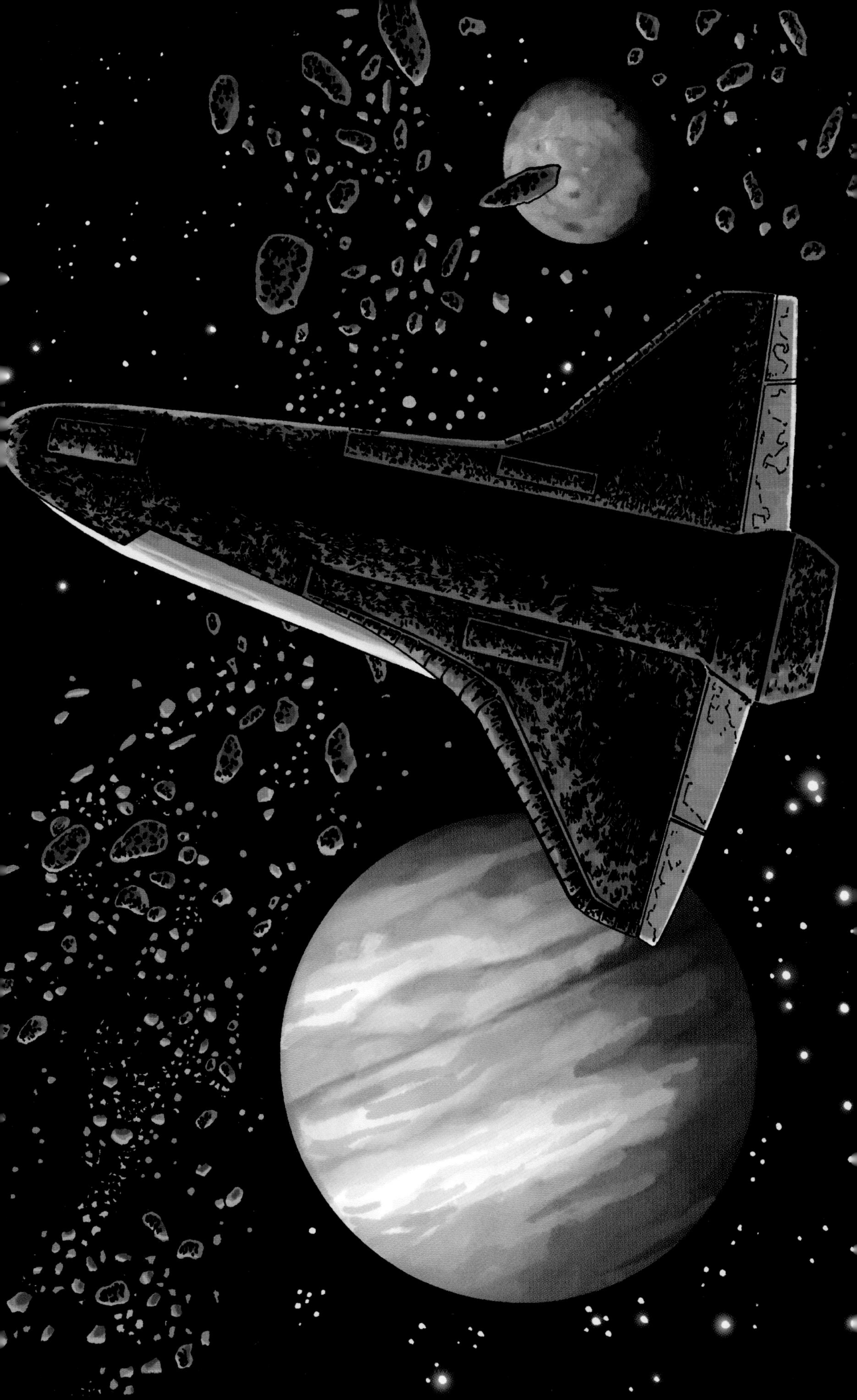

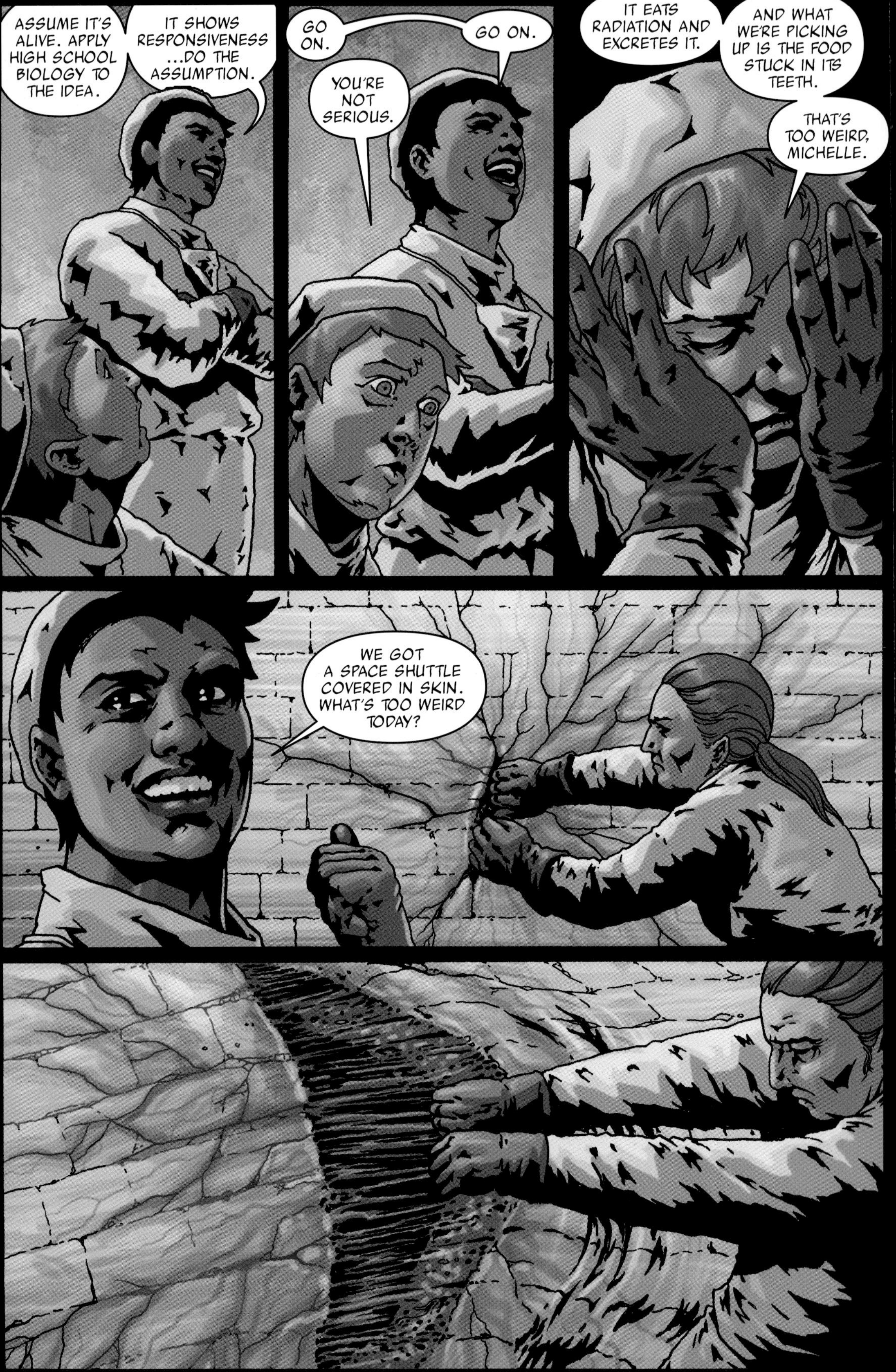
ASSUME IT'S ALIVE. APPLY HIGH SCHOOL BIOLOGY TO THE IDEA.
IT SHOWS RESPONSIVENESS ...DO THE ASSUMPTION.
GO ON.
GO ON.
YOU'RE NOT SERIOUS.
IT EATS RADIATION AND EXCRETES IT.
AND WHAT WE'RE PICKING UP IS THE FOOD STUCK IN ITS TEETH.
THAT'S TOO WEIRD, MICHELLE.
WE GOT A SPACE SHUTTLE COVERED IN SKIN. WHAT'S TOO WEIRD TODAY?

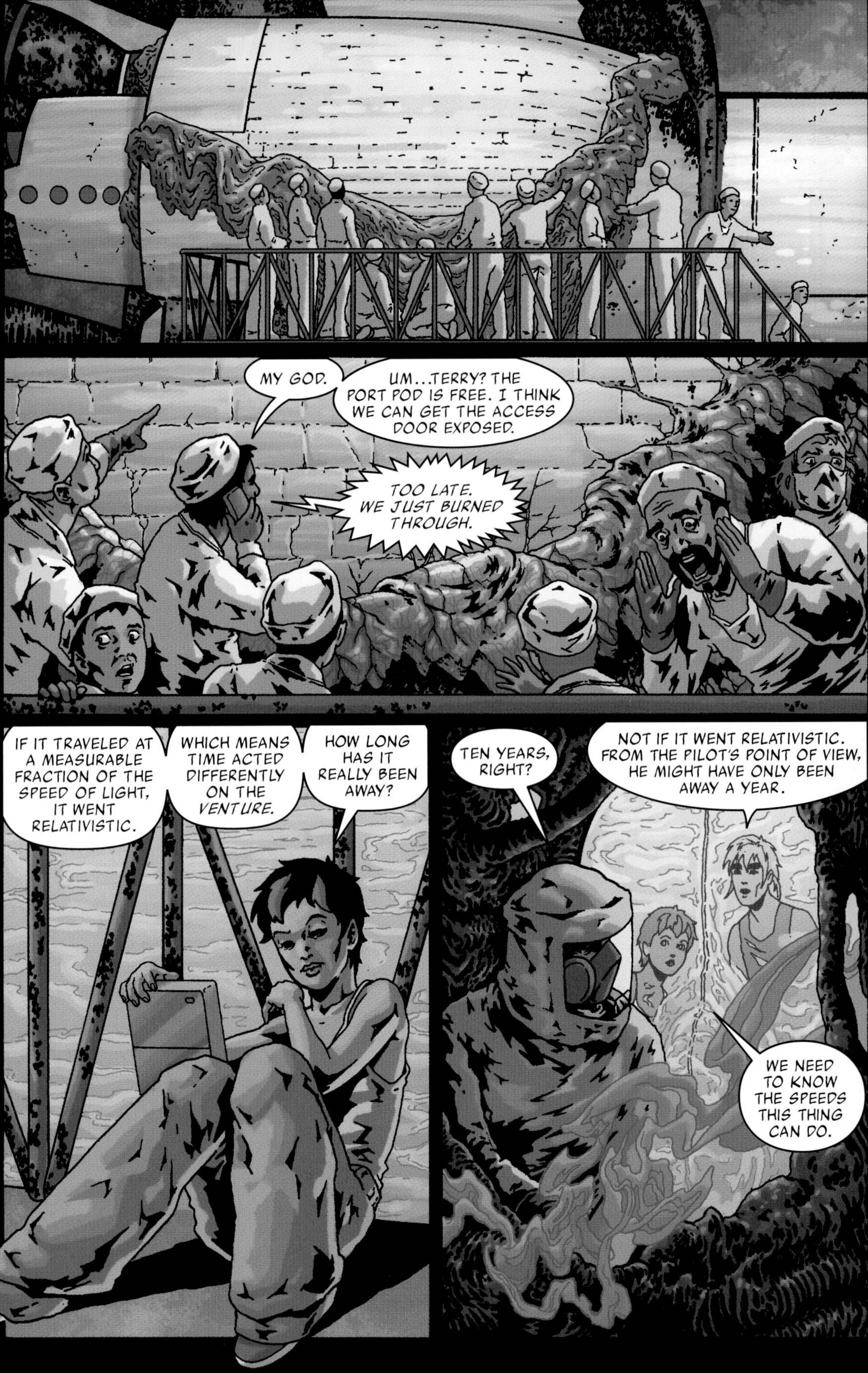
MY GOD.
UM...TERRY? THE PORT POD IS FREE. I THINK WE CAN GET THE ACCESS DOOR EXPOSED.
TOO LATE. WE JUST BURNED THROUGH.
IF IT TRAVELED AT A MEASURABLE FRACTION OF THE SPEED OF LIGHT, IT WENT RELATIVISTIC.
WHICH MEANS TIME ACTED DIFFERENTLY ON THE *VENTURE.*
HOW LONG HAS IT REALLY BEEN AWAY?
TEN YEARS, RIGHT?
NOT IF IT WENT RELATIVISTIC. FROM THE PILOT'S POINT OF VIEW, HE MIGHT HAVE ONLY BEEN AWAY A YEAR.
WE NEED TO KNOW THE SPEEDS THIS THING CAN DO.

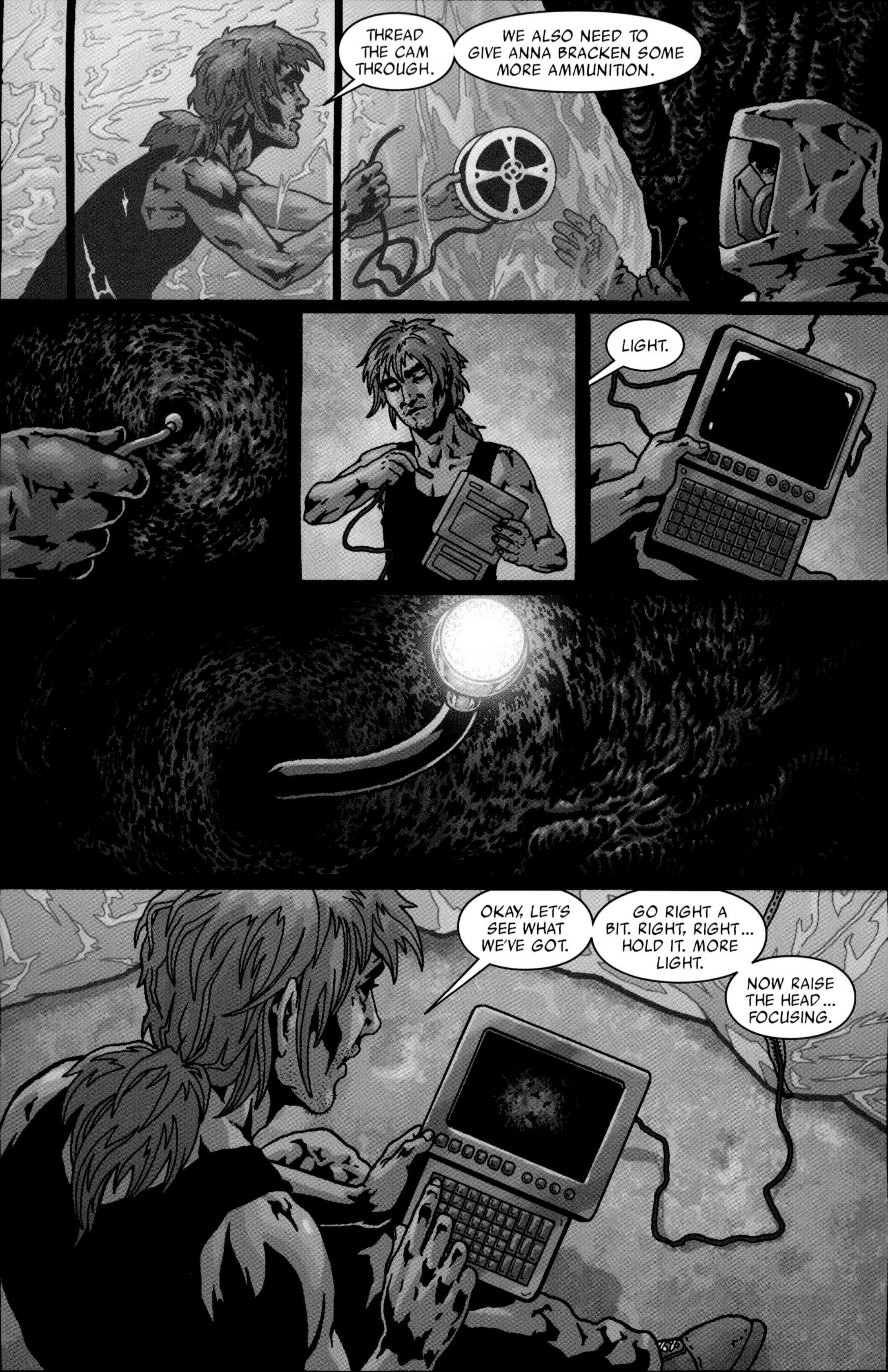
THREAD THE CAM THROUGH.
WE ALSO NEED TO GIVE ANNA BRACKEN SOME MORE AMMUNITION.
LIGHT.
OKAY, LET'S SEE WHAT WE'VE GOT.
GO RIGHT A BIT. RIGHT, RIGHT... HOLD IT. MORE LIGHT.
NOW RAISE THE HEAD... FOCUSING.

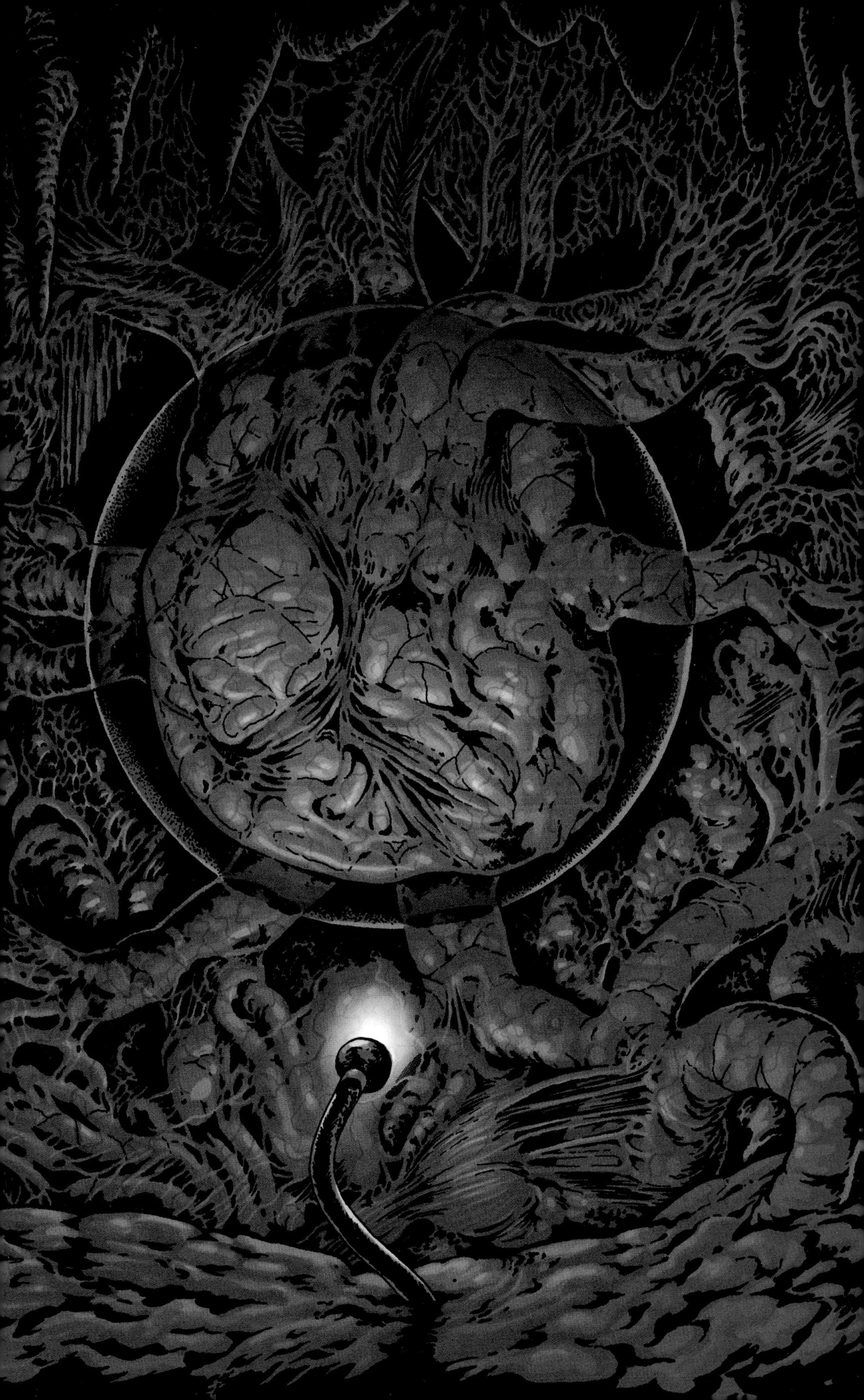

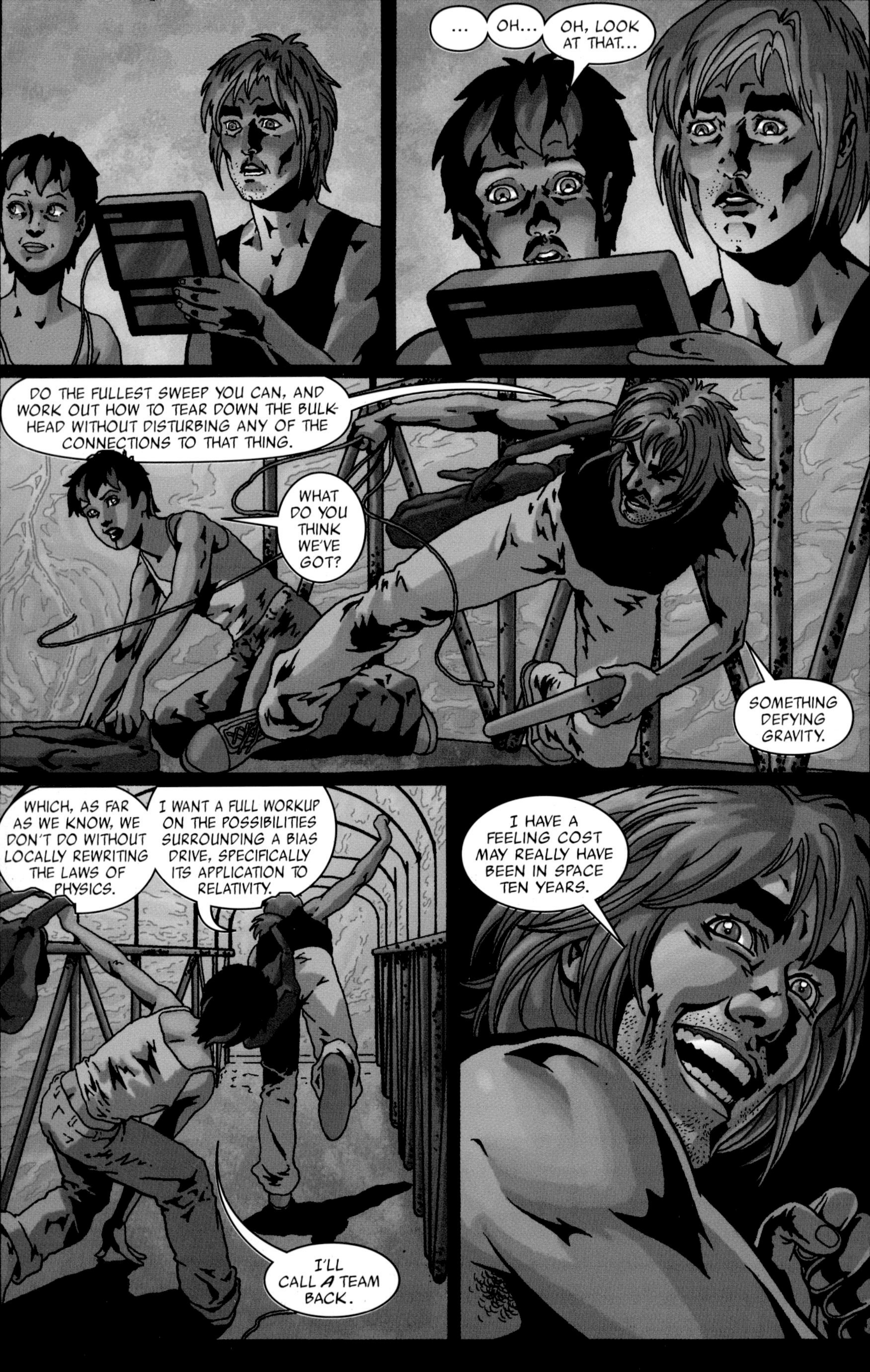
...
OH...
OH, LOOK AT THAT...
DO THE FULLEST SWEEP YOU CAN, AND WORK OUT HOW TO TEAR DOWN THE BULK-HEAD WITHOUT DISTURBING ANY OF THE CONNECTIONS TO THAT THING.
WHAT DO YOU THINK WE'VE GOT?
SOMETHING DEFYING GRAVITY.
WHICH, AS FAR AS WE KNOW, WE DON'T DO WITHOUT LOCALLY REWRITING THE LAWS OF PHYSICS.
I WANT A FULL WORKUP ON THE POSSIBILITIES SURROUNDING A BIAS DRIVE, SPECIFICALLY ITS APPLICATION TO RELATIVITY.
I'LL CALL A TEAM BACK.
I HAVE A FEELING COST MAY REALLY HAVE BEEN IN SPACE TEN YEARS.

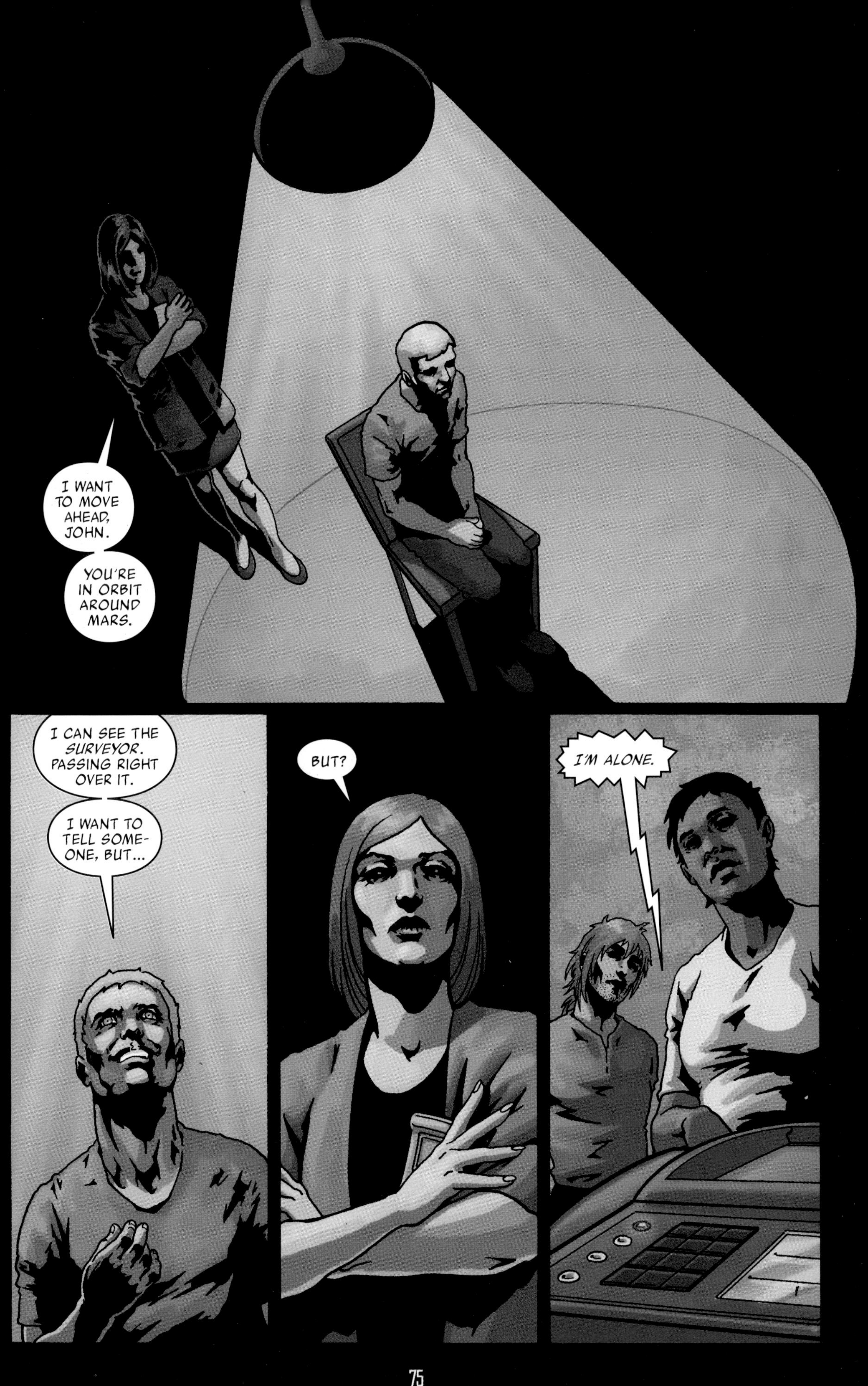
I WANT TO MOVE AHEAD, JOHN.
YOU'RE IN ORBIT AROUND MARS.
I CAN SEE THE *SURVEYOR*. PASSING RIGHT OVER IT.
I WANT TO TELL SOME-ONE, BUT...
BUT?
I'M ALONE.

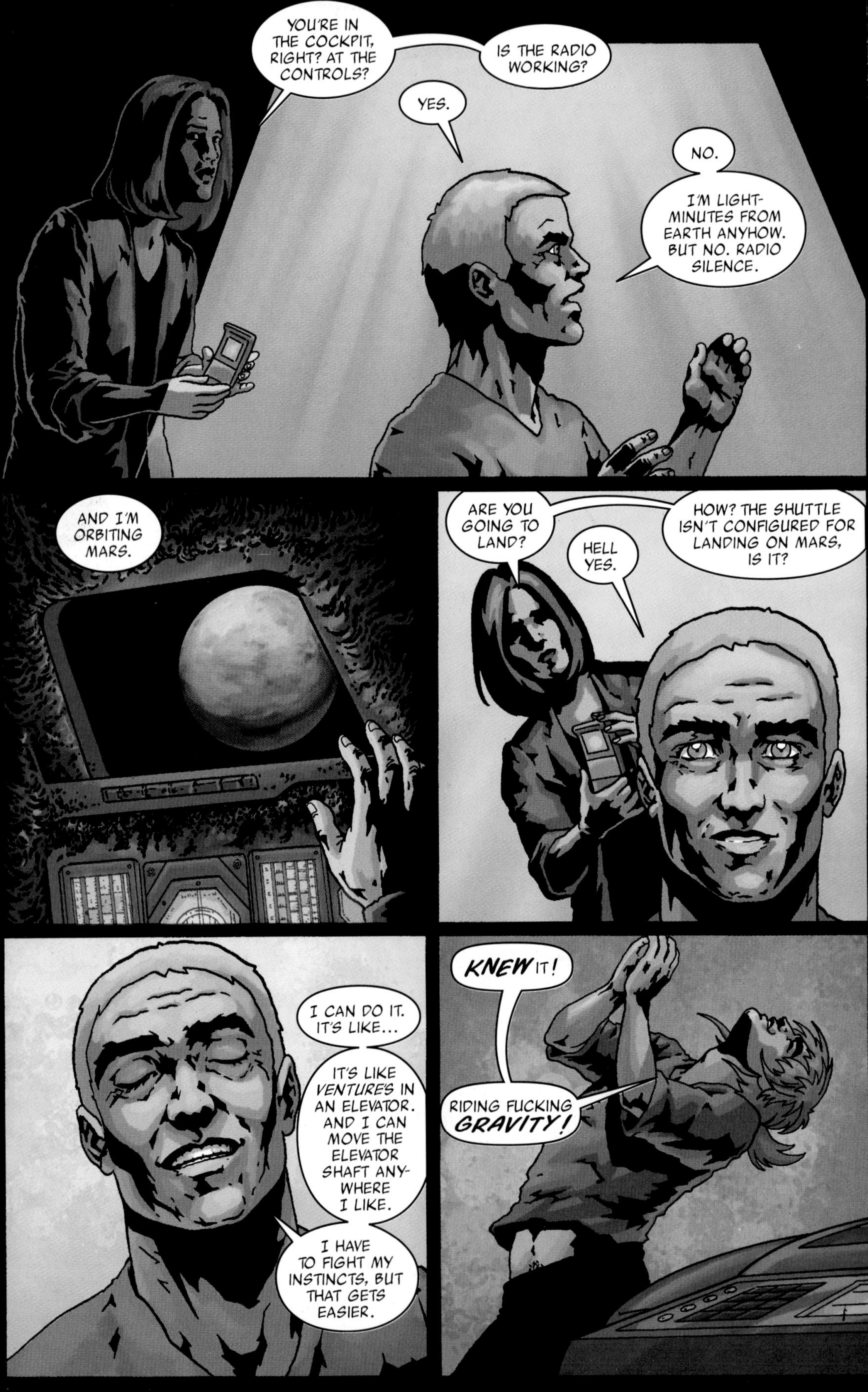
YOU'RE IN THE COCKPIT, RIGHT? AT THE CONTROLS?
IS THE RADIO WORKING?
YES.
NO.
I'M LIGHT-MINUTES FROM EARTH ANYHOW. BUT NO. RADIO SILENCE.
AND I'M ORBITING MARS.
ARE YOU GOING TO LAND?
HOW? THE SHUTTLE ISN'T CONFIGURED FOR LANDING ON MARS, IS IT?
HELL YES.
I CAN DO IT. IT'S LIKE...
IT'S LIKE *VENTURE'S* IN AN ELEVATOR. AND I CAN MOVE THE ELEVATOR SHAFT ANYWHERE I LIKE.
I HAVE TO FIGHT MY INSTINCTS, BUT THAT GETS EASIER.
KNEW IT!
RIDING FUCKING **GRAVITY**!

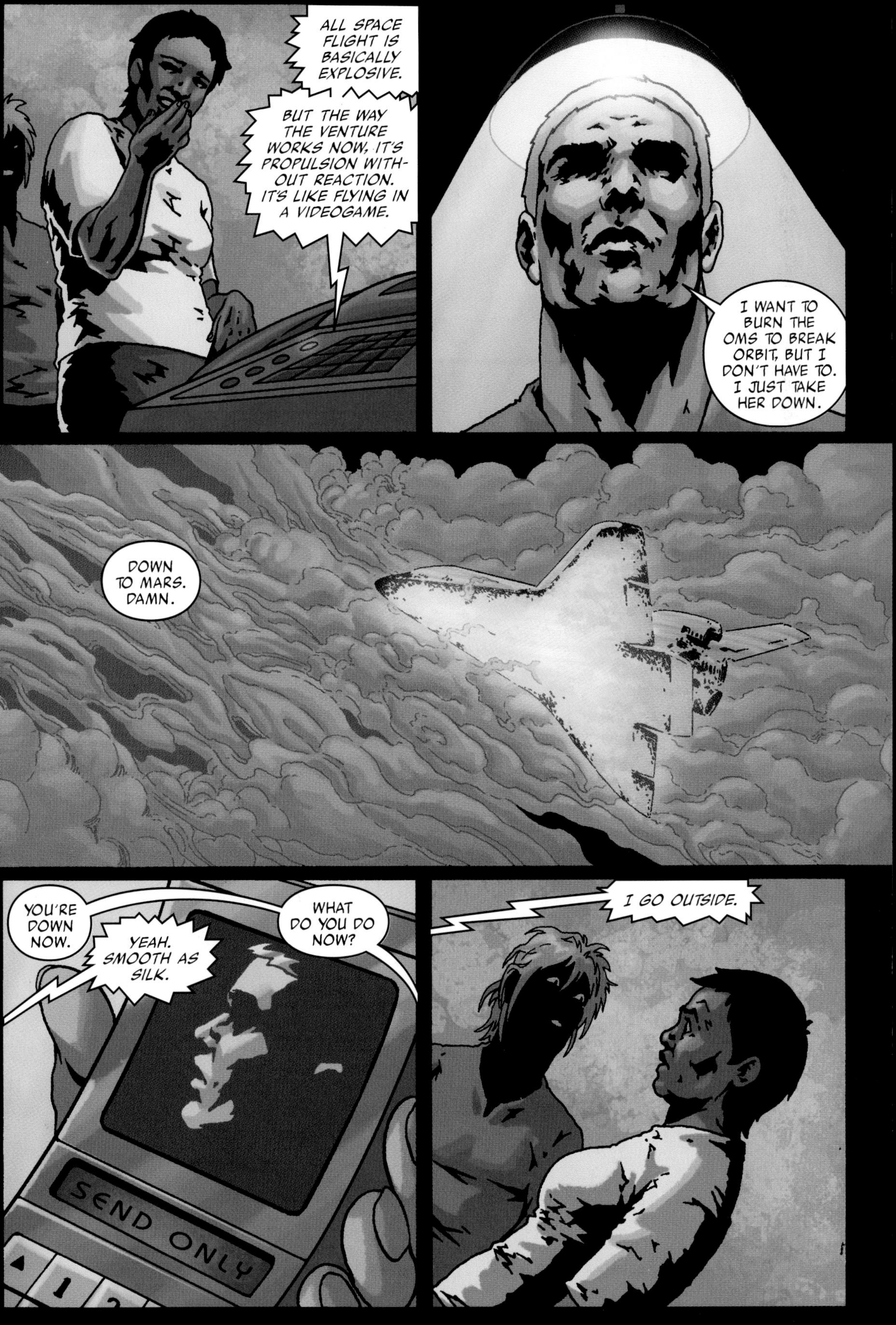
ALL SPACE FLIGHT IS BASICALLY EXPLOSIVE.
BUT THE WAY THE VENTURE WORKS NOW, IT'S PROPULSION WITH-OUT REACTION. IT'S LIKE FLYING IN A VIDEOGAME.
I WANT TO BURN THE OMS TO BREAK ORBIT, BUT I DON'T HAVE TO. I JUST TAKE HER DOWN.
DOWN TO MARS. DAMN.
YOU'RE DOWN NOW.
YEAH. SMOOTH AS SILK.
WHAT DO YOU DO NOW?
SEND ONLY
I GO OUTSIDE.

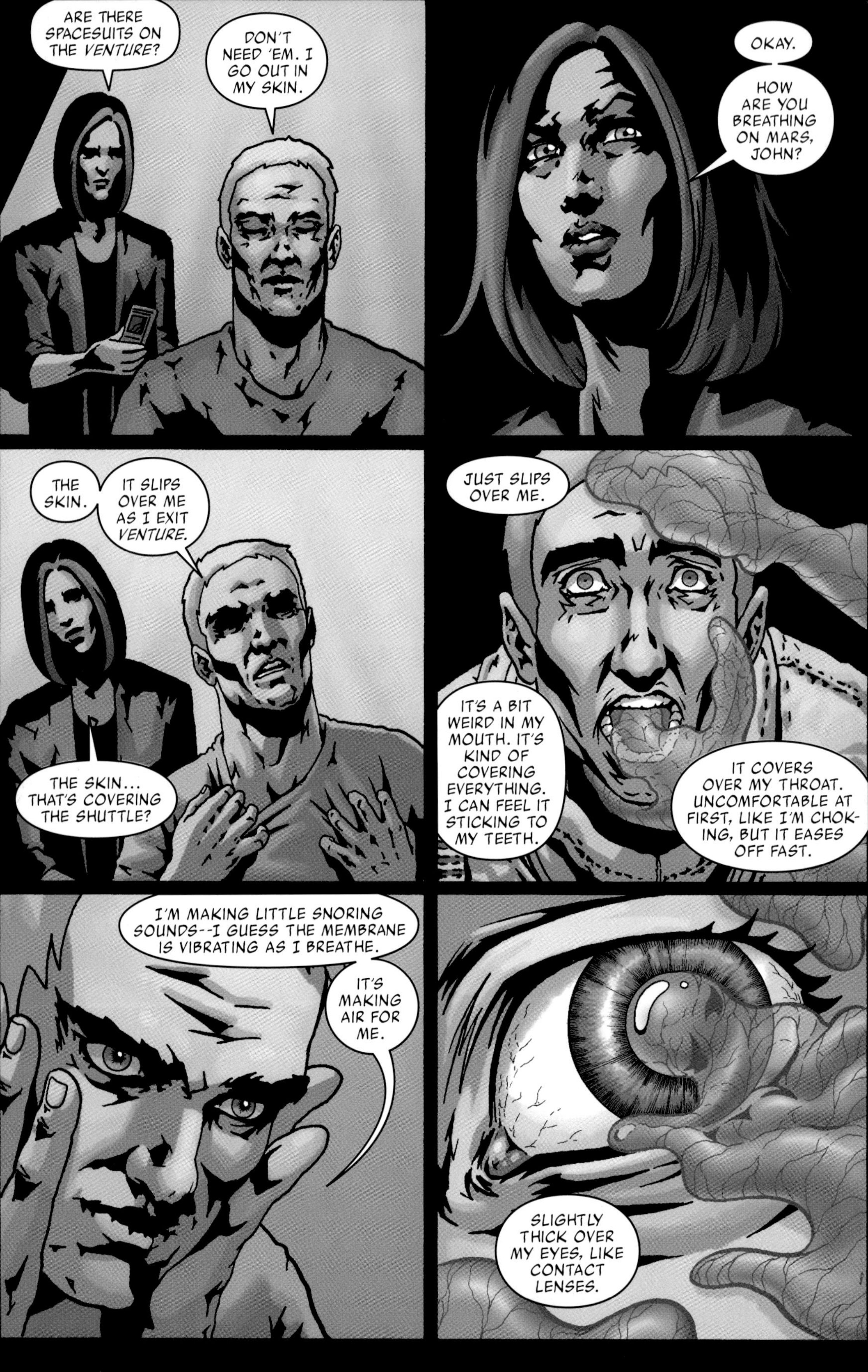
ARE THERE SPACESUITS ON THE *VENTURE*?
DON'T NEED 'EM. I GO OUT IN MY SKIN.
OKAY.
HOW ARE YOU BREATHING ON MARS, JOHN?
THE SKIN.
IT SLIPS OVER ME AS I EXIT *VENTURE*.
THE SKIN... THAT'S COVERING THE SHUTTLE?
JUST SLIPS OVER ME.
IT'S A BIT WEIRD IN MY MOUTH. IT'S KIND OF COVERING EVERYTHING. I CAN FEEL IT STICKING TO MY TEETH.
IT COVERS OVER MY THROAT. UNCOMFORTABLE AT FIRST, LIKE I'M CHOKING, BUT IT EASES OFF FAST.
I'M MAKING LITTLE SNORING SOUNDS--I GUESS THE MEMBRANE IS VIBRATING AS I BREATHE.
IT'S MAKING AIR FOR ME.
SLIGHTLY THICK OVER MY EYES, LIKE CONTACT LENSES.

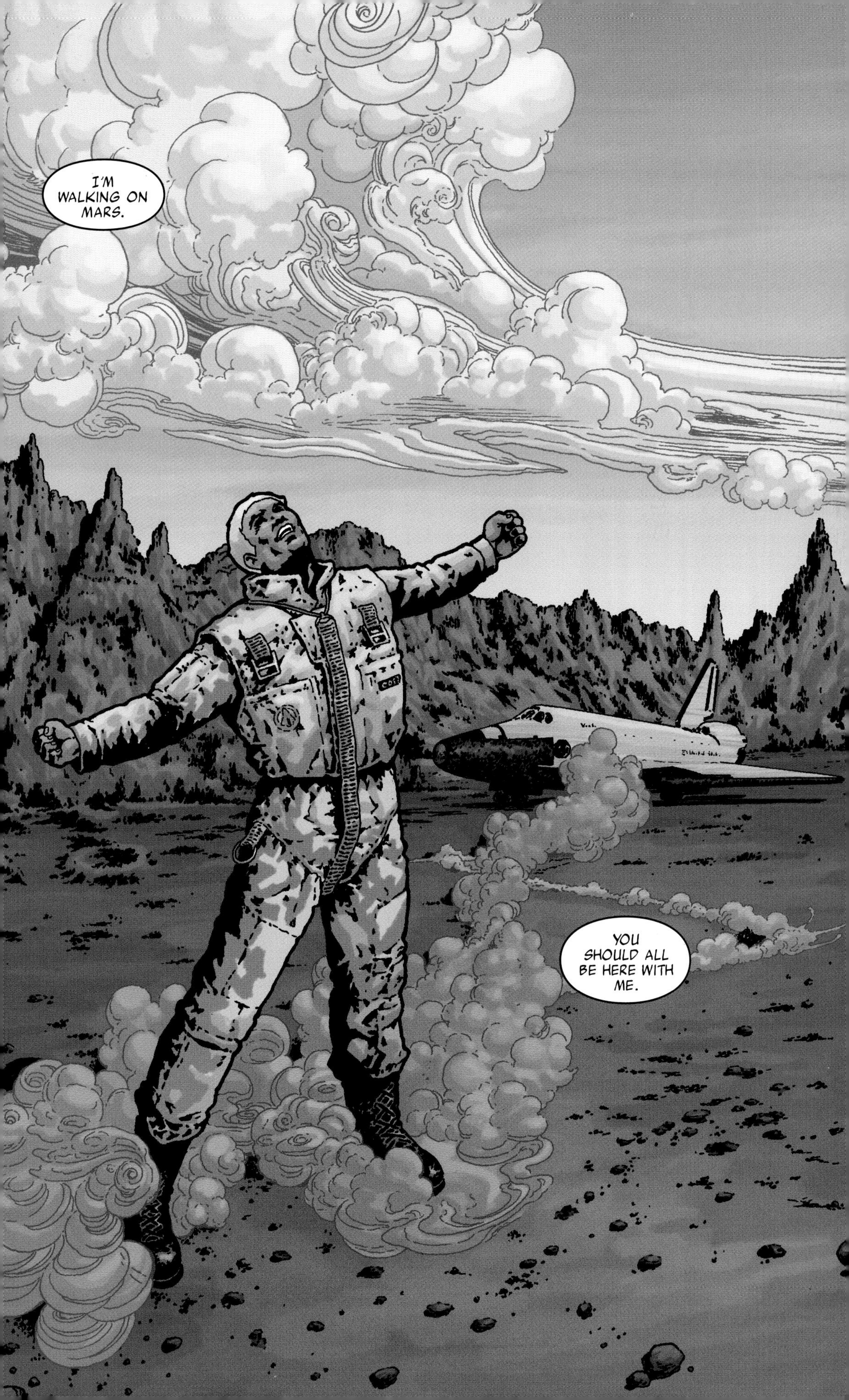
I'M WALKING ON MARS.
YOU SHOULD ALL BE HERE WITH ME.

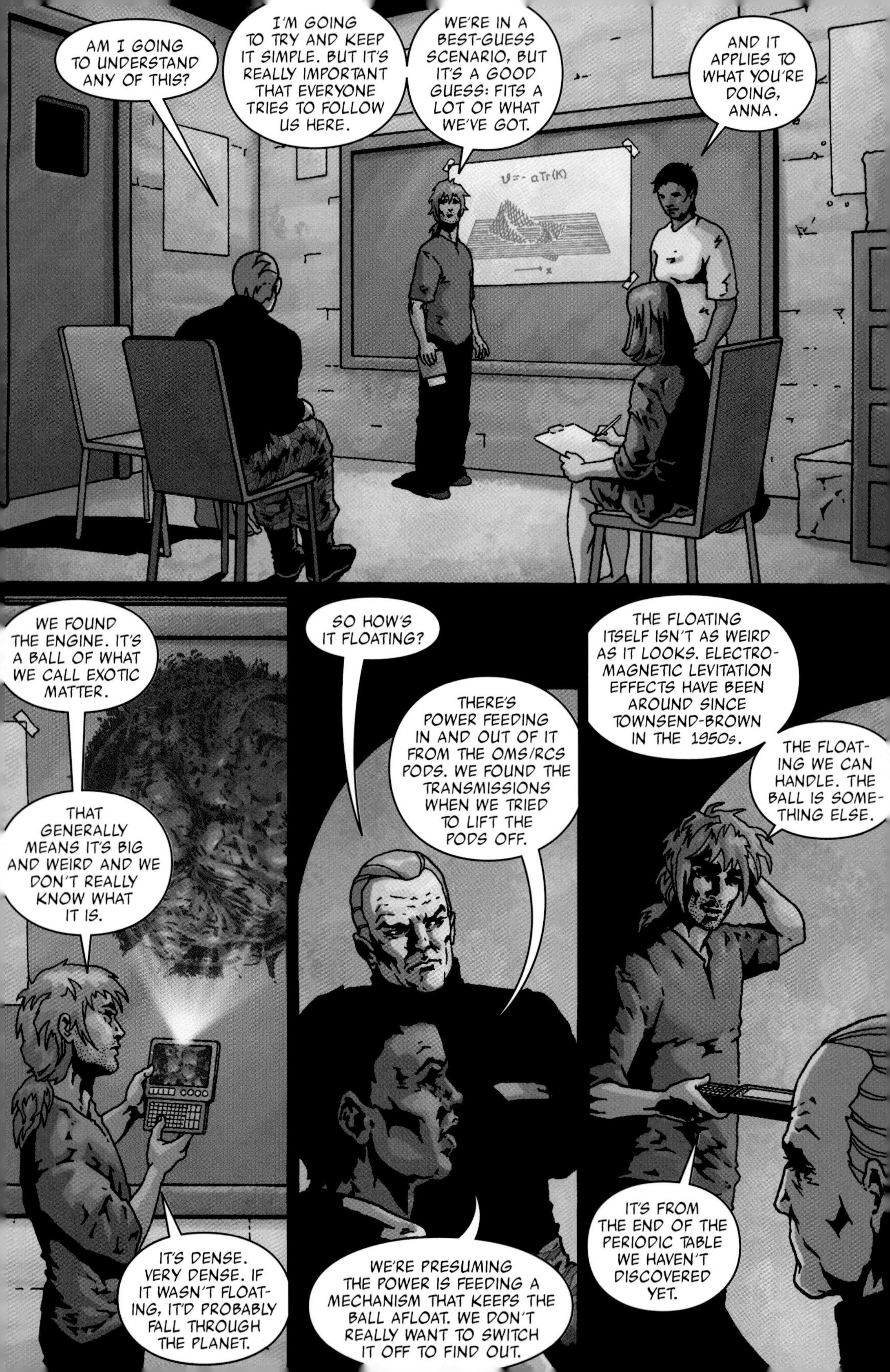
AM I GOING TO UNDERSTAND ANY OF THIS?
I'M GOING TO TRY AND KEEP IT SIMPLE. BUT IT'S REALLY IMPORTANT THAT EVERYONE TRIES TO FOLLOW US HERE.
WE'RE IN A BEST-GUESS SCENARIO, BUT IT'S A GOOD GUESS: FITS A LOT OF WHAT WE'VE GOT.
AND IT APPLIES TO WHAT YOU'RE DOING, ANNA.
U=- aTr(K)
WE FOUND THE ENGINE. IT'S A BALL OF WHAT WE CALL EXOTIC MATTER.
THAT GENERALLY MEANS IT'S BIG AND WEIRD AND WE DON'T REALLY KNOW WHAT IT IS.
IT'S DENSE. VERY DENSE. IF IT WASN'T FLOATING, IT'D PROBABLY FALL THROUGH THE PLANET.
SO HOW'S IT FLOATING?
THERE'S POWER FEEDING IN AND OUT OF IT FROM THE OMS/RCS PODS. WE FOUND THE TRANSMISSIONS WHEN WE TRIED TO LIFT THE PODS OFF.
WE'RE PRESUMING THE POWER IS FEEDING A MECHANISM THAT KEEPS THE BALL AFLOAT. WE DON'T REALLY WANT TO SWITCH IT OFF TO FIND OUT.
THE FLOATING ITSELF ISN'T AS WEIRD AS IT LOOKS. ELECTROMAGNETIC LEVITATION EFFECTS HAVE BEEN AROUND SINCE TOWNSEND-BROWN IN THE 1950s.
THE FLOATING WE CAN HANDLE. THE BALL IS SOMETHING ELSE.
IT'S FROM THE END OF THE PERIODIC TABLE WE HAVEN'T DISCOVERED YET.

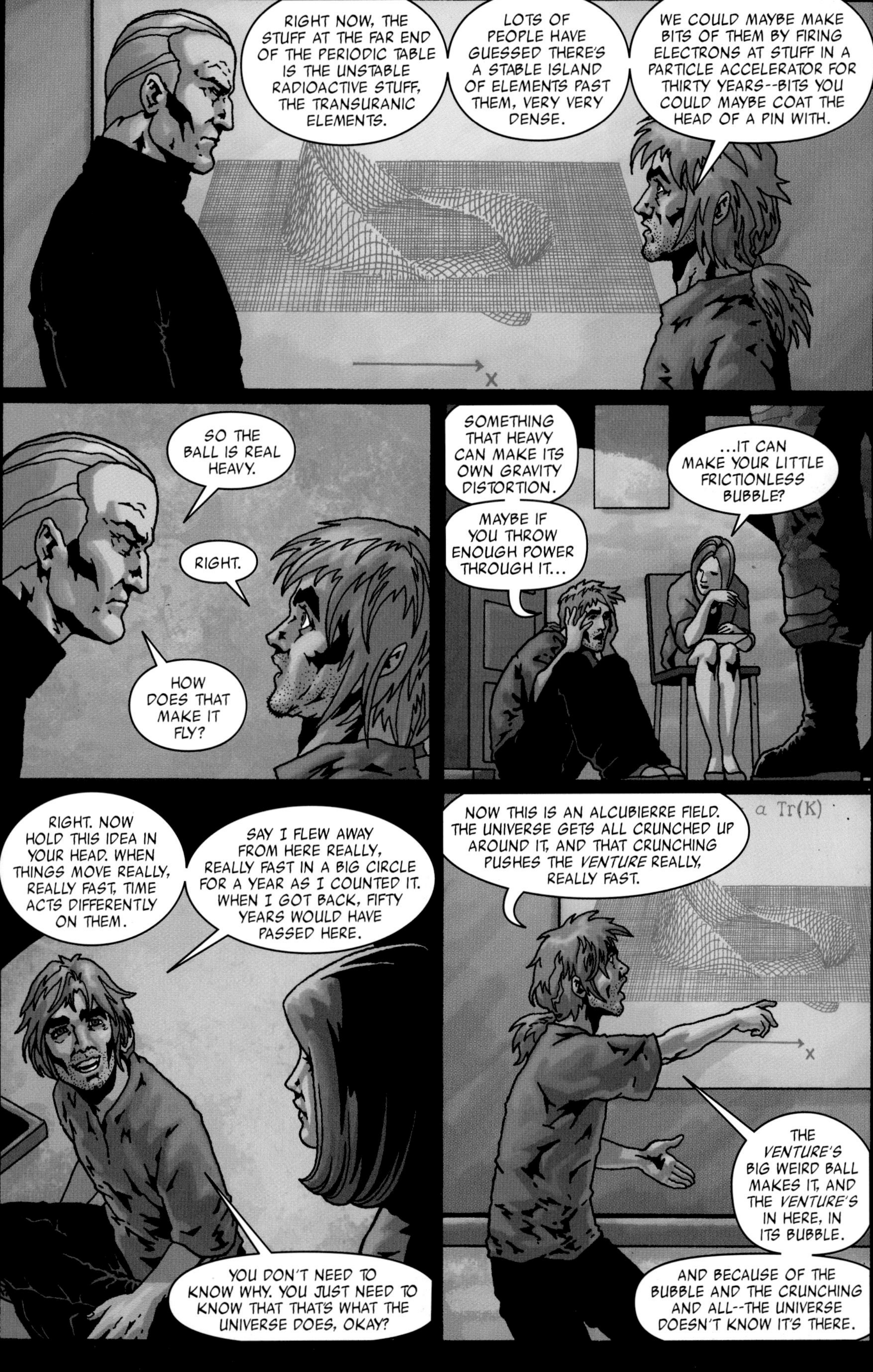

RIGHT NOW, THE STUFF AT THE FAR END OF THE PERIODIC TABLE IS THE UNSTABLE RADIOACTIVE STUFF, THE TRANSURANIC ELEMENTS.
LOTS OF PEOPLE HAVE GUESSED THERE'S A STABLE ISLAND OF ELEMENTS PAST THEM, VERY VERY DENSE.
WE COULD MAYBE MAKE BITS OF THEM BY FIRING ELECTRONS AT STUFF IN A PARTICLE ACCELERATOR FOR THIRTY YEARS--BITS YOU COULD MAYBE COAT THE HEAD OF A PIN WITH.
x
SO THE BALL IS REAL HEAVY.
RIGHT.
HOW DOES THAT MAKE IT FLY?
SOMETHING THAT HEAVY CAN MAKE ITS OWN GRAVITY DISTORTION.
...IT CAN MAKE YOUR LITTLE FRICTIONLESS BUBBLE?
MAYBE IF YOU THROW ENOUGH POWER THROUGH IT...
RIGHT. NOW HOLD THIS IDEA IN YOUR HEAD. WHEN THINGS MOVE REALLY, REALLY FAST, TIME ACTS DIFFERENTLY ON THEM.
SAY I FLEW AWAY FROM HERE REALLY, REALLY FAST IN A BIG CIRCLE FOR A YEAR AS I COUNTED IT. WHEN I GOT BACK, FIFTY YEARS WOULD HAVE PASSED HERE.
YOU DON'T NEED TO KNOW WHY. YOU JUST NEED TO KNOW THAT THAT'S WHAT THE UNIVERSE DOES, OKAY?
NOW THIS IS AN ALCUBIERRE FIELD. THE UNIVERSE GETS ALL CRUNCHED UP AROUND IT, AND THAT CRUNCHING PUSHES THE *VENTURE* REALLY, REALLY FAST.
a Tr(K)
x
THE *VENTURE'S* BIG WEIRD BALL MAKES IT, AND THE *VENTURE'S* IN HERE, IN ITS BUBBLE.
AND BECAUSE OF THE BUBBLE AND THE CRUNCHING AND ALL--THE UNIVERSE DOESN'T KNOW IT'S THERE.

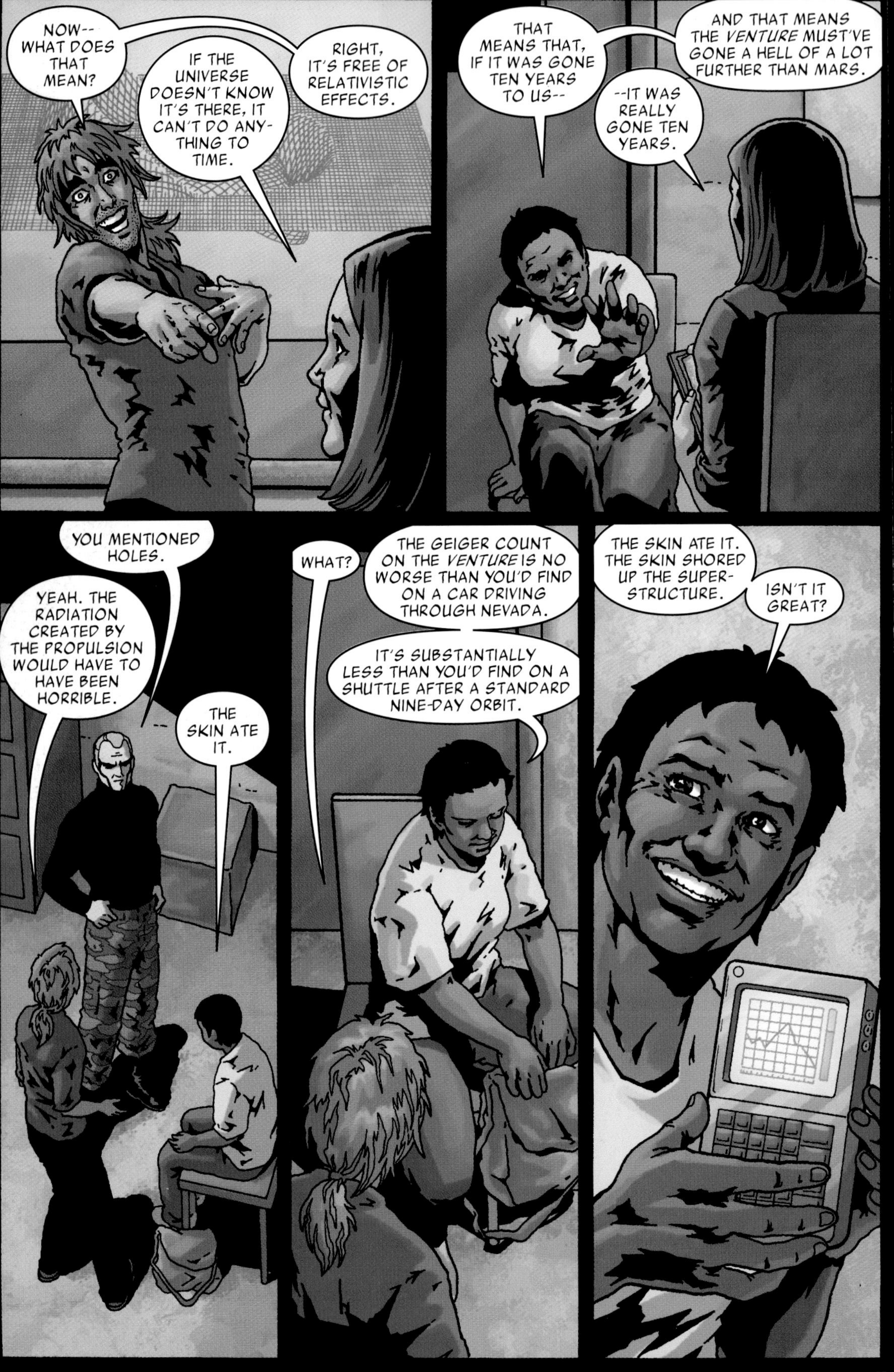
NOW-- WHAT DOES THAT MEAN?
IF THE UNIVERSE DOESN'T KNOW IT'S THERE, IT CAN'T DO ANYTHING TO TIME.
RIGHT, IT'S FREE OF RELATIVISTIC EFFECTS.
THAT MEANS THAT, IF IT WAS GONE TEN YEARS TO US--
--IT WAS REALLY GONE TEN YEARS.
AND THAT MEANS THE VENTURE MUST'VE GONE A HELL OF A LOT FURTHER THAN MARS.
YOU MENTIONED HOLES.
YEAH. THE RADIATION CREATED BY THE PROPULSION WOULD HAVE TO HAVE BEEN HORRIBLE.
THE SKIN ATE IT.
WHAT?
THE GEIGER COUNT ON THE VENTURE IS NO WORSE THAN YOU'D FIND ON A CAR DRIVING THROUGH NEVADA.
IT'S SUBSTANTIALLY LESS THAN YOU'D FIND ON A SHUTTLE AFTER A STANDARD NINE-DAY ORBIT.
THE SKIN ATE IT. THE SKIN SHORED UP THE SUPERSTRUCTURE.
ISN'T IT GREAT?

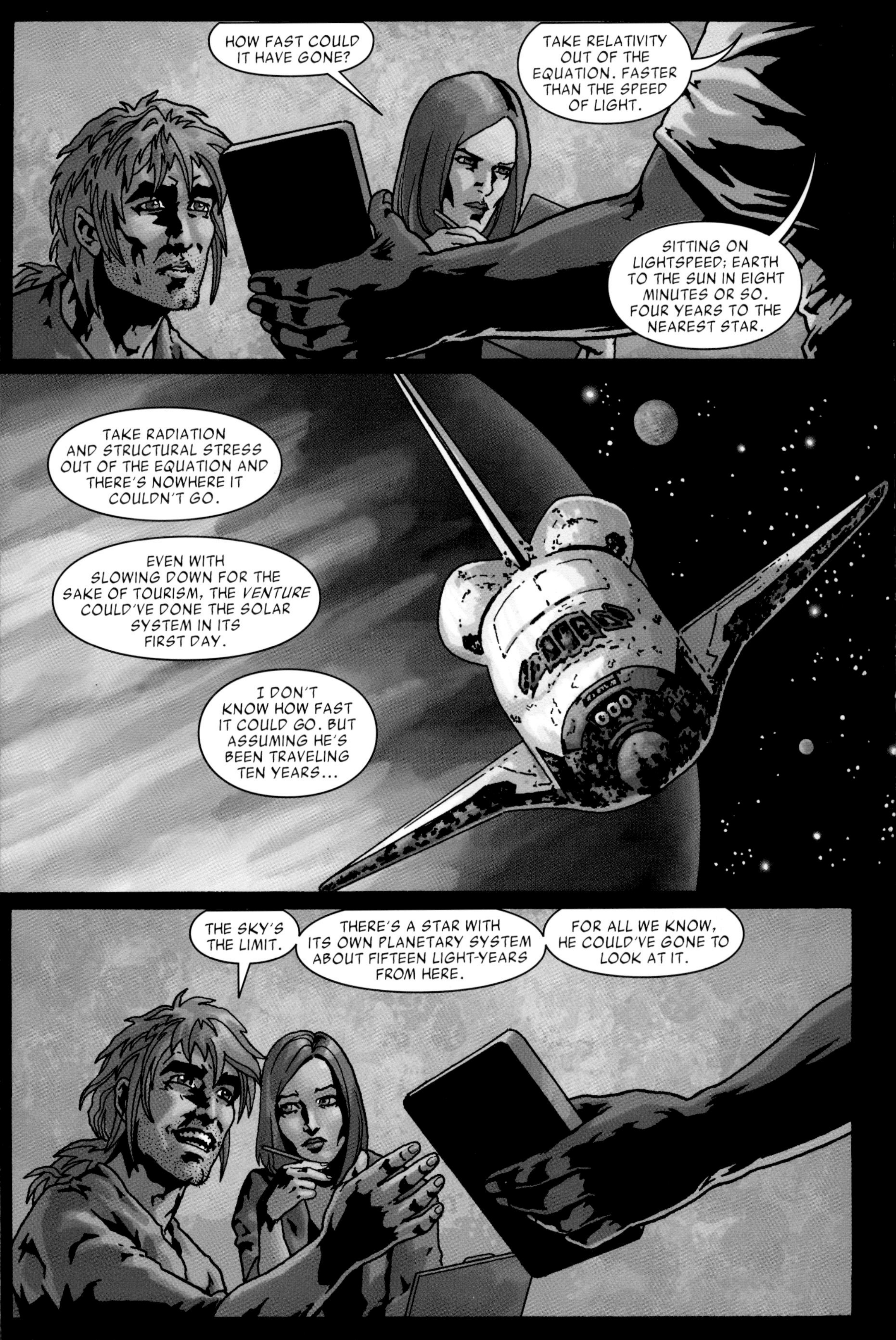
HOW FAST COULD IT HAVE GONE?
TAKE RELATIVITY OUT OF THE EQUATION. FASTER THAN THE SPEED OF LIGHT.
SITTING ON LIGHTSPEED; EARTH TO THE SUN IN EIGHT MINUTES OR SO. FOUR YEARS TO THE NEAREST STAR.
TAKE RADIATION AND STRUCTURAL STRESS OUT OF THE EQUATION AND THERE'S NOWHERE IT COULDN'T GO.
EVEN WITH SLOWING DOWN FOR THE SAKE OF TOURISM, THE *VENTURE* COULD'VE DONE THE SOLAR SYSTEM IN ITS FIRST DAY.
I DON'T KNOW HOW FAST IT COULD GO. BUT ASSUMING HE'S BEEN TRAVELING TEN YEARS...
THE SKY'S THE LIMIT.
THERE'S A STAR WITH ITS OWN PLANETARY SYSTEM ABOUT FIFTEEN LIGHT-YEARS FROM HERE.
FOR ALL WE KNOW, HE COULD'VE GONE TO LOOK AT IT.

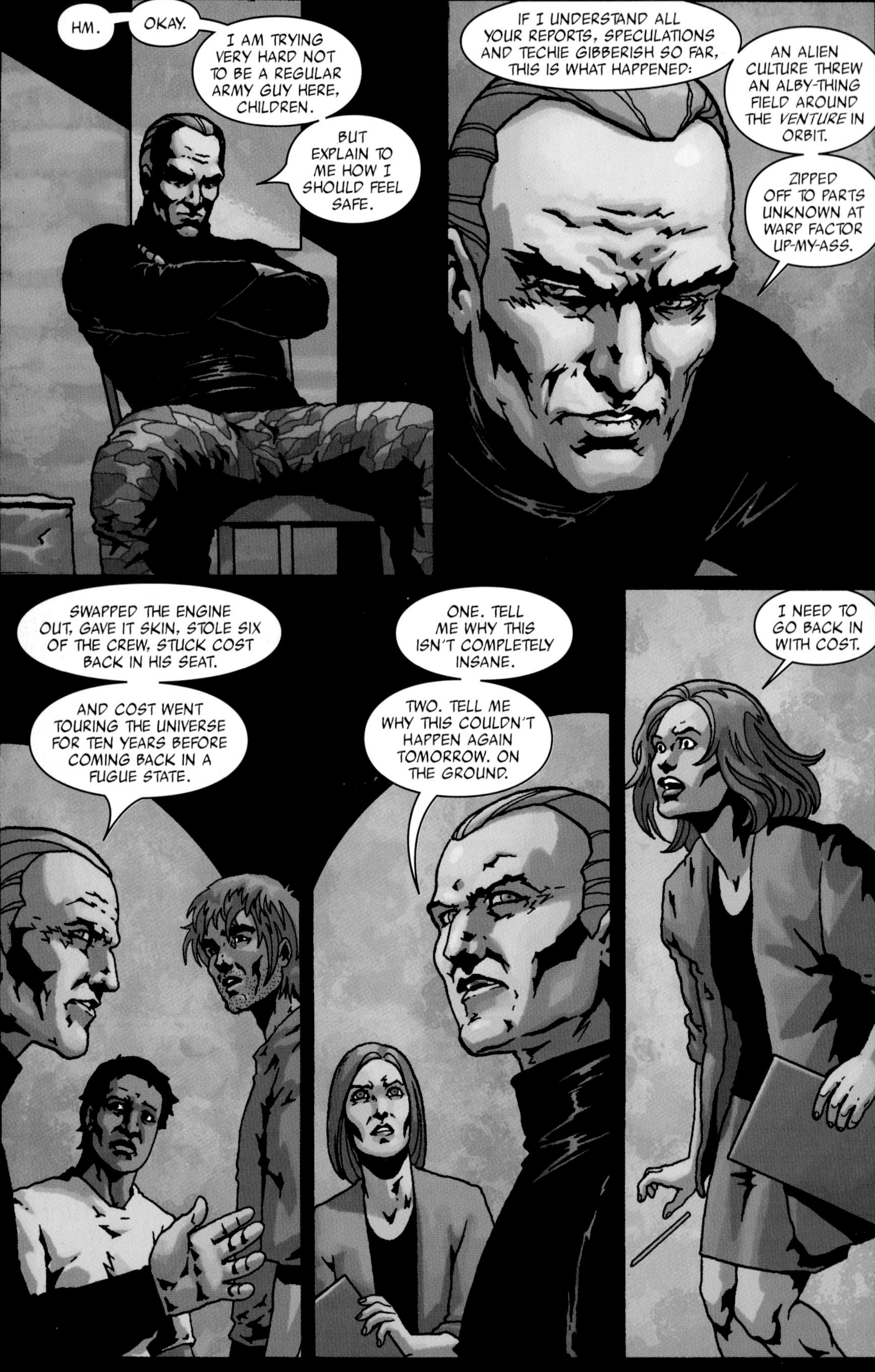
HM.
OKAY.
I AM TRYING VERY HARD NOT TO BE A REGULAR ARMY GUY HERE, CHILDREN.
BUT EXPLAIN TO ME HOW I SHOULD FEEL SAFE.
IF I UNDERSTAND ALL YOUR REPORTS, SPECULATIONS AND TECHIE GIBBERISH SO FAR, THIS IS WHAT HAPPENED:
AN ALIEN CULTURE THREW AN ALBY-THING FIELD AROUND THE *VENTURE* IN ORBIT.
ZIPPED OFF TO PARTS UNKNOWN AT WARP FACTOR UP-MY-ASS.
SWAPPED THE ENGINE OUT, GAVE IT SKIN, STOLE SIX OF THE CREW, STUCK COST BACK IN HIS SEAT.
AND COST WENT TOURING THE UNIVERSE FOR TEN YEARS BEFORE COMING BACK IN A FUGUE STATE.
ONE. TELL ME WHY THIS ISN'T COMPLETELY INSANE.
TWO. TELL ME WHY THIS COULDN'T HAPPEN AGAIN TOMORROW. ON THE GROUND.
I NEED TO GO BACK IN WITH COST.

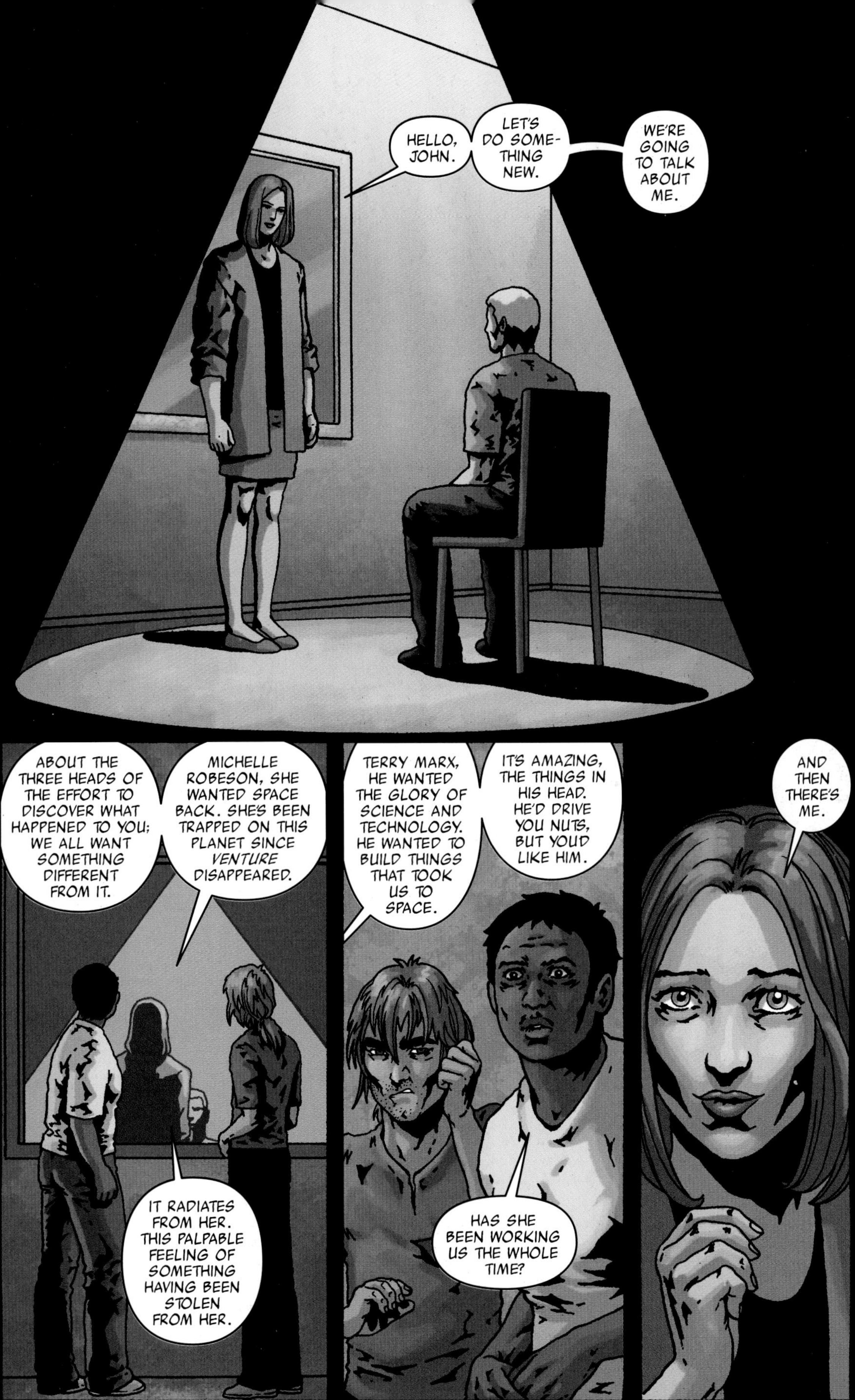
HELLO, JOHN.
LET'S DO SOME-THING NEW.
WE'RE GOING TO TALK ABOUT ME.
ABOUT THE THREE HEADS OF THE EFFORT TO DISCOVER WHAT HAPPENED TO YOU; WE ALL WANT SOMETHING DIFFERENT FROM IT.
MICHELLE ROBESON, SHE WANTED SPACE BACK. SHE'S BEEN TRAPPED ON THIS PLANET SINCE *VENTURE* DISAPPEARED.
IT RADIATES FROM HER. THIS PALPABLE FEELING OF SOMETHING HAVING BEEN STOLEN FROM HER.
TERRY MARX, HE WANTED THE GLORY OF SCIENCE AND TECHNOLOGY. HE WANTED TO BUILD THINGS THAT TOOK US TO SPACE.
IT'S AMAZING, THE THINGS IN HIS HEAD. HE'D DRIVE YOU NUTS, BUT YOU'D LIKE HIM.
HAS SHE BEEN WORKING US THE WHOLE TIME?
AND THEN THERE'S ME.

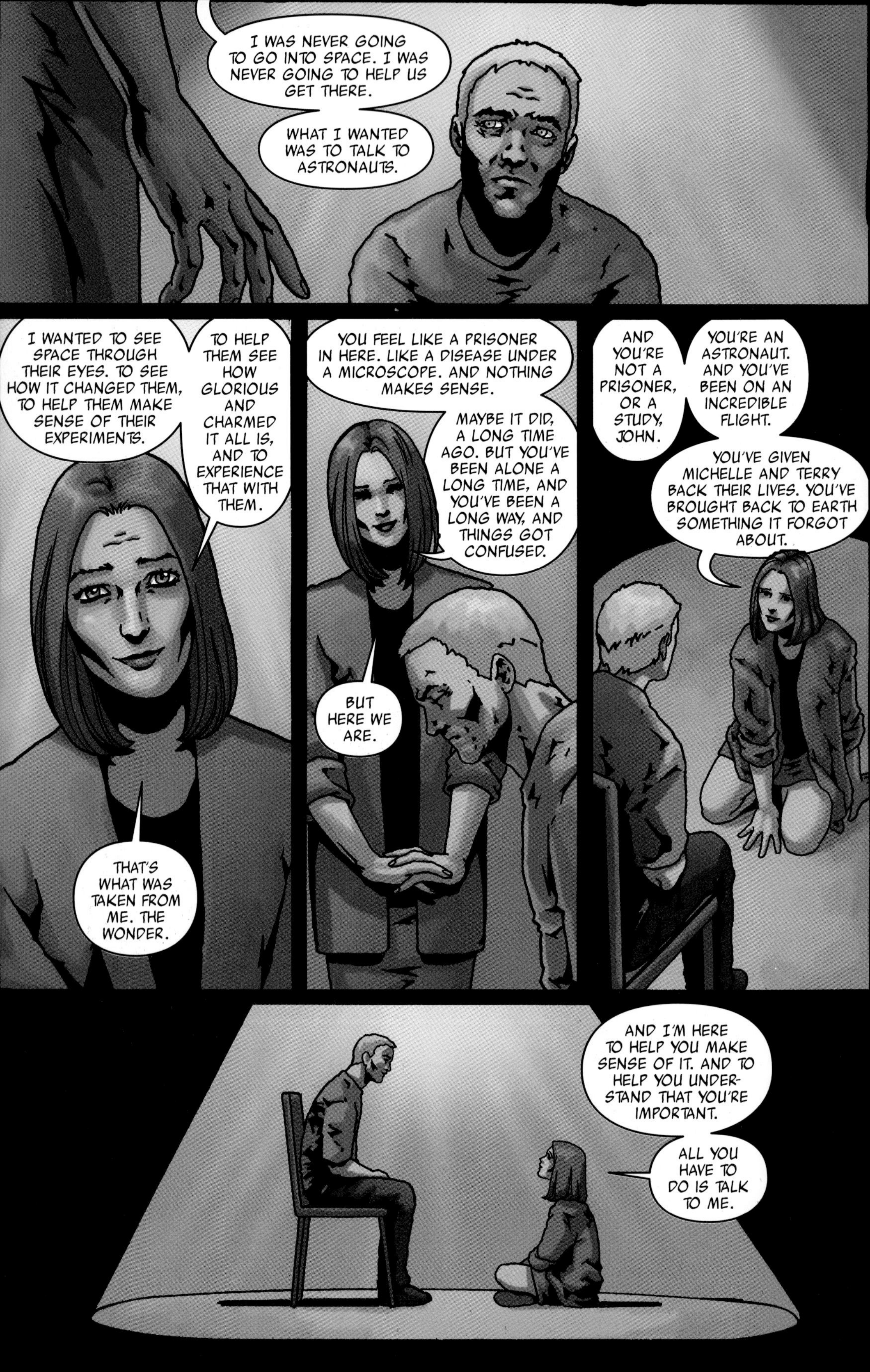
I WAS NEVER GOING TO GO INTO SPACE. I WAS NEVER GOING TO HELP US GET THERE.
WHAT I WANTED WAS TO TALK TO ASTRONAUTS.
I WANTED TO SEE SPACE THROUGH THEIR EYES. TO SEE HOW IT CHANGED THEM, TO HELP THEM MAKE SENSE OF THEIR EXPERIMENTS.
TO HELP THEM SEE HOW GLORIOUS AND CHARMED IT ALL IS, AND TO EXPERIENCE THAT WITH THEM.
THAT'S WHAT WAS TAKEN FROM ME. THE WONDER.
YOU FEEL LIKE A PRISONER IN HERE. LIKE A DISEASE UNDER A MICROSCOPE. AND NOTHING MAKES SENSE.
MAYBE IT DID, A LONG TIME AGO. BUT YOU'VE BEEN ALONE A LONG TIME, AND YOU'VE BEEN A LONG WAY, AND THINGS GOT CONFUSED.
BUT HERE WE ARE.
AND YOU'RE NOT A PRISONER, OR A STUDY, JOHN.
YOU'RE AN ASTRONAUT. AND YOU'VE BEEN ON AN INCREDIBLE FLIGHT.
YOU'VE GIVEN MICHELLE AND TERRY BACK THEIR LIVES. YOU'VE BROUGHT BACK TO EARTH SOMETHING IT FORGOT ABOUT.
AND I'M HERE TO HELP YOU MAKE SENSE OF IT. AND TO HELP YOU UNDERSTAND THAT YOU'RE IMPORTANT.
ALL YOU HAVE TO DO IS TALK TO ME.

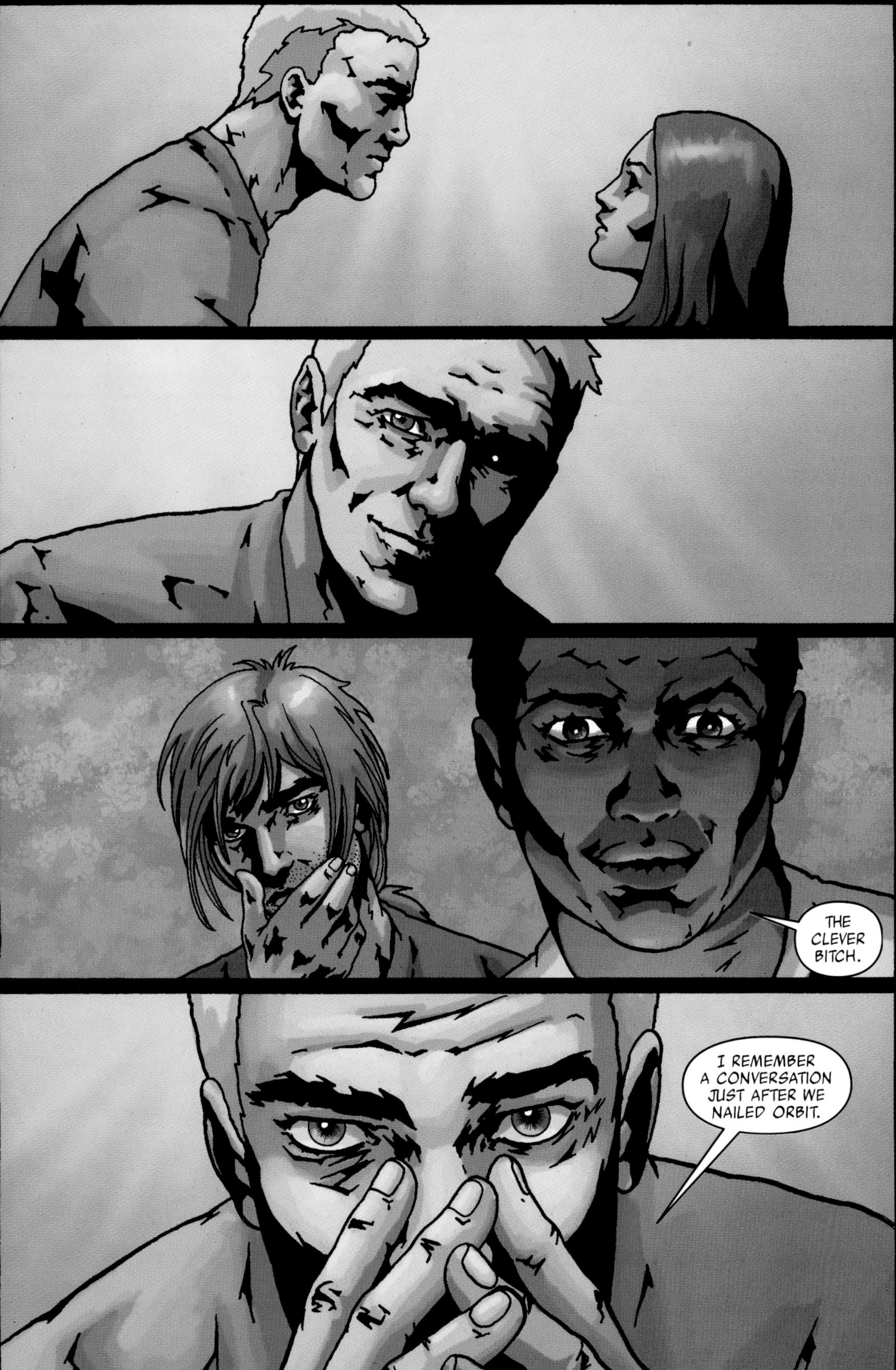
THE CLEVER BITCH.
I REMEMBER A CONVERSATION JUST AFTER WE NAILED ORBIT.

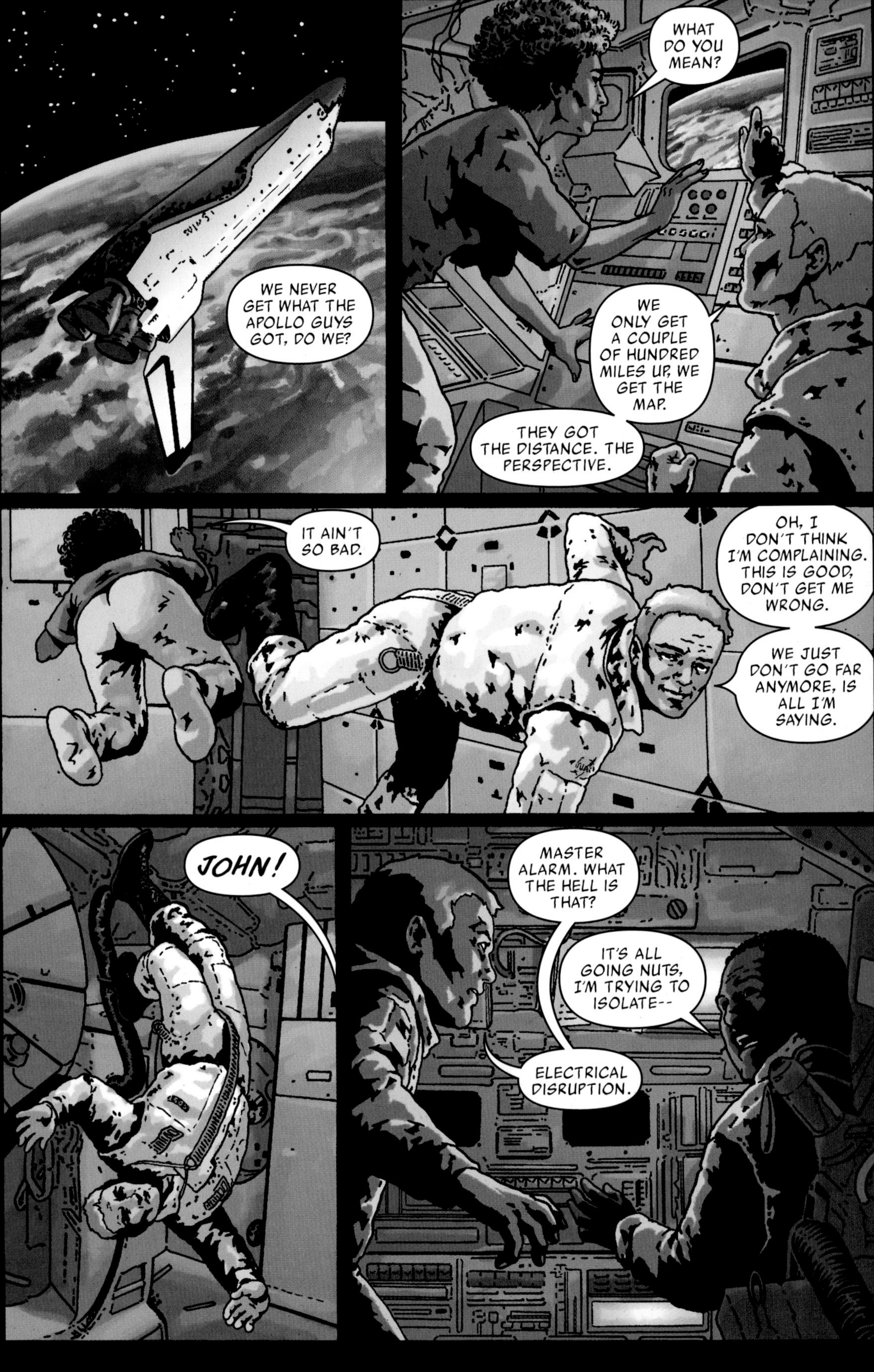
WE NEVER GET WHAT THE APOLLO GUYS GOT, DO WE?
WHAT DO YOU MEAN?
THEY GOT THE DISTANCE. THE PERSPECTIVE.
WE ONLY GET A COUPLE OF HUNDRED MILES UP, WE GET THE MAP.
IT AIN'T SO BAD.
OH, I DON'T THINK I'M COMPLAINING. THIS IS GOOD, DON'T GET ME WRONG.
WE JUST DON'T GO FAR ANYMORE, IS ALL I'M SAYING.
JOHN!
MASTER ALARM. WHAT THE HELL IS THAT?
IT'S ALL GOING NUTS, I'M TRYING TO ISOLATE--
ELECTRICAL DISRUPTION.

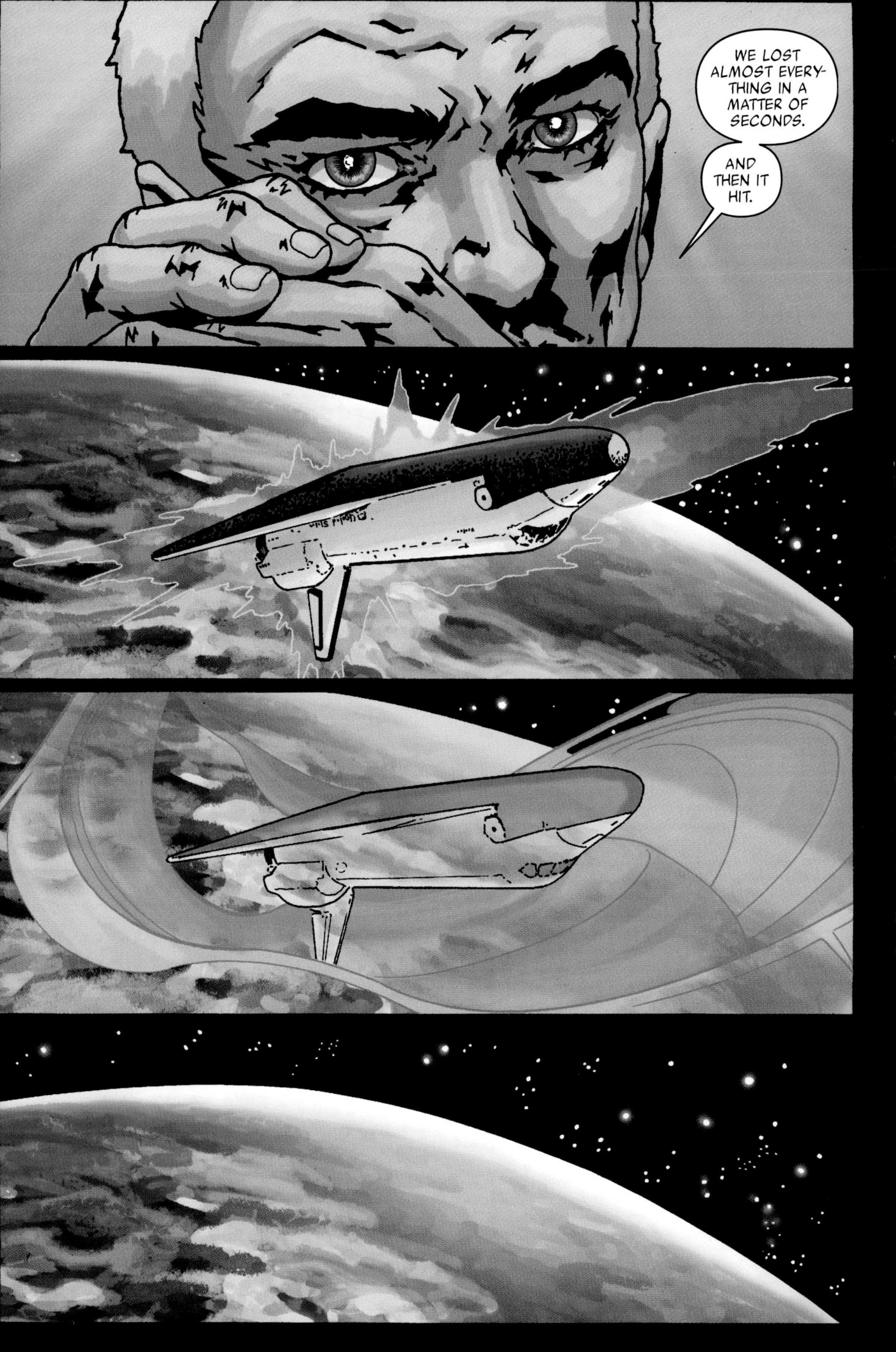
WE LOST ALMOST EVERY-THING IN A MATTER OF SECONDS.
AND THEN IT HIT.

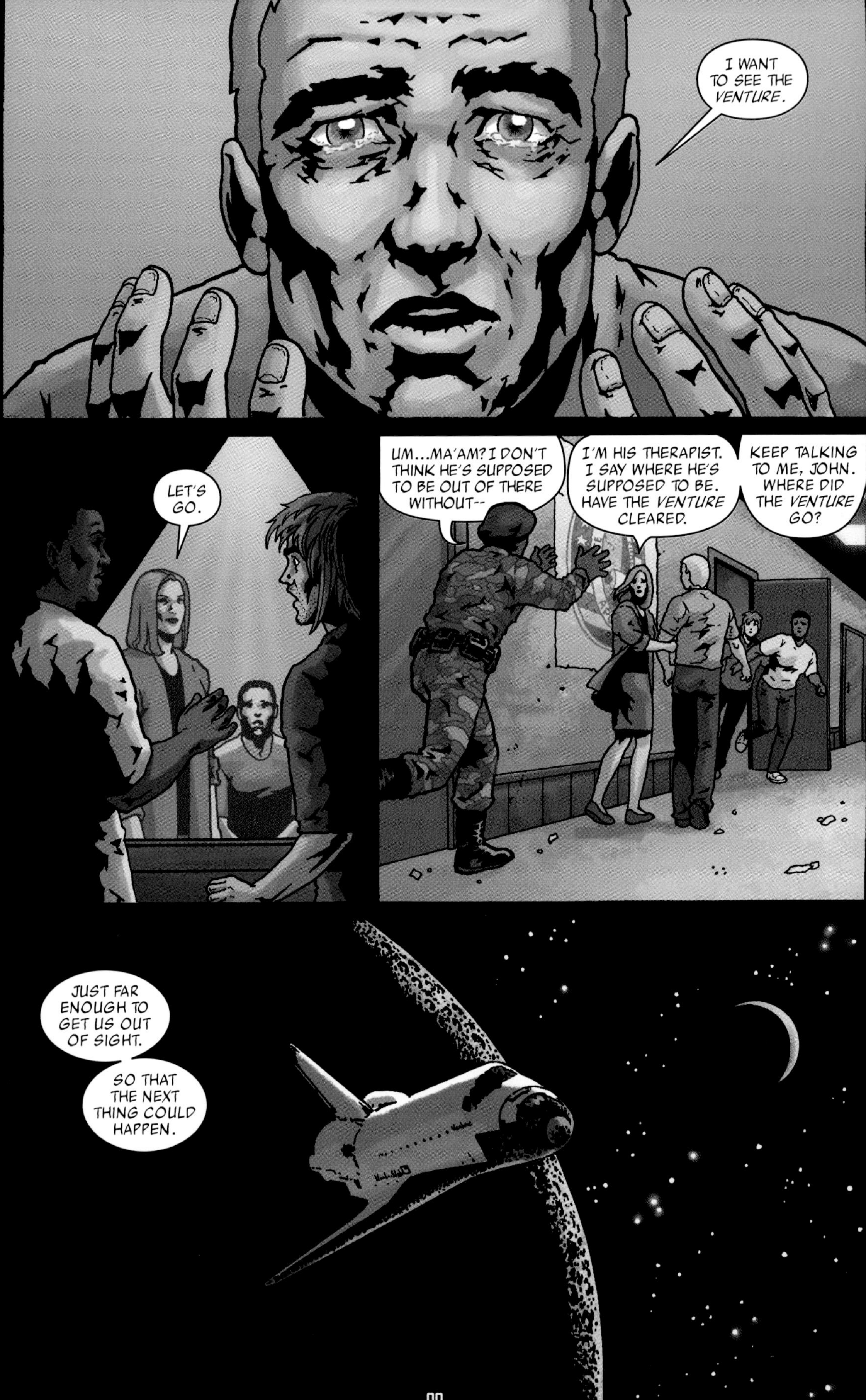
I WANT TO SEE THE VENTURE.
LET'S GO.
UM...MA'AM? I DON'T THINK HE'S SUPPOSED TO BE OUT OF THERE WITHOUT--
I'M HIS THERAPIST. I SAY WHERE HE'S SUPPOSED TO BE. HAVE THE VENTURE CLEARED.
KEEP TALKING TO ME, JOHN. WHERE DID THE VENTURE GO?
JUST FAR ENOUGH TO GET US OUT OF SIGHT.
SO THAT THE NEXT THING COULD HAPPEN.

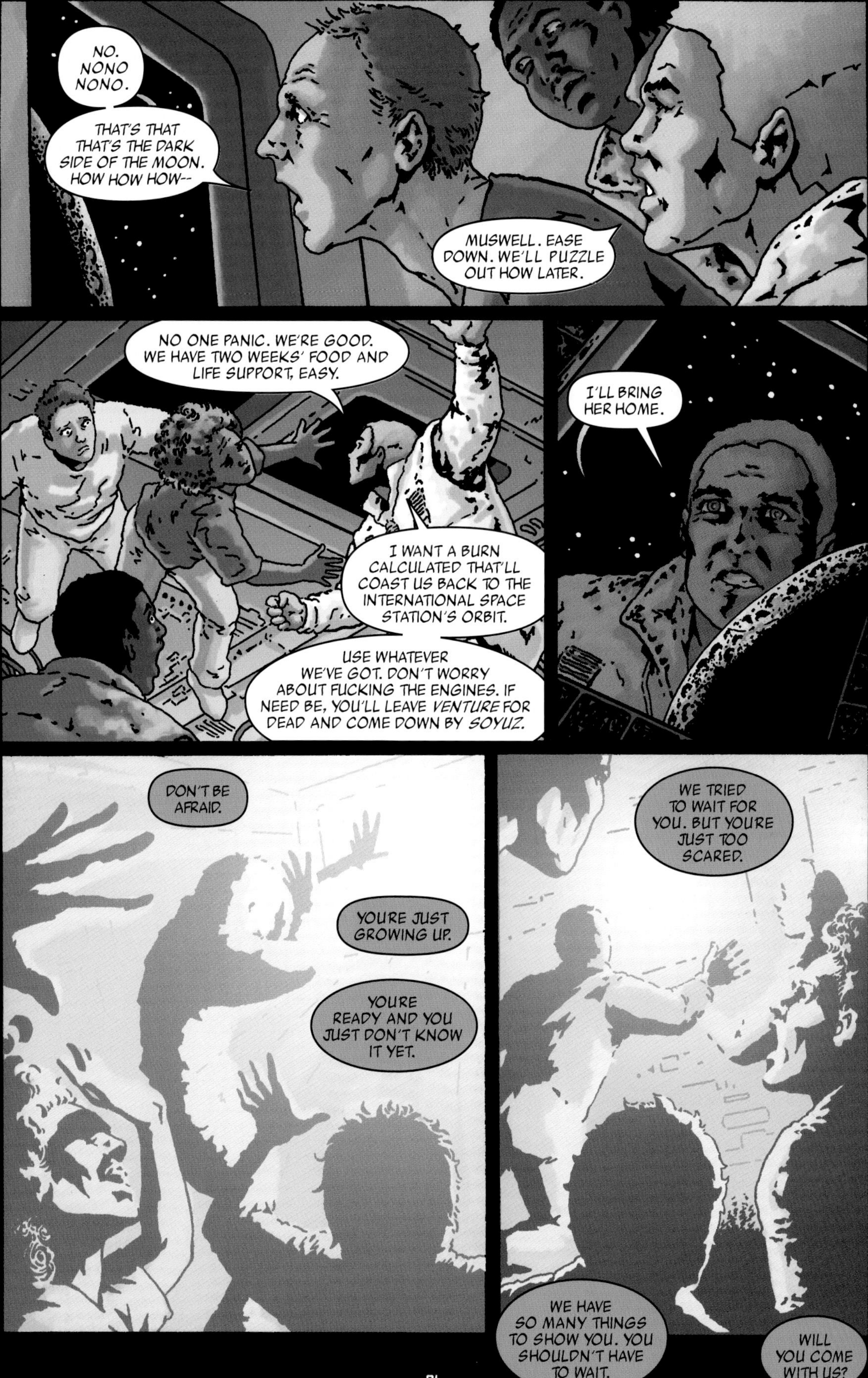
NO. NONO NONO.
THAT'S THAT THAT'S THE DARK SIDE OF THE MOON. HOW HOW HOW--
MUSWELL. EASE DOWN. WE'LL PUZZLE OUT HOW LATER.
NO ONE PANIC. WE'RE GOOD. WE HAVE TWO WEEKS' FOOD AND LIFE SUPPORT, EASY.
I WANT A BURN CALCULATED THAT'LL COAST US BACK TO THE INTERNATIONAL SPACE STATION'S ORBIT.
USE WHATEVER WE'VE GOT. DON'T WORRY ABOUT FUCKING THE ENGINES. IF NEED BE, YOU'LL LEAVE VENTURE FOR DEAD AND COME DOWN BY SOYUZ.
I'LL BRING HER HOME.
DON'T BE AFRAID.
YOU'RE JUST GROWING UP.
YOU'RE READY AND YOU JUST DON'T KNOW IT YET.
WE TRIED TO WAIT FOR YOU. BUT YOU'RE JUST TOO SCARED.
WE HAVE SO MANY THINGS TO SHOW YOU. YOU SHOULDN'T HAVE TO WAIT.
WILL YOU COME WITH US?

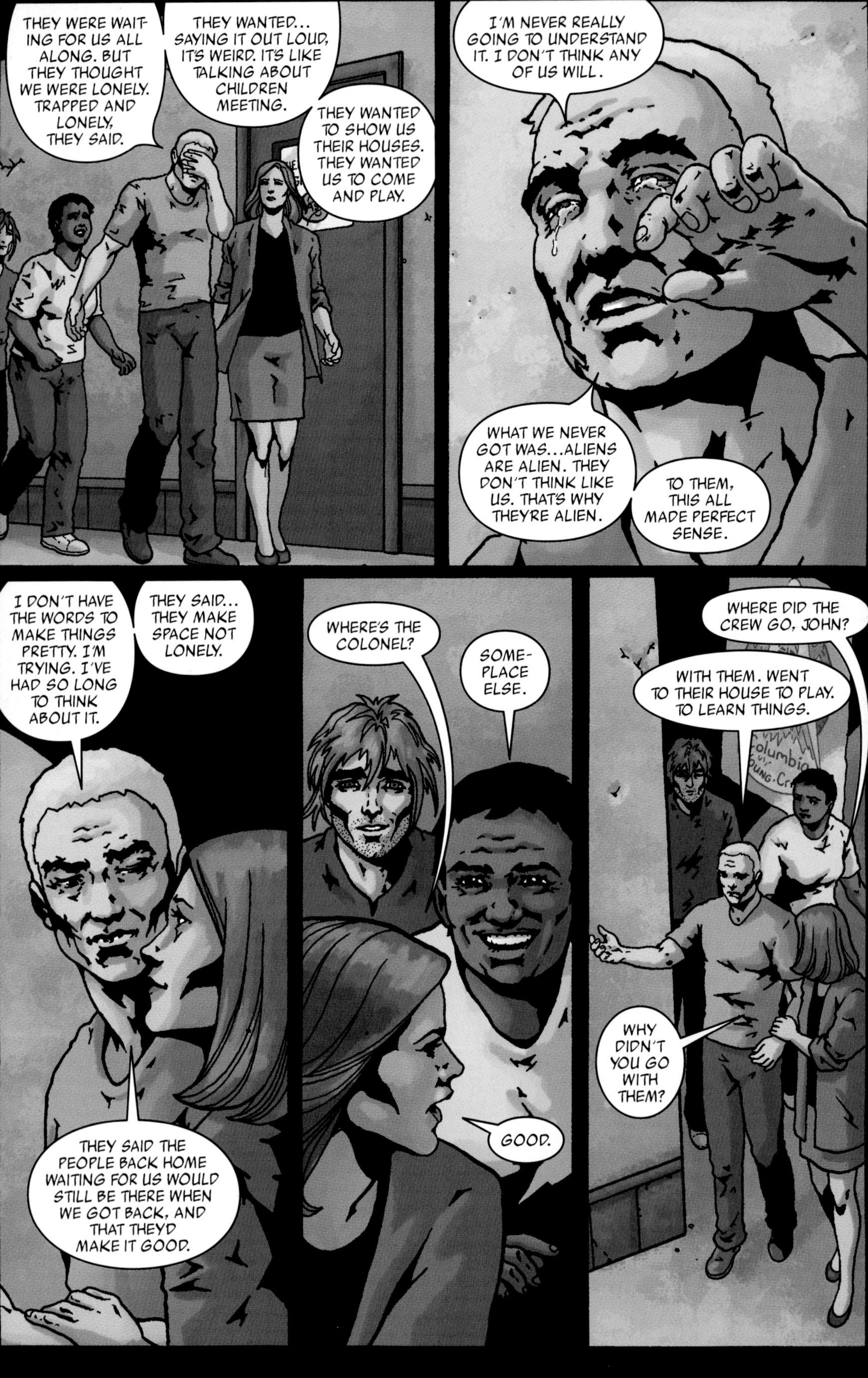
THEY WERE WAIT-ING FOR US ALL ALONG. BUT THEY THOUGHT WE WERE LONELY. TRAPPED AND LONELY, THEY SAID.
THEY WANTED... SAYING IT OUT LOUD, IT'S WEIRD. IT'S LIKE TALKING ABOUT CHILDREN MEETING.
THEY WANTED TO SHOW US THEIR HOUSES. THEY WANTED US TO COME AND PLAY.
I'M NEVER REALLY GOING TO UNDERSTAND IT. I DON'T THINK ANY OF US WILL.
WHAT WE NEVER GOT WAS...ALIENS ARE ALIEN. THEY DON'T THINK LIKE US. THAT'S WHY THEY'RE ALIEN.
TO THEM, THIS ALL MADE PERFECT SENSE.
I DON'T HAVE THE WORDS TO MAKE THINGS PRETTY. I'M TRYING. I'VE HAD SO LONG TO THINK ABOUT IT.
THEY SAID... THEY MAKE SPACE NOT LONELY.
THEY SAID THE PEOPLE BACK HOME WAITING FOR US WOULD STILL BE THERE WHEN WE GOT BACK, AND THAT THEY'D MAKE IT GOOD.
WHERE'S THE COLONEL?
SOME-PLACE ELSE.
GOOD.
WHERE DID THE CREW GO, JOHN?
WITH THEM. WENT TO THEIR HOUSE TO PLAY. TO LEARN THINGS.
WHY DIDN'T YOU GO WITH THEM?

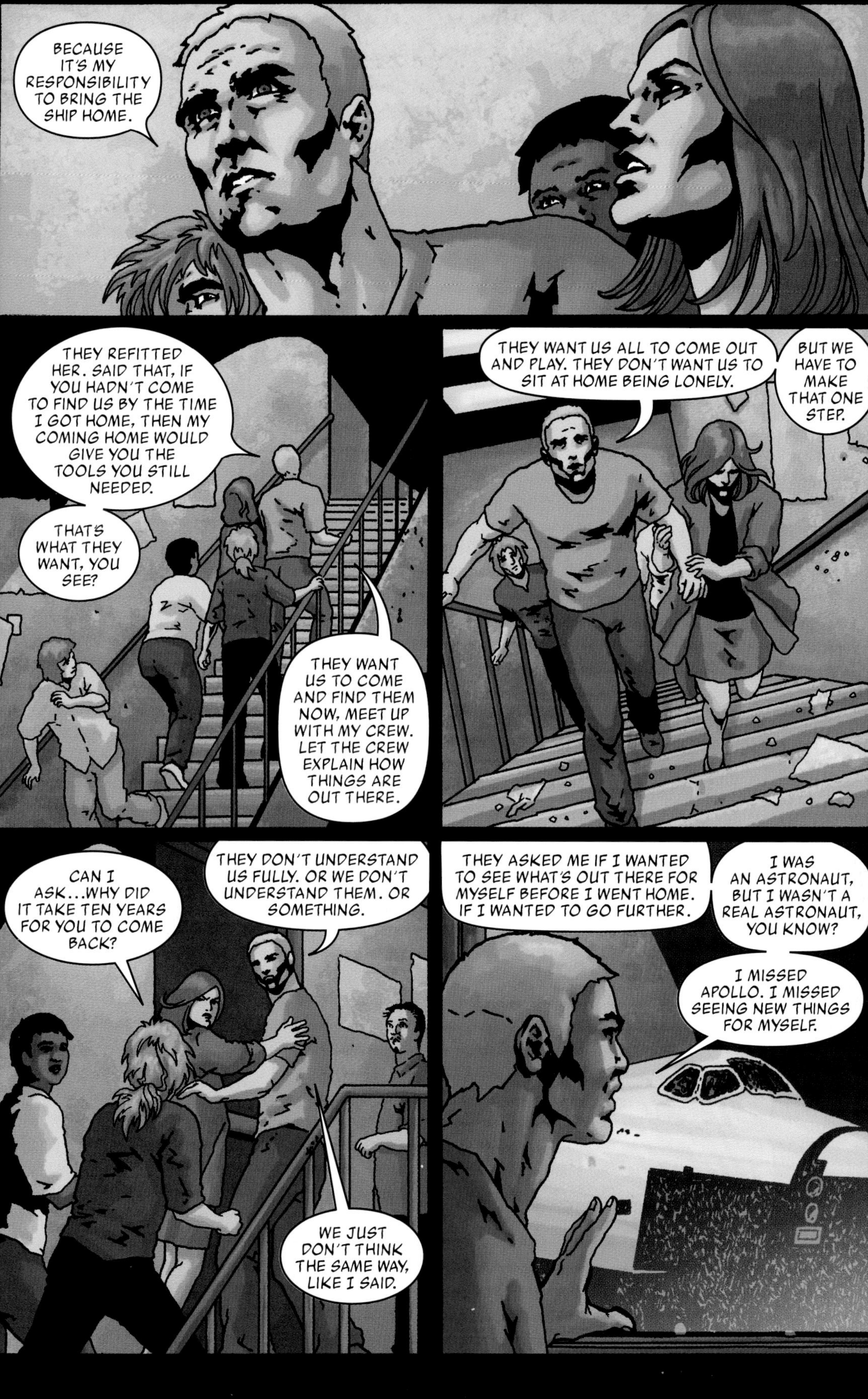
BECAUSE IT'S MY RESPONSIBILITY TO BRING THE SHIP HOME.
THEY REFITTED HER. SAID THAT, IF YOU HADN'T COME TO FIND US BY THE TIME I GOT HOME, THEN MY COMING HOME WOULD GIVE YOU THE TOOLS YOU STILL NEEDED.
THAT'S WHAT THEY WANT, YOU SEE?
THEY WANT US TO COME AND FIND THEM NOW, MEET UP WITH MY CREW. LET THE CREW EXPLAIN HOW THINGS ARE OUT THERE.
THEY WANT US ALL TO COME OUT AND PLAY. THEY DON'T WANT US TO SIT AT HOME BEING LONELY.
BUT WE HAVE TO MAKE THAT ONE STEP.
CAN I ASK...WHY DID IT TAKE TEN YEARS FOR YOU TO COME BACK?
THEY DON'T UNDERSTAND US FULLY. OR WE DON'T UNDERSTAND THEM. OR SOMETHING.
WE JUST DON'T THINK THE SAME WAY, LIKE I SAID.
THEY ASKED ME IF I WANTED TO SEE WHAT'S OUT THERE FOR MYSELF BEFORE I WENT HOME. IF I WANTED TO GO FURTHER.
I WAS AN ASTRONAUT, BUT I WASN'T A REAL ASTRONAUT, YOU KNOW?
I MISSED APOLLO. I MISSED SEEING NEW THINGS FOR MYSELF.

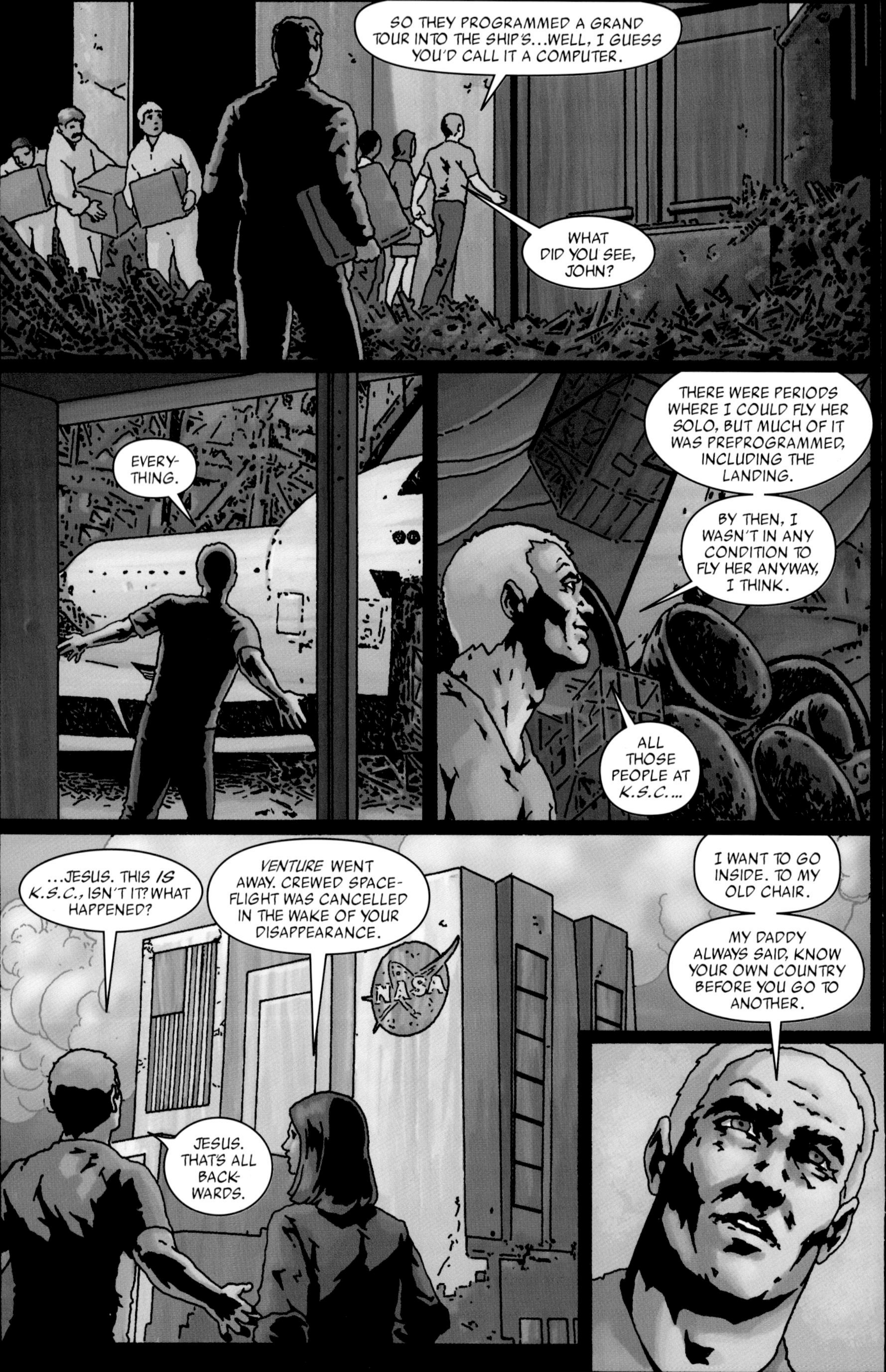
SO THEY PROGRAMMED A GRAND TOUR INTO THE SHIP'S...WELL, I GUESS YOU'D CALL IT A COMPUTER.
WHAT DID YOU SEE, JOHN?
EVERY-THING.
THERE WERE PERIODS WHERE I COULD FLY HER SOLO, BUT MUCH OF IT WAS PREPROGRAMMED, INCLUDING THE LANDING.
BY THEN, I WASN'T IN ANY CONDITION TO FLY HER ANYWAY, I THINK.
ALL THOSE PEOPLE AT K.S.C....
...JESUS. THIS *IS* K.S.C., ISN'T IT? WHAT HAPPENED?
VENTURE WENT AWAY. CREWED SPACE-FLIGHT WAS CANCELLED IN THE WAKE OF YOUR DISAPPEARANCE.
NASA
JESUS. THAT'S ALL BACK-WARDS.
I WANT TO GO INSIDE. TO MY OLD CHAIR.
MY DADDY ALWAYS SAID, KNOW YOUR OWN COUNTRY BEFORE YOU GO TO ANOTHER.

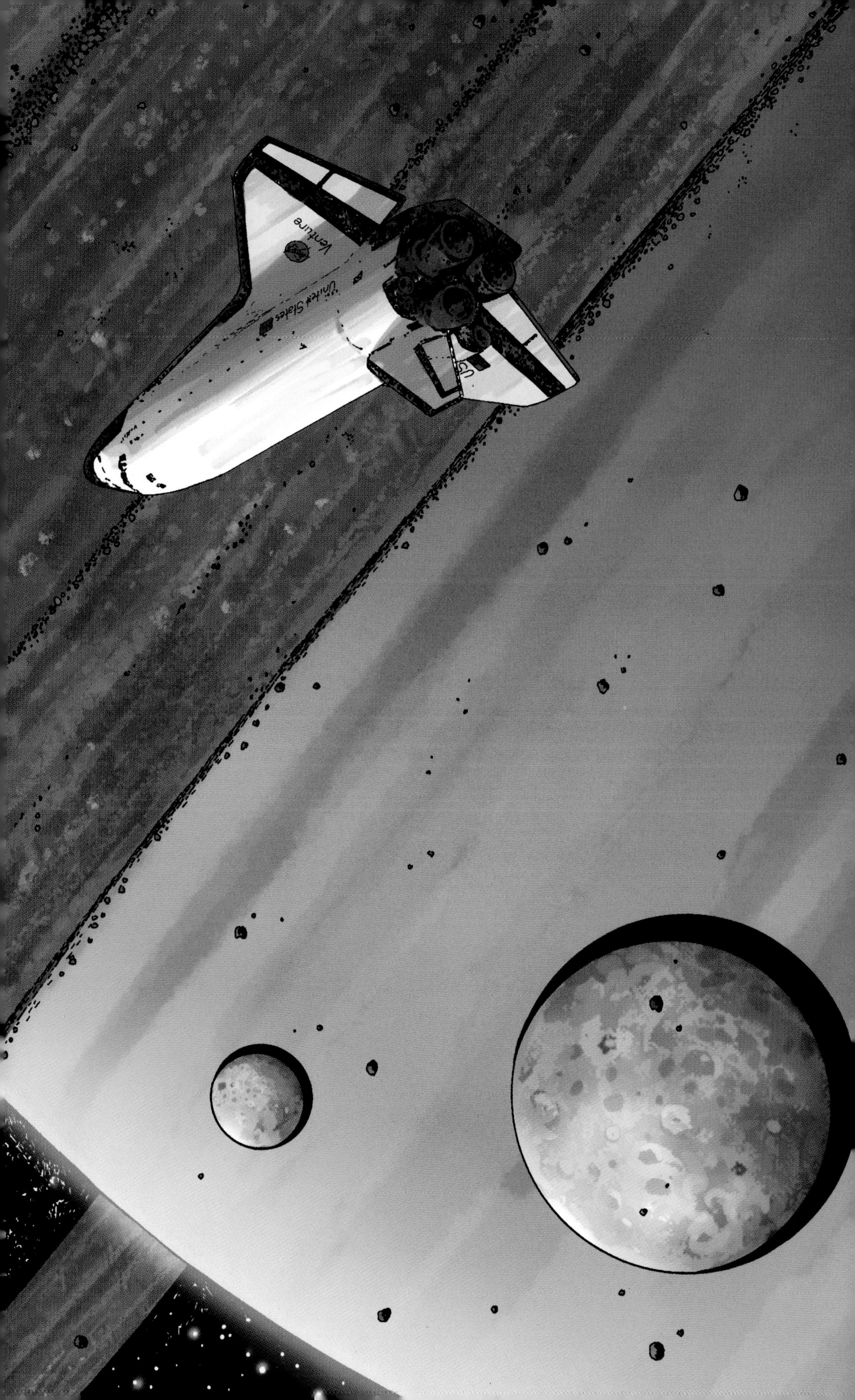
Venture
United States
USA

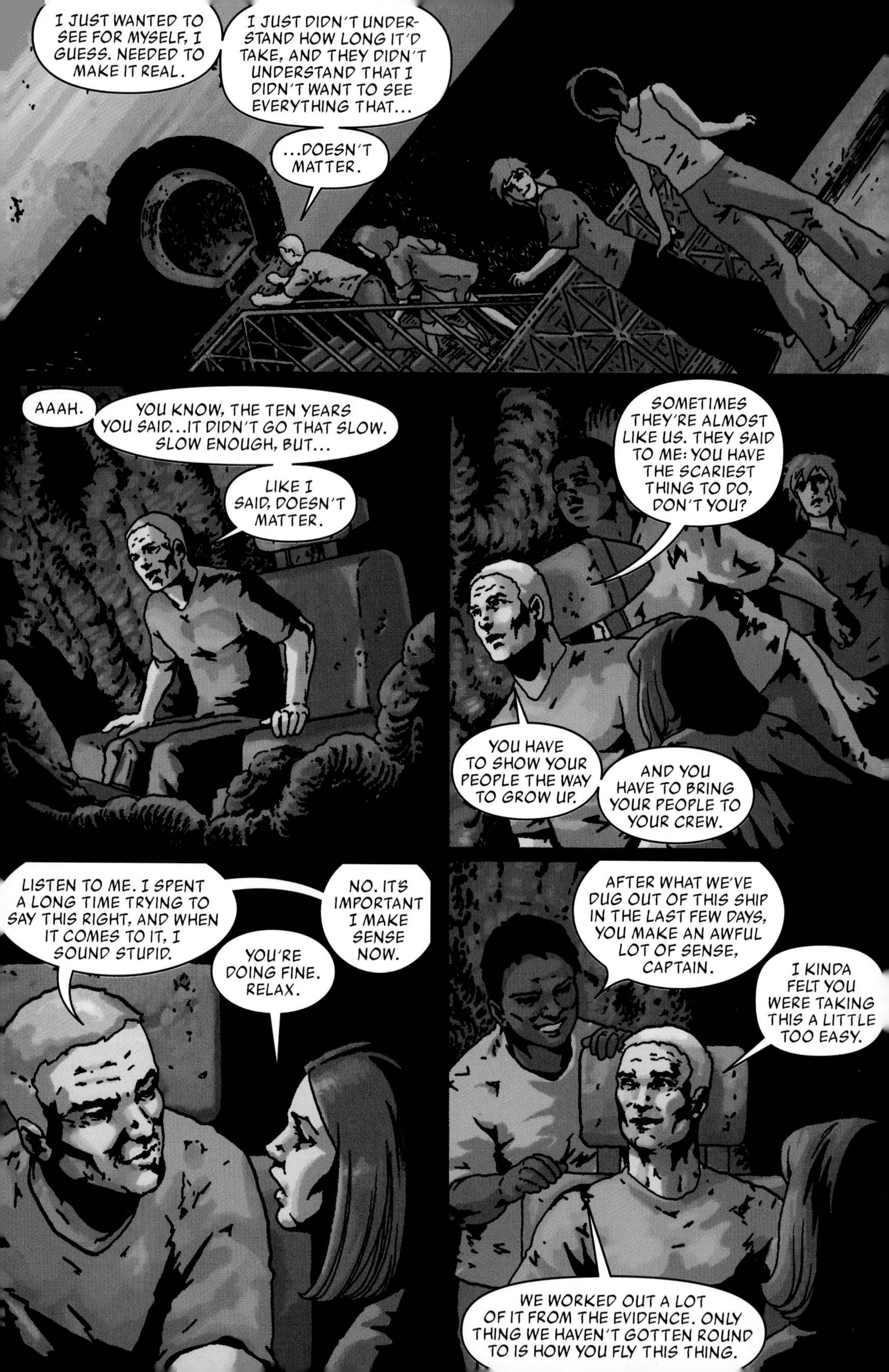
I JUST WANTED TO SEE FOR MYSELF, I GUESS. NEEDED TO MAKE IT REAL.
I JUST DIDN'T UNDERSTAND HOW LONG IT'D TAKE, AND THEY DIDN'T UNDERSTAND THAT I DIDN'T WANT TO SEE EVERYTHING THAT...
...DOESN'T MATTER.
AAAH.
YOU KNOW, THE TEN YEARS YOU SAID...IT DIDN'T GO THAT SLOW. SLOW ENOUGH, BUT...
LIKE I SAID, DOESN'T MATTER.
SOMETIMES THEY'RE ALMOST LIKE US. THEY SAID TO ME: YOU HAVE THE SCARIEST THING TO DO, DON'T YOU?
YOU HAVE TO SHOW YOUR PEOPLE THE WAY TO GROW UP.
AND YOU HAVE TO BRING YOUR PEOPLE TO YOUR CREW.
LISTEN TO ME. I SPENT A LONG TIME TRYING TO SAY THIS RIGHT, AND WHEN IT COMES TO IT, I SOUND STUPID.
YOU'RE DOING FINE. RELAX.
NO. IT'S IMPORTANT I MAKE SENSE NOW.
AFTER WHAT WE'VE DUG OUT OF THIS SHIP IN THE LAST FEW DAYS, YOU MAKE AN AWFUL LOT OF SENSE, CAPTAIN.
I KINDA FELT YOU WERE TAKING THIS A LITTLE TOO EASY.
WE WORKED OUT A LOT OF IT FROM THE EVIDENCE. ONLY THING WE HAVEN'T GOTTEN ROUND TO IS HOW YOU FLY THIS THING.

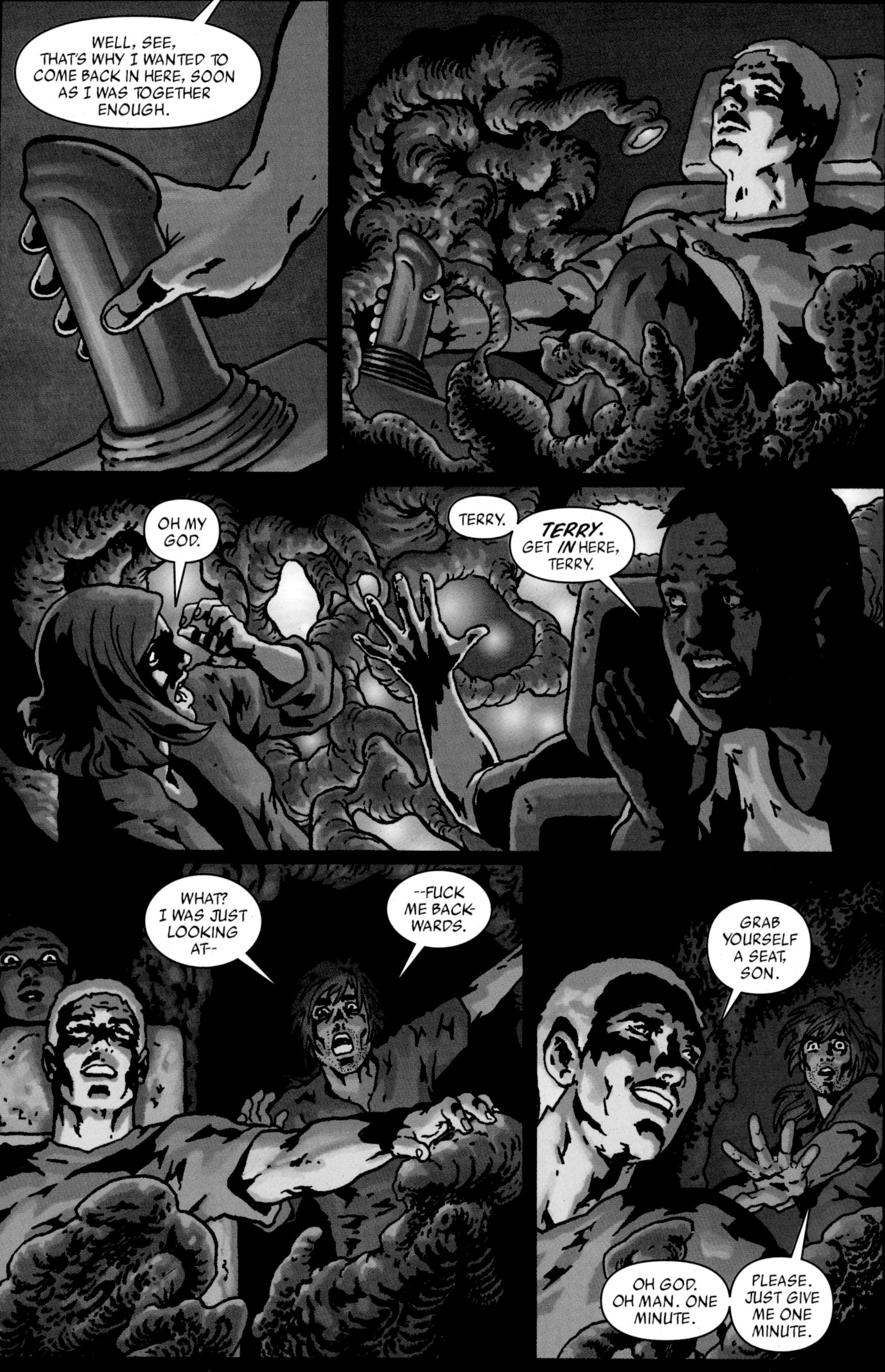
WELL, SEE, THAT'S WHY I WANTED TO COME BACK IN HERE, SOON AS I WAS TOGETHER ENOUGH.
OH MY GOD.
TERRY.
TERRY. GET IN HERE, TERRY.
WHAT? I WAS JUST LOOKING AT-
--FUCK ME BACK-WARDS.
GRAB YOURSELF A SEAT, SON.
OH GOD. OH MAN. ONE MINUTE.
PLEASE. JUST GIVE ME ONE MINUTE.

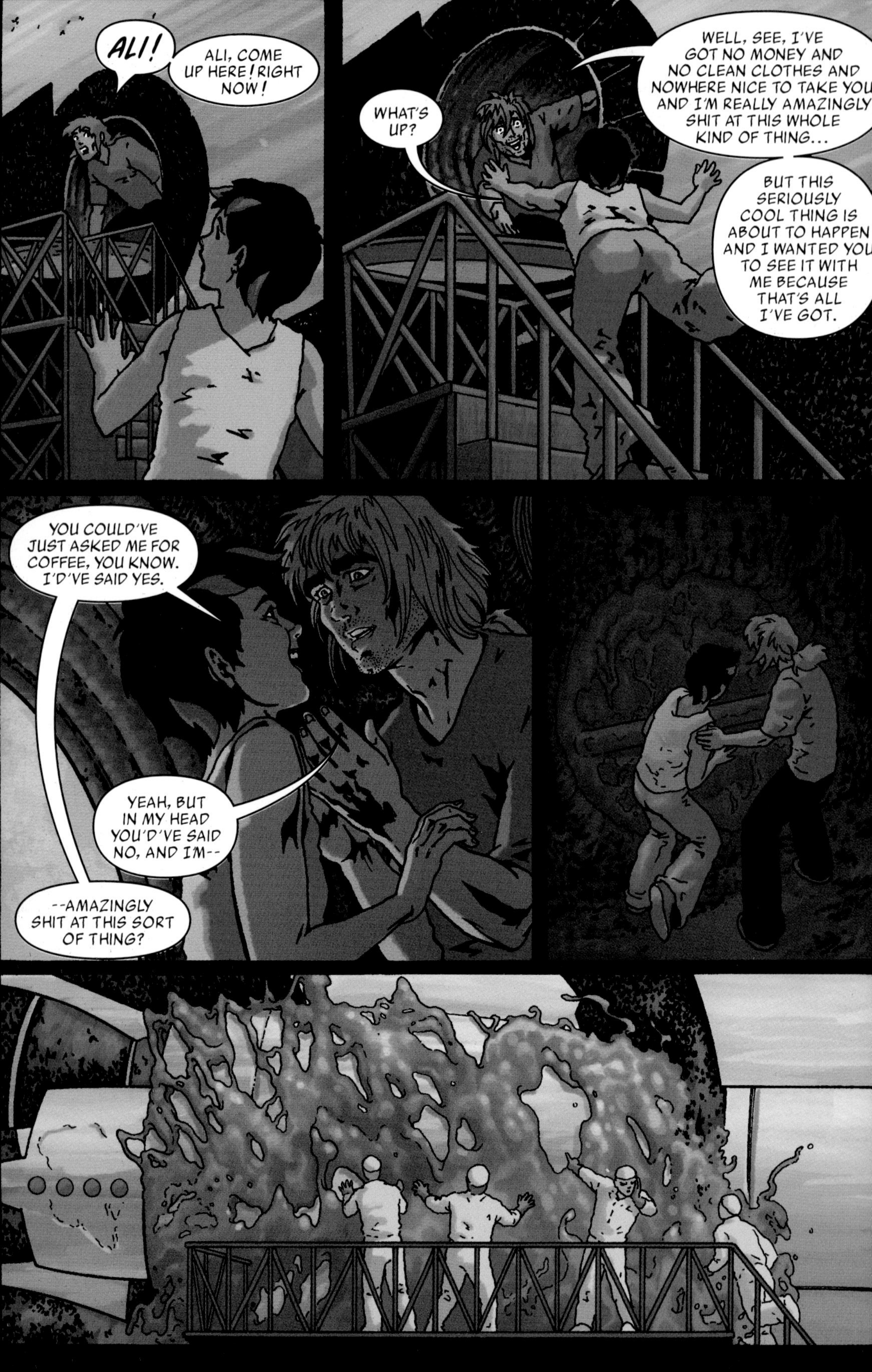
ALI!
ALI, COME UP HERE! RIGHT NOW!
WHAT'S UP?
WELL, SEE, I'VE GOT NO MONEY AND NO CLEAN CLOTHES AND NOWHERE NICE TO TAKE YOU AND I'M REALLY AMAZINGLY SHIT AT THIS WHOLE KIND OF THING...
BUT THIS SERIOUSLY COOL THING IS ABOUT TO HAPPEN AND I WANTED YOU TO SEE IT WITH ME BECAUSE THAT'S ALL I'VE GOT.
YOU COULD'VE JUST ASKED ME FOR COFFEE, YOU KNOW. I'D'VE SAID YES.
YEAH, BUT IN MY HEAD YOU'D'VE SAID NO, AND I'M--
--AMAZINGLY SHIT AT THIS SORT OF THING?

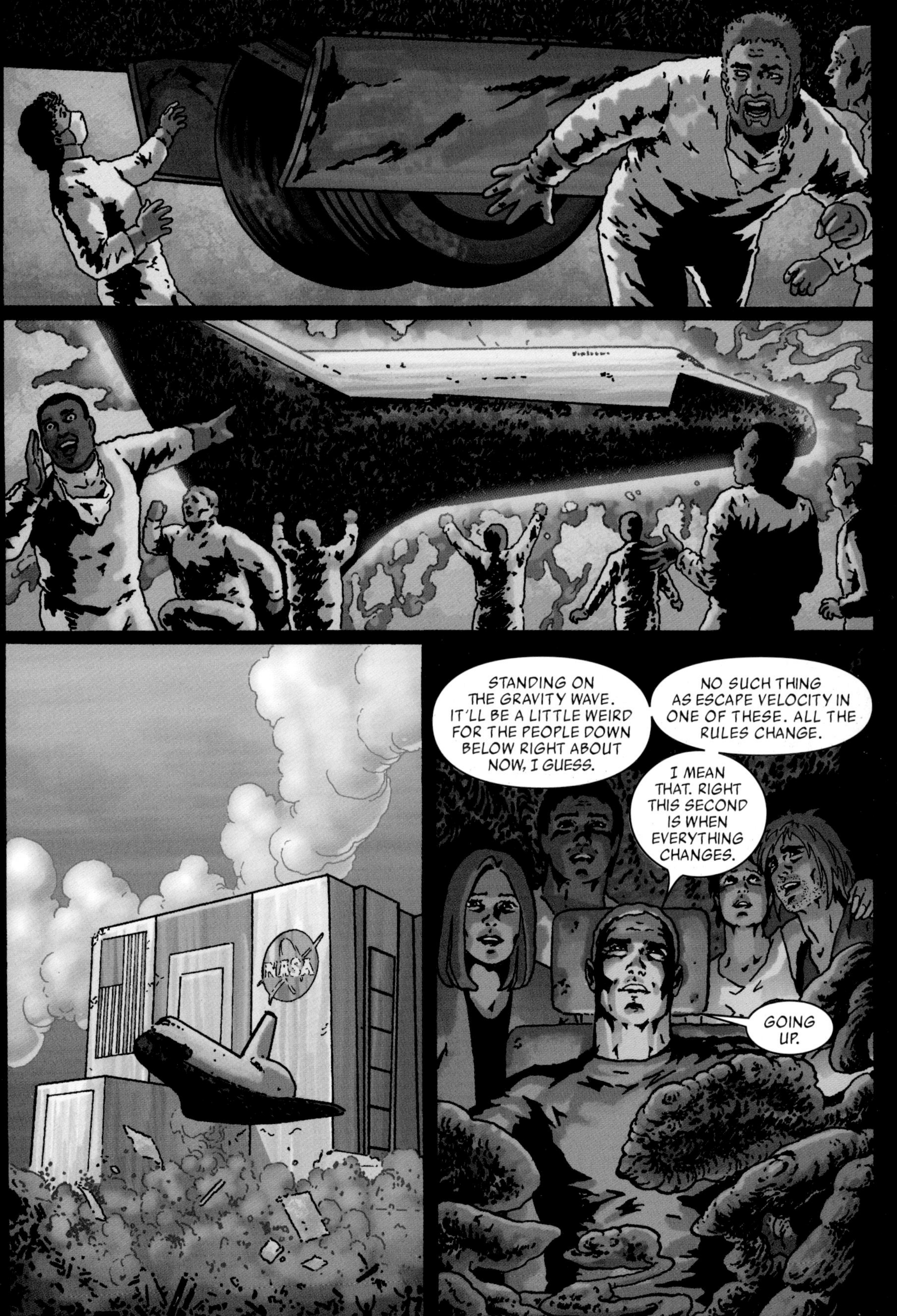
STANDING ON THE GRAVITY WAVE. IT'LL BE A LITTLE WEIRD FOR THE PEOPLE DOWN BELOW RIGHT ABOUT NOW, I GUESS.
NO SUCH THING AS ESCAPE VELOCITY IN ONE OF THESE. ALL THE RULES CHANGE.
I MEAN THAT. RIGHT THIS SECOND IS WHEN EVERYTHING CHANGES.
GOING UP.

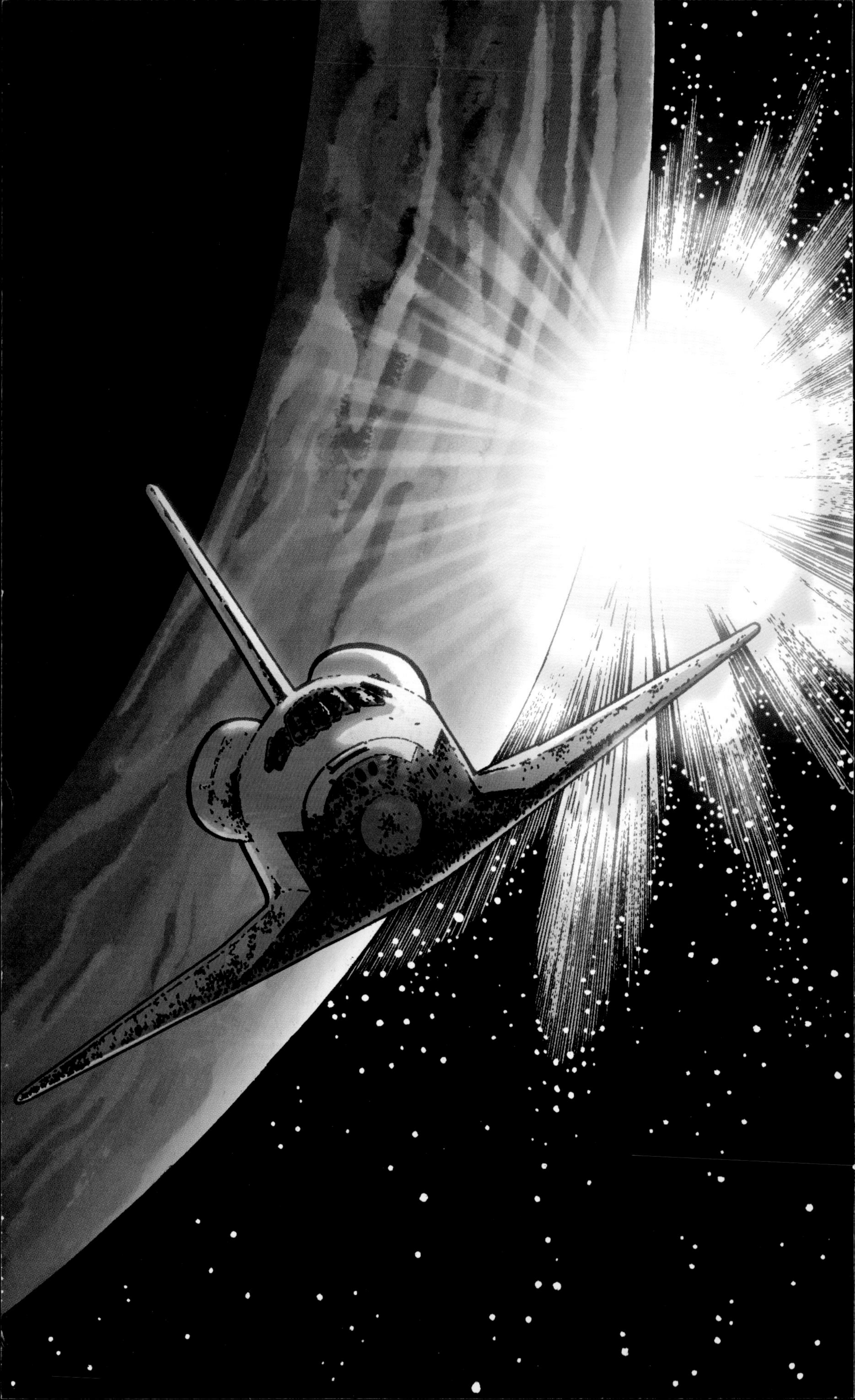